STRANGER
THAN
FICTION

STRANGER THAN FICTION

FICTION

THE LIFE OF EDGAR WALLACE, THE MAN WHO CREATED KING KONG

NEIL CLARK

The
History
Press

Front and back cover illustrations: © Getty Images

First published 2014

The History Press
The Mill, Brimscombe Port
Stroud, Gloucestershire, GL5 2QG
www.thehistorypress.co.uk

British Library Cataloguing in Publication Data.
A catalogue record for this book is available from the British Library.

ISBN 978 0 7524 9882 9

Typesetting and origination by The History Press
Printed in Great Britain

CONTENTS

ACKNOWLEDGEMENTS

Thanks to my family: my mother Joan for her encouragement, reading through the book at various stages, and for her suggestions; my wife Zsuzsanna and father Roy for all their help and support.

Thank you to Dunja Sharif of the Bodleian Library, Oxford, for help and assistance with accessing the Hogan collection of Wallace material. Thanks to Roger Wilkes for his work on listing all the material.

Thanks to my commissioning editor, Mark Beynon, and all who have worked on the book at The History Press.

All biographers owe a debt to those who have written about the subject previously, and I would like to thank Selina Hastings, daughter and literary executor of the late Margaret Lane, for kindly giving me permission to quote, without restriction, from her mother's 1938 biography of Edgar Wallace and also to reprint photographs from the book.

Thank you to Swami Dayatmananda of the Ramakrishna Vedanta Centre, Bourne End, Buckinghamshire for permission to include a photograph of what used to be Edgar Wallace's house, Chalklands. Thanks also to Wheeler Winston Dixon and Sharla Clute of the SUNY Press and Mr Duff Hart-Davis for permissions. With grateful thanks to Reverend Michael Boultbee for permission to include his letter about his childhood recollections of Edgar Wallace, written in 1975.

I am grateful for the advice of Sir Rupert Mackeson and the Society of Authors.

I am indebted to the British Library, British Newspaper Archive, Jonathan Horne (special collections) at the University of Leeds, and the special collections at the University of Sussex and Oxfordshire Library services.

INTRODUCTION

Truth is stranger than fiction, and has need to be, since most fiction is founded on truth.

Edgar Wallace, *The Man Who Knew*, 1919

It is one of the most famous scenes in motion picture history. A gigantic ape, roaring defiantly, stands at the top of the Empire State Building and is attacked from all sides by fire from circling aeroplanes. *King Kong* caused a sensation when it first appeared on cinema screens in 1933, becoming the first film to open at the world's two largest theatres – the Radio City Music Hall, and the Roxy, in New York – simultaneously. 'The Strangest Story Ever Conceived by Man ... the greatest film the world will ever see,' the publicity declared. 'For once the catch-lines were right,' wrote film historian Denis Gifford, 'in the history of horror movies, indeed of movies, *King Kong* still towers above them all.'[1]

More than eighty years on, the story of how the eponymous gorilla is captured on a remote island and taken to New York, where he escapes and causes havoc, still packs a punch. It's not just a thrilling adventure tale and horror story, but a romance too – a modern reworking of 'Beauty and the Beast' that never fails to touch our emotions. There have been two film remakes, in 1976 and 2005, and a new musical version opened in Melbourne, Australia, in 2013 to widespread critical acclaim. In 1991, the 1933 film was deemed to fit the criteria of being 'culturally, historically or aesthetically significant' by the US Library of Congress, and was selected for preservation in the National Film Registry. But, while almost everyone knows the story of *King Kong*, and its place in cinematic history is assured, what is less well known is the almost equally fantastic tale of his English co-creator, who tragically died in Hollywood at the moment of his greatest and most enduring success. Writing the screenplay for *Kong* was the last major piece of work for Edgar Wallace, a man who packed into his relatively short time on earth enough achievements and experiences to fill several lives over.

Wallace worked as a printer's assistant; a milk roundsman; a newspaper seller; a plasterer's labourer; a soldier; a ship's cook and captain's boy on a Grimsby fishing trawler; a boot and shoe shop assistant; a rubber factory worker; a newspaper reporter; a foreign correspondent; a racing tipster; a columnist; a special constable; and a film producer and director.

The illegitimate son of a travelling actress, who left school at the age of 12 with no formal qualifications, he was also, at one point, the most widely read author in the world. Wallace made his name writing fast-paced thrillers, detective stories and tales of adventure. He wrote more than 170 books, and his work was translated into more than thirty languages. More films were made from his books than those of any other twentieth-century writer. He was the publishing sensation of the 1920s – in one year in that decade, one out of every four fiction books bought in England was by Edgar Wallace. If that wasn't enough, he also wrote twenty-three plays, sixty-five sketches and almost 1,000 short stories. 'Wallace brought the art of popular entertainment to a pitch which never before had been achieved by any other writer,' wrote his 1938 biographer, Margaret Lane.[2]

Edgar Wallace's work was devoured by people of all classes, nationalities and political persuasions. Among his millions of fans were King George V, British Prime Minister Stanley Baldwin, a president of the United States, and a certain Adolf Hitler who, it is said, owned copies of all of Wallace's books.

The man born in poverty in south-east London, and whose mother gave him away to foster parents when he was just over a week old, became one of the biggest celebrities in Britain in the first third of the twentieth century.

He cut a flamboyant figure, chain-smoking cigarettes from his trademark 10in-long cigarette holder and being chauffeur-driven round London in a yellow Rolls-Royce. Wallace worked hard and played hard and was renowned not just for his industry but for his incredible generosity which knew no bounds. It was this open-handedness which meant that, despite his high income, Wallace died heavily in debt. However, he wouldn't have minded too much as he was a man with big ambitions who did everything on a grand scale. The covers of his books often carried the proud boast of the publisher: 'It is impossible not to be thrilled by Edgar Wallace.' As I hope to prove, it is also impossible not to be thrilled – and inspired – by Edgar Wallace's extraordinary life story.

1

A BIRTH IN GREENWICH

He lived for some extraordinary reason in Greenwich, in a side street that runs parallel with the river.

Edgar Wallace, *The Twister*, 1928

The year 1875 was one of the most eventful of the Victorian era. It was the year that Britain acquired a majority interest in the Suez Canal, Captain Webb became the first person to swim the Channel, William Gladstone resigned as Liberal Party leader and Gilbert & Sullivan's earliest surviving opera, *Trial by Jury*, was premiered. Although life was still harsh for most people, things were improving – at least for those living in towns and cities.

Among the important pieces of legislation passed that year by Benjamin Disraeli's reforming ministry was the Artisans' Dwelling Act which enabled local authorities to purchase and demolish slums and insanitary property; and a ground-breaking Public Health Act which compelled local authorities to ensure adequate drainage and sewage disposal, and to collect refuse on a regular basis. Later in 1875, another sign of progress – Joseph Bazalgette completed his thirty-year construction of London's sewers.

If we could magically go back in a time machine to the London of 1875, we'd no doubt marvel at the 'new' big thing in transport – horse-drawn trams on rails, which since 1870 had been challenging the supremacy of the horse bus. We'd also be curious to see lamplighters, carrying long poles with wicks at the end to light the gas lamps which lit the city's streets, and 'public disinfectors' clad in white coats, dragging handcarts into which they would put contaminated clothing and other materials.

We'd be surprised at just how lively street life was compared to today, with the thoroughfares full of hawkers selling everything from fresh strawberries and jellied eels to medicines. If we fancied some entertainment, we'd have no shortage of options – in 1875 there were no fewer than 375 music halls in Greater London.

Some things from the modern world we would recognise. For example, in 1875 the London Underground, the oldest such railway in the world, was already 12 years old, although the Metropolitan and District lines are the only ones we would know today.

In 1875, London was, of course, not only the capital of Britain but the centre of a vast empire, which would continue to expand over the next half-century. It was into this great imperial metropolis, at No. 7 Ashburnham Grove, in an unremarkable street of terrace houses in Greenwich, that the subject of our story was born on Thursday, 1 April 1875.

The boy was born out of wedlock. His mother was Polly Richards, a kind-hearted travelling actress, and his father, Richard Horatio Edgar, was an actor and the son of Miss Marriott, the manageress of the theatre company for which Polly worked, and was already betrothed to another. Miss Marriot did not know of her son's affair, putting Polly in a bind. Due to rejoin her theatre company in Yorkshire on 10 April, without the means to bring up the child herself, and determined to keep the identity of the boy's father a secret, she had no option but to look for foster parents for her child. So it was that just a few days after his birth, the baby boy, wrapped in a white shawl, was taken from No. 7 Ashburnham Grove to his new parents, a fish porter and his wife who lived a few blocks away.

What odds would have been given that the child, born in such unpromising circumstances, would become the most-read author in the world, that this illegitimate son of a poor travelling actress would one day enjoy fabulous wealth, own a yellow Rolls-Royce and a string of racehorses, would know and hobknob with peers of the realm, and would entertain his guests lavishly at his own private box at Royal Ascot?

The phrase 'rags to riches' tends to be overused, but the story of Edgar Wallace is, in many ways, the ultimate rags-to-riches tale.

2

THE STORY OF POLLY RICHARDS

Holbrook had no illusions about the theatrical profession; he knew something of their lives, knew something of their terrific struggle for existence which went on all the time, except for a few favourites of the public …

Edgar Wallace, *The Hand of Power*, 1927

Polly Richards, Edgar Wallace's mother, was literally a woman of many parts. She was born Mary Jane Blair, in White Street, in the St Thomas sub-district of Liverpool in March 1843. Her father was James Blair, whose occupation was recorded as 'mariner' on her birth certificate, and her mother, Charlotte Blair, nee Duffye.

Polly worked as a small-part actress and dancer, and in 1867 married a merchant service skipper named Captain Richards. But the marriage was ill-fated, and in January 1868, on his first voyage after his marriage, Captain Richards became ill and died, leaving Polly a widow and eight months pregnant at the age of 24. Polly had no option but to return to the stage (she changed her first name to 'Marie'), but life was a terrible struggle. 'How she weathered those first years of widowhood, living precariously on the fringes of the theatre, depositing her baby first with one lodging house keeper and then another while she worked, one can only guess; but with no beauty and no outstanding talent to recommend her she must have had a tedious and embittering struggle,' suggests Margaret Lane, Edgar's biographer.[1]

Nietzsche's adage that 'that which does not kill us makes us stronger' comes to mind when we consider how Polly got through those years. She did survive; showing the same sort of perseverance demonstrated by her celebrated son whenever he met with what looked like insurmountable setbacks.

Polly's lucky break came in 1872, when she met her saviour, the remarkable Alice Marriott, one of the mid-Victorian era's best known Shakespearean actresses, and owner of a travelling theatre company. At the time Polly, in the words of Margaret Lane, 'had reached the lowest ebb of disillusion and poverty, and was almost starving'.[2] Aged 29, she was living with her child,

Josephine, as a lodger in a cottage behind a public house which was next door to the Theatre Royal in Williamson Square, Liverpool. Miss Marriott and her company had come to play at the Theatre Royal which, in 1872, was celebrating its centenary. We don't know the exact circumstances of the meeting between Marriott and Polly, but we do know that the kindly older woman took pity on the out-of-work and out-of-luck actress, and took her to her own lodgings and offered her work in her own company. Polly acted small parts in plays and also worked as a dresser.

There was, of course, the problem of what was to become of Polly's little girl, Josephine, who was aged just 6 years. Miss Marriott suggested that she be put into the Sailors' Infant Orphan Asylum in Snaresbrook and, when a vacancy occurred there, 'Joey' was duly sent off. Unsurprisingly, she was unhappy in her new environment and went on a hunger strike, causing great alarm to the orphanage authorities, who wrote to Polly requesting that she remove her child. Polly went to the orphanage by train and brought Joey back. Now, it wasn't just Polly Richards who became part of Miss Marriott's company, but her daughter too, and they both proved popular additions to the troupe. Lane quoted the testimony of Adeline, one of Miss Marriott's two grown-up daughters, who told how the new recruit, 'for all her sardonic reserve of manner, somehow contrived to be the life and soul of dressing-room parties, keeping them all in a roar with funny and improbable stories which she told with a disarming air of gravity and truth, watching her audience from under heavy eyelids, her face impassive.'[3] It was later said of Polly's son that he was the best raconteur in London, another quality he seems to have inherited from his mother.

The other two members of the Marriott company requiring mention are her husband, Robert Edgar, and her son, Richard Horatio Edgar. Like many husbands of strong, determined women, Robert Edgar seems to have been something of a waster. Given the formal title of 'manager', he blew much of the money his wife had earned on foolish financial speculations; thereby preventing his spouse from living out her final years in the comfortable retirement her hard work and her talent deserved.

Richard Edgar was handsome and charming; a talented actor in comedy roles, but also rather lazy and something of a lothario. His devoted mother was keen for her son to settle down, and decided to use Polly as a match-maker. In the autumn of 1873, Polly presented a pretty young actress called Jenny Taylor, whom she had befriended on a trip to Scotland. Jenny passed Miss Marriott and her son's seal of approval and was taken on as member of the company. The script should have continued with Richard Edgar and Jenny getting engaged, marrying and living happily ever after but, if that had happened, we would have no story. Richard and Jenny *did* get engaged and *did* get married[4] but, before that, something else happened. The circumstances are unclear, but what we do know is that sometime in the spring or early summer of 1874 Richard Edgar had a sexual encounter with Polly Richards. So that, at the very time that Richard and her friend Jenny were announcing their engagement, Polly found herself pregnant – with the child of her patron's son.

It is easy for us to imagine what might have been going on in Polly's mind at this moment. She could tell Miss Marriott everything about the child and who the father was, but that would surely have sabotaged the wedding between Richard and Jenny. She might also have invoked the ire of Miss Marriott, even though that kindly woman would probably have shown her forgiveness. Polly decided the wisest course of action was to keep schtum, even though that would almost certainly mean her having to discard her child after it was born.

At Christmas, she absented herself from the company and took lodgings in Greenwich. Heavily pregnant, she not unsurprisingly failed to attend Richard and Jenny's wedding, which took place in late March. Just a week after his marriage on 1 April 1875, Richard's son, and the subject of our story, was born. Polly and Richard's little boy was baptised by a curate named V.P. Hobson in St Alfeges Church, Greenwich, on 11 April. He was given the name 'Richard Horatio Edgar Wallace' with Walter Wallace, comedian, recorded as his father and 'Mary Jane Wallace' as his mother.

So, who was Walter Wallace? 'No amount of research has yielded a clue to the mysterious "Walter Wallace, comedian" in the Greenwich Register, and it is more than probable that he never existed,' wrote Margaret Lane,[5] who noted that no one still living at the time of writing her book (1938), and who was associated with the Greenwich Theatre or Polly Richards, could remember such a person. Today, we have computer technology and websites like FreeBMD[6] to help us search for people born after 1837.

Records show that ten people named simply 'Walter Wallace' were born between June 1838 and December 1854, with a further five having their second names given. It is perfectly possible that Polly Richards could have come across one of these 'Walter Wallaces' in her life and decided to make him the father of her child, but the likeliest explanation is that she simply made the name up, giving her son a fictitious father who could never be traced.

Having had her child baptised, Polly now had to place him with foster parents. Lane tells us that Polly's midwife had recommended a fish porter and his wife, George and Clara Freeman, who had already brought up ten children of their own and who lived about a mile away in a four-roomed cottage in Norway Court, Deptford. Lane tells us that Polly went round to 'interview' Clara Freeman. 'The cottage, though overcrowded, was spotlessly clean, and Polly was received in a dark but proudly kept front parlour with plants in the window and a fringed cloth on the table.'[7] Payment of 5s a week for the child's upkeep was agreed, and the deal was done.

In Edgar Wallace's own version, though, it was the Freemans who made the first move:

> Happily, there was a philanthropist who heard of my plight, and having for the workhouse the loathing which is the proper possession of the proud poor, he dispatched Clara to fetch me. 'She's adopted', said Mr Freeman, an autocrat in his way. Nor when he discovered that he had been mistaken as to my sex did he vary his humane decision.[8]

Why is there a discrepancy between the accounts of Margaret Lane and Wallace, on how he came to be adopted? It is revealing that Wallace's mother gets no mention at all in his autobiography, written in 1926, and it is likely that he still felt hurt over her actions. For Wallace, it was the Freemans who came to the rescue of a discarded child, while from Lane's point of view, Polly Richards comes over as dutiful for making sure her son had a good home.

Whatever the precise steps were, after the agreement was made between Polly and the Freemans, Milly, one of the Freeman children, visited Ashburnham Grove the following morning to take little Richard Horatio Edgar Wallace away to his new home. What Polly must have felt at bidding farewell to her baby we can only imagine, but she had little time to feel sorry for herself as she desperately needed to earn money. She left Greenwich for Huddersfield to rejoin Miss Marriott's company, playing at the Theatre Royal.

3

A DOCKLANDS CHILDHOOD

Somewhere in the east the sun was rising, but the skies were dark and thick; lamps burnt on river and shore. Billingsgate Market was radiant with light, and over the wharves where cargo-boats were at anchor white arc lights stared like stars.

Edgar Wallace, *The India Rubber Men*, 1929

Clara Freeman and her husband welcomed the new addition to their family with 'the total generosity of the very poor', to use the memorable phrase of the journalist James Cameron, the writer and presenter of a BBC documentary on Edgar Wallace which was broadcast in 1976.[1]

George Freeman was a strict but kindly man who worked as a fish porter in Billingsgate Market, to where he would head at three o'clock every morning, come rain or shine. He was not only a Freeman by name, but also a 'freeman of the City of London', a liveryman of the Haberdashers' company, who proudly claimed that he could trace his ancestry back through 500 years of city records. He was certainly a respected local figure. 'He never did a crooked thing in his life … He lived a Christian life, was just to all men, fearless – he could not lie', Wallace later wrote of his adopted father.

A photograph of Mr Freeman with his bowler hat, waistcoat and overcoat, cravat and goatee beard confirms the impression of a decent, serious man – the very model of Victorian propriety. Occasionally though, this devout paragon would let his hair down. 'He used to "break out" about twice a year and drink brandy,' Wallace recalled, 'then was the Testament laid reverently aside, and he would fight any man of any size and beat him. Once he fought for two hours, perilously, on the edge of a deep cutting.'

His wife, Clara, who bore him ten children, was described by Wallace as 'the gentlest mother who ever lived.' The photograph (Plate No. 3) of her shows a shortish woman with a serious but kindly face, dressed in a bonnet and mantle. Someone who, like her husband, could no doubt be strict when the need arose but, like George, had a heart of gold.

Dick Freeman – the name his foster parents gave him – was surrounded by warmth and affection in his new home, but his time at the Freemans' could have come to a relatively early end when he was just 2 years old. Polly came to visit, to see her child, and returned again not long afterwards. It was during this second visit that she told Mrs Freeman that she could no longer afford to pay Dick's keep and so had made arrangements for her son to be 'taken in somewhere'. The prospect of her beloved foster child going to an orphanage appalled Mrs Freeman, and her daughter Clara, who was present at the meeting, and they offered to formally adopt the child. So it was that little Dick Freeman became an official member of the family.

Polly still kept visiting Dick frequently throughout his childhood, according to her granddaughter, Grace Fairless: 'I heard from her own lips that he had been taken by her to see his sister [Josephine] at school, and [s]he told me how he had looked up to her and thought how sweet she was because she had given him sixpence for himself.'[2]

Of the Freeman children, it was Clara who became Dick's closest ally. Like her sisters, Clara had been sent off at the age of 12 into domestic service – the standard fate which befell girls of her class at that time. Margaret Lane surmises that Clara championed the cause of her little brother because she had so little youth of her own and 'saw in the adopted boy possibilities of a richer and more promising life than she would ever know.'[3] Clara would renew her friendship with Dick when she returned to her parental home during intervals between jobs. They would go for walks together by the river and explore the environs.

Although Norway Court and the surrounding area was far from salubrious, it was nevertheless an interesting place for a young boy to grow up. 'Greenwich had a maritime flavour in those days. It was a town of blue-jerseyed men, and in every other house in our neighbourhood was the model of a full-rigged ship,' Wallace recalled. 'That riverside landscape was the first he [Wallace] ever knew', wrote James Cameron, 'Exploring the grey edges of the Thames, the tidal river where the ships still came. All the wharves and alleys and by-ways of Deptford and Bermondsey, all the waterfront smells of spice and sail cloths – that was the background of life – sombrely exciting.'

Billingsgate fish market[4] where his foster father worked as a fish porter[5] played an important part in Wallace's early life. When he was old enough, Dick would sometimes accompany Mr Freeman to work. 'How those men worked!' he recalled, 'Their hobnailed boots rattling over the slippery pavement of the market – along the planks that spanned between wharf and GIC boats that lay alongside.' Dick would stand and watch at the quayside as the boats unloaded their catches: 'Ice-rimed boats from Grimsby, tubby eel boats from Holland, big ship and little ship. "Collectors" that had come rolling from the Dogger Bank with their holds packed with silvery fish that was officially "alive".'

It was this colourful, bustling, Thameside world, with ships sailing to and from exotic parts of the world and its warehouses laden with tea and spices and sailors singing shanties in bars, which arguably first fired Dick Freeman's imagination and his lifelong love of adventure. Growing up in London's docklands not only gave him a taste for travel, it also started his enduring fascination with crime. 'My first vivid recollection in life is one of a sort of possessive pride in prison vans. The gloomy Black Maria that rumbled up the Greenwich Road every afternoon,' he wrote.

The Freeman sons were often in trouble with the police – which wasn't hard in those days, when the working classes didn't have to do too much to feel the long arm of the law. 'All his life he hated policemen and he had a passion for fighting them,' Wallace said of his step-brother Harry. When he was 10, Dick was involved in criminal activity for the first time and he became an associate member of a gang of burglars. 'I never took part in any of the raids carried out by a desperado very little older than myself, but I received a little of the loot and regretted it was not more useful,' he confessed many years later.

Afterwards, though, he found himself on the right side of the law. He was approached by a man who asked Dick to buy cigarettes for him, a penny's worth at a time. He gave Dick 'nice new florins'. Dick took one of the florins to a policeman, and asked him if the money was 'snide' i.e. counterfeit. The policeman broke the coin with his finger and thumb and pronounced it snide. The cigarette buyer was arrested, and the magistrate duly praised Dick, saying he was a smart little boy. The incident led to a historic first, as the *News of the World* report of the crime was the first of many times that Dick Freeman was to see his name in print. The little boy who would one day be a Fleet Street legend, under the name of 'Edgar Wallace', had made his newspaper debut.

After the young Dick Freeman had attended infant classes, at St Peter's Infant School in Thames Street, the Freemans moved from Norway Court to Camberwell. For Dick, that meant going to Reddin's Road Board School. Primary education had only been established on a national basis by the Education Act of 1870, passed by the Liberal government of William Gladstone. The Act established 'School Boards' which were empowered to provide schools paid for out of the local rates in areas where there was inadequate provision. Although the Act had its critics, there's no doubting the impact it made. We see this dramatic transformation with Edgar Wallace's own family – he went on to become a great writer, while neither of his beloved foster parents could write.

Not that Dick greatly appreciated the effects of the 1870 Education Act at the time, 'Every morning when I turned the corner of Reddin's Road, Peckham, and saw the board school still standing where it did, I was filled with a helpless sense of disappointment,' he wrote. The 'big yellow barracks of a place' was, for Wallace, and no doubt for other children too, a grim, uninviting place. '… and the fires that were never lit, and the evil blackboard where godlike teachers, whose calligraphy is still my envy, wrote words of fearful length. The drone of the classrooms, the humourless lessons, the agonies of mental arithmetic and the seeming impossibilities of the written variety.'

It was common for there to be as a many as fifty children in one class, and the building itself was gradually sinking, having been built – so the story went – on an old rubbish tip. It was all a far cry from the modern schools of today with their computers and comfortable centrally-heated classrooms, but, as much as the young Dick Freeman hated his board school days, there were positives too. He learnt to write his name, to the great pride of his father. 'George gave me a penny and carried the scrawl to the market for the admiration of his friends,' he recalled.

And not all lessons were to be dreaded. The brightest school day of all for Dick was when a teacher named Mr Newton read out stories from *The Arabian Nights* to the class:

> The colour of the beauty of the East stole through the foggy windows of Reddin's Road School. Here was a magic carpet indeed that transported forty none too cleanly little boys into the palace of the Caliphs, through the spicy bazaars of Bagdad, hand in hand, with the king of kings.

Wallace was not the only writer to be inspired by *The Arabian Nights*; others include Sir Arthur Conan Doyle, Tolstoy, Alexander Dumas, Wilkie Collins and many romantic poets.

It was also at board school that Dick was first introduced to the works of William Shakespeare, starting a lifelong love affair with the works of 'The Bard of Avon'. 'I learnt whole scenes of *Macbeth* and *Julius Caesar* and *Hamlet* and could recite them with gusto on every, and any, excuse.'

It was clear to George and Clara that young Dick Freeman had a talent worth nurturing. Their other children had left school at 10, but the Freemans agreed to Dick staying on until he was 12. Once again, this demonstrated their kind-heartedness as it meant they would have to wait another two years before their foster son brought a wage in to the household.

Not that Dick wasn't kept busy outside of the classroom. He helped his parents out as much as he could, and did most of the shopping. 'Up before breakfast, and with a mat bag ranging the Old Kent Road for the day's provisions … A pound of sixpenny "pieces" from Mills the butcher, two penn'orth of potatoes from the greengrocer's, a parsnip and a penn'orth of carrots – I came to have a violent antipathy to Irish stew,' he recalled. After he'd done the shopping, it was time to head off for school.

In the second chapter of his autobiography, Wallace lists what he learnt at board school. It's an interesting historical document, as it shows us the sort of things that a working-class child in Britain would have been learning in the 1880s:

Geography: Roughly, the shape of England; nothing about the United States, nothing about the railway systems of Europe. I learnt that China had two great rivers, the Yangtze-kiang and Hoangho, but which is which I can't remember. I knew the shape of Africa and that it was an easy map to draw. I knew nothing about France except Paris was on the Seine. I knew the shape of Italy was like a top-booted leg, and that India was in the shape of a pear; but except that there had been a mutiny in that country, it was terra incognita to me.

History: The ancient Britons smeared themselves with woad and paddled round in basket-shaped boats. William the Conqueror came to England in 1066. Henry VIII had seven – or was it eight? – wives. King Charles was executed for some obscure reason, and at a vague period of English history there was a War of the Roses.

Chemistry: If you put a piece of heated wire in oxygen – or was it hydrogen – it glowed very brightly. If you blow a straw into lime water, the water becomes cloudy.

Religion: No more than I learnt at Sunday school.

Drawing: Hours of hard work I made an attempt to acquire proficiency in an art for which I had no aptitude.

Arithmetic: As far as decimals. In those days book-keeping was not learnt at school. You might say that all the knowledge I acquired from my lessons in arithmetic was the ability to tot columns of figures with great rapidity.

Wallace then gave his general reflections on a board school education:

I think I would undertake to teach in a month more geography than I learnt in six years.

… the system is as wrong as it can well be, and hour after hour of time is wasted in inculcating into a class of fifty, knowledge which is of no interest whatever except to possibly two or three.

It's important to note that board school was not the only 'school' which Dick attended at this time. There was also Sunday school[6] where children not only learnt stories from the Bible, but played games, acted in plays, sang songs and generally had a very enjoyable time. It was at Sunday school that Wallace learnt the story of 'Christie's Old Organ'. 'The moral of the story was that one ought to be kind to people less fortunate than oneself,' he later recalled. It certainly made a big impact on Dick – someone who, when he grew up, would become renowned for his generosity. 'The complex introduced into my mental system by "Christie's Old Organ" has cost me thousands of pounds,' he ruefully reflected, 'I have often wished I had begun my course of reading with "Jack Sheppard".'

Wallace, throughout his life, was never religious, yet he enjoyed the more relaxed atmosphere at Sunday school far more than his days at Reddin's Road. Every year there was the annual excursion, where the children who were regular scholars would get a day out in the country – including food – for sixpence. Dick loved these trips, so he decided to get on as many of them as he could. One became a 'regular' scholar by being on the books of a Sunday school for one month, so Dick, with characteristic resourcefulness, set out to enrol in as many different Sunday schools as he could. 'In the course of the years I worked almost every Sunday school in the neighbourhood,' he recalled.

As deficient as was the education which Dick Freeman – and other working-class children of his generation – received in the 1880s, the combination of Sunday school and board school was still a marked improvement on what had gone before. In the thirty years' existence of the school boards, some 2.5 million new places in new buildings were provided. Let's suppose that the 1870 Education Act had not been passed, and that a nationwide system of elementary education had not come into effect for, say, another twenty years – then the phenomenon of Edgar Wallace, the illegitimate working-class son of a travelling actress, who rose to become the most widely read author of the world, would simply not have happened.

Before Wallace, one can think of no prolific writer who came from his social background. He was the trailblazer for a class of people who, for centuries, had no voice. They had stories to tell, stories at least as interesting as the upper or middle classes, but they were unable to write them down. W.E. Forster's Act did not go far enough – we had to wait until 1902 before local education authorities were empowered to provide secondary schools – but it did at least ensure that a whole new generation of working-class children learned to read and write, and had exposure to classic literature. In *The Naval Treaty*, by Sir Arthur Conan Doyle, Sherlock Holmes is travelling with Dr Watson on a train going past Clapham Junction, 'Look at those big, isolated clumps of buildings rising up above the slates, like brick islands in a lead-coloured sea.' Holmes declares. 'The Board schools', Dr Watson replies. 'Lighthouses, my boy! Beacons of the future!' exclaims Holmes, 'Capsules with hundreds of bright little seeds in each, out of which will spring the wiser better England of the future.'

As we have seen, Dick Freeman's working career began while he was still at school, running early morning errands for his parents. In the summer holidays of 1886, when he was 11, he embarked on another job – selling newspapers at Ludgate Circus. He didn't tell his parents. He sold copies – on a sale or return basis – of *The Echo*, which he described as 'a bilious-looking sheet that was remarkable for its high moral tone and the accuracy of its tips.' His pitch was outside Cook's Travel Agency, very close to the wall which today carries a bronze plaque to his memory. He later wrote:

> It was an enthralling experience. I stood in the very centre of London. Past me rumbled the horse buses, the drays and wagons of the great metropolis. I saw great men, pointed out to me by a queer old gentleman in a frowsy overcoat and top hat who haunted Ludgate Circus. Sala – Mr Lawson, who owned the Telegraph ... Henry Irving driving in a hansom cab with a beautiful lady called Ellen Terry (they were coming from St Paul's). I was very happy and grateful that I had the opportunity of seeing such people.

Dick loved his job, but he still had one more year of school to go. So, whenever he could, he played truant in the afternoons when the new school term began and made his way up to Ludgate Circus. Selling newspapers in the winter was not as much fun as in the summer, trade was slack and there was the cold to deal with too. Always the great improviser, Dick found a novel method of keeping warm. As he stamped his feet he would recite the quarrel scene from *Julius Caesar*. What, I wonder, would the purchasers of the *Echo* have thought of the young lad, quoting word for word from the works of William Shakespeare?

Dick's earnings averaged about 3s a week – which he spent on ginger beer, toffees and the theatre. But he got from the experience far more than that. Selling newspapers had kindled in him a love for newsprint – and for the sights and sounds of Fleet Street. In a little café, close to the Glengall Arms where Mr Freeman would go drinking, Dick would indulge in his love of the written word with the proprietress, a young woman called Mrs Anstee, who shared his passion for books and newspapers. They would read out loud to each other – and formed quite a bond.

Today, a friendship between a 12-year-old boy and a young married woman, brought together by their love of reading, might seem rather strange, but this was the 1880s, an age where reading for pleasure – and for self-improvement – was becoming hugely popular.

Margaret Lane records that when the Free Library in the Old Kent Road opened, Wallace would carry round the books he'd borrowed, 'selected at random from the library catalogue', to show to Mrs Anstee.[7] He did the same with the second-hand books he bought. Mrs Anstee cut an attractive figure, and was a big influence on Dick. 'She was the best and most stimulating companion possible for a child aching for something to try his wits upon, and with no one, beside herself, to encourage his eccentric appetite for reading', says Lane.[8]

Going to Mrs Anstee's shop also brought Dick closer to the world of the theatre. Her husband, Fred, was a part-time scene-shifter at the Gaiety Theatre in the Strand. Dick would sometimes go to work with him to run errands and do odd jobs. His love of the theatre was so great that he would do anything just to be inside the building. Mr Anstee was also able, sometimes, to get complimentary tickets to shows, and so Dick was able to go and watch performances from the gallery with Mrs Anstee. It wasn't the only source of free tickets, sometimes he'd get them from Polly Richards too, and when the tickets arrived he'd go off to watch shows with Mrs Freeman, who was just as excited as he was. Even when there were no free tickets going, Dick would still save up and use any money he had to indulge his passion.

Queen Victoria's Golden Jubilee was celebrated in 1887, and there was a special treat from Her Majesty for the board school children – a day off school to enjoy the occasion. 'I went to Hyde Park labelled, drank sweet lemonade, cheered the wrong lady in the royal procession, and was awarded a jubilee mug shaped like a truncated cone.' Wallace recalled, 'I won three others in the train home by tossing, but I had to surrender them to the enraged parents who were waiting at Peckham Rye to welcome the adventurers home.'

With his school days coming to an end and the world of full-time work looming, George and Clara Freeman decided to give their adopted son a holiday. Again, this shows their wonderfully generous nature. Neither the Freemans nor their children had ever had a holiday in their lives – but this didn't stop them wanting Dick to enjoy things they had done without. A nephew of George Freeman's – a certain Mr Frisby – had moved to Dewsbury in Yorkshire, where he had a confectionary store. He came back down to London with his daughter, Lizzie, who was appearing at a choir festival at the Crystal Palace, and paid a visit to the Freemans. Frisby took a shine to Dick and suggested that, when his schooling had finished, the boy go up to Dewsbury for a holiday.

For Dick, it was his first trip out of the capital. He spent a happy three weeks in the confectioner's shop – what a treat for a sweet-toothed boy of 12! – and enjoyed playing with the Frisbys' seven daughters. He was also taken down a coal mine – Combs Pit – another big adventure. The Frisbys were sorry to see Dick go, and Dick himself was sad to return to London, having found West Yorkshire a very exciting place indeed. But now, after his summer holiday, it was time for him to enter the world of work in earnest.

4

THE UNIVERSITY OF LIFE

Of his life in London as a boy little is known. He worked, that is certain. But he was never more than two or three months in any one job. I have traced him to printers, shoemakers, and milk vendors. He seemed to be consumed with a spirit of restlessness which made the monotony of any form of employment maddening.

Edgar Wallace, *Eve's Island*, 1926

Before Dick began work, he had to secure a copy of his birth certificate to show to his employers. Freeman was now 'Richard Horatio Edgar Wallace' and he took great pride in writing his new name.

His experiences as a newcomer in the labour market of late 1880s London tells us much about the grim working and employment conditions that ordinary people had to put up with 130 years ago, in what was the richest country in the world. Dick's first full-time job was working in a printing factory, which made paper bags, in Newington Causeway. He was paid 5s a week, but during the first three weeks of his employment, 5s was deducted from his wages as a guarantee that he would not leave without giving due notice.

The work itself involved Dick standing by a lithographic machine from eight o'clock in the morning until five o'clock at night, taking off the paper bags as they were printed. Although he wore a black apron, his face still grew black as the day progressed. When bags with gold lettering were printed, he would come home with 'gold' dust on his boots.

One day Dick failed to turn up for work. When he came the next day he was paid the money owing to him and shown the door. The company refused to return to him the 5s deposit. Most young men, faced with this ending to their first job, would have been cowed and accepted their 'punishment' without too much argument, but Dick – to his credit – was having none of it. He reported the matter to the first policeman he met – 'a fat man with cheeks that overhung his neck' – and the sympathetic law enforcer told him that the company was in the wrong. 'They've got no right to keep your money and you can't sign anything away because you're a minor,' PC Harry Curtis-Bennett declared. Wallace told the policeman that he was indeed 12 on his last birthday, but notwithstanding the new information, he was advised to take out a summons. Wallace went to the magistrates' court, told them about his case and then took out a summons – which cost him 1s – against his former employer. He conducted his own case in court, won the lawsuit – and got back his 5s.

This incident is revealing, since it shows to us once again the extraordinary self-confidence that Dick possessed. How many 12-year-old working-class boys would have had the courage to take their former employer to court, and to conduct the case themselves? Throughout his life, whether as Dick Freeman or Edgar Wallace, he refused to be intimidated or depressed by any obstacles or setbacks – on the contrary, he saw them as challenges to be overcome.

His experience in court also cemented his belief that, however unjust individual employers might be, the British justice system was essentially a fair one. We have already seen that he was praised as a smart little boy by a magistrate in the case of the snide florins, now here he was winning a court case all on his own. His experience also strengthened his positive view of the police force. 'I have always had a blind faith in the police,' he wrote, when recalling the incident. When Dick left the courtroom having won his case, a policeman with a broken nose approached him and asked if he had used to be called Freeman. Dick admitted that he had. 'Your brother Harry done that,' the policeman declared, pointing to his broken nose; but there were no hard feelings – Dick and the policeman went to have a cup of tea together in a café, and the latter paid.

Dick next found another job as a printer's boy – this time with a company called Riddle and Couchman's. This one he enjoyed rather more than his first job. 'I was in the paper store and it was very interesting,' he wrote. 'Have you seen electric sparks come from between two sheets of paper after they have been hauled under a hydraulic press? Did you know that you could cut your finger to the bone on the sharp edge of paper?' he asked the readers of his autobiography.

Again, though, the job didn't last long. There were strikes, and all the boys – except Dick – walked out. That didn't go down too well with his fellow workers, and Dick made a 'dramatic exit' from his workplace by way of the paper chute. 'The boys were enthusiastic but I was out of work.' Undaunted, he got another job with a printers. This one lasted for all of two weeks. The company in question printed railway timetables, and Dick had to carry large parcels of railway printing to various offices. Unsurprisingly, he didn't feel that he had found his life's vocation. When he left this job, Wallace decided to go back to his 'old love' – selling newspapers. 'W.H. Smith provided me with a peaked cap, and on the wind-swept railway platform at Ludgate Hill and St Paul's I promoted the sale of newspapers in a perfectly respectable manner.'

But this was a tough assignment too – there could have been few colder spots in the whole of London than where Dick had his pitch. It wasn't long before he swapped the job for one working in a cheap boot and shoe shop in Peckham, which at least had the benefit of being indoors. Dick's main responsibility was to mark the soles of new shoes with their selling prices, he wrote:

> It was one of those multiple shops with branches in various poor districts. On Saturday nights you could earn an extra shilling by attaching yourself to one of the branches. In a clean, white apron, I sold tins of blacking to the ladies of Peckham, and tins of dubbin to the horny-handed male saunterers. I drew attention to delightful slippers for women, and hooked down dangling hob-nailed boots for the inspection of hardier citizens.

Although the job was a reasonably secure one, and not as physically arduous as ones which had preceded it, Dick soon grew bored of it. He handed in his notice and got a job working as a 'hand' in a rubber factory in Camberwell. 'I, who had started life as a furtive seller of newspapers, had found my proper place in the industrial scheme.' The job involved making mackintosh cloth. The hours were long, but it was an educational experience for Dick to say the least:

> At the rubber works was a bitter man who taught me something. He was bitter about everything – his home, his work, the beef sandwiches his wife packed for him, my incompetence (I was his assistant), his grinding employer. I sat down one morning in the breakfast hour and puzzled through, without assistance, to the genesis of bitterness. I was so full of my unaided discovery that I fell upon him the moment he came in from the yard. 'You're sorry for yourself', I said, with the air of a savant revealing a great discovery. He was carrying a great roll of damask and hit me over the head with it. Thus I learnt two things: never to be sorry for yourself; never to tell people unpalatable truths unless you are in a position to hit them back.

Dick also learnt how to get drunk on the cheap at the factory. 'Rubber was dissolved in naphtha. By leaning over the vat in which the process was in operation and breathing in the naphtha fumes, it was possible to get pleasantly and even hilariously intoxicated,' he explained. But there was a downside too, 'You could also get dead. I had many a pleasant jag until one day it made me very sick.'

It was while working at the Camberwell rubber factory that Dick tried his hand at writing poetry for the first time. He composed rhymed couplets, poking fun at his self-pitying boss. Unsurprisingly, it didn't go down too well and another job ended. It was back to shoes again – this time making boot heels by pasting scraps of leather together in a mould. But, while work was a large part of his life, it was not the only part. Whenever he had any spare time, he would indulge his love of reading. 'When I left school I continued my reading education with the aid of penny dreadfuls and very wholesome and moral stories they were,' he recalled in a 1926 article entitled 'The University of Life':[1]

> There was a series called 'Handsome Harry' and another called 'Jack Harkaway'; both made me hungrier for further conquests of the written word. I read everything that Henty wrote. Ballantyne was another potent influence, notably 'The Young Fur Traders.' Then I came upon Jules Verne, to have my imagination stimulated by 'The Clipper in the Clouds.' Those writers did more for the past two generations than many a man who has had monuments put up to him since.

There were other activities too to keep him fully occupied. The temperance movement's aim was to rid the scourge of alcoholism from working-class communities by encouraging people to take the 'pledge' to abstain from drinking the 'Demon Run' and other noxious liquids. The movement was at its peak in the 1890s, and Dick, through his best friend Willie Ramsey – another printer's boy – was introduced to it. As Margaret Lane explains, there were solid reasons why the movement would have appealed to Dick:

> Dick himself in his younger days had spent hours, miserable and peevish, standing outside the swing doors of saloons, waiting for 'Father' to reappear and be steered home and his ears were filled with the moan of Mrs Freeman. Harry Hanford, Clara's milkman husband, alternated blithely between crusading teetotalism and passionate bouts of drink, and 'old Campbell,' the umbrella-maker across the road, could always be relied on to entertain the boy with hair-raising stories of eternal fires awaiting the drunkard.[2]

At the age of 15, Dick signed 'the pledge'. 'As I did not even know the taste of strong drink, I signed readily,' he wrote. In any case, Dick, with his wonderful imagination, positive mindset and unquenchable appetite for life, did not have the sort of character which seeks solace in alcohol. Life was exciting enough as it was – so why seek to be transported to another world by getting drunk? As we shall see later, he did become a man of addictions – smoking around eighty cigarettes a day, and drinking numerous cups of tea – but tobacco and caffeine were substances which kept him in the here and now, and didn't leave him with a sore head in the morning.

The Christ Church Bermondsey Temperance Society wasn't all about lecturing people about the evils of alcohol, there was a lighter side to it too. There were dances held in the winter and there were cricket and football teams attached to the society. Dick and Willie Ramsey spent their Saturday afternoons in both summer and winter playing for the teams. There were political meetings, and it was here that Dick – who just forty years later would be a Parliamentary Candidate himself – first experienced the rough and tumble of politics. Those who think politics is a dirty enough game today may be relieved to know that it was no less dirty in the 1880s. Dick and Willie were paid 1s a night to canvass for the local Rotherhithe Liberal and Radical Association, and part of their duties involved helping to break up any local Conservative meetings. Dick was to stay loyal to the Liberals all his life.

The Temperance Society wasn't Dick's only outside interest, he and Willie also enrolled in the local St John Ambulance Brigade. There, they learnt first aid and how to roll bandages and set splints. 'It was good enough fun at the time and something to do, but for Dick at least this amateur training was to prove important,' records Margaret Lane, 'several years later, bored with the heavy routine of army life, he was to remember his own deftness with splints and bandages and the flattering approval of the St John Ambulance instructor, and apply for a transfer that permanently affected his life.'[3]

One is impressed with the sense of purpose that Dick possessed, and the way he put every experience to good use. He was already gathering, consciously or not, material which he would use when it came to writing his stories. The real-life 'Kidbrooke Murder Case' could have been the spark that kindled Dick's interest in detective fiction. The grisly murder of a domestic servant, Jane Maria Clouson, took place four years before Dick had been born, but was still unsolved at the time he and his best pal Willie were keen to play 'detectives'. Clouson had been found by a policeman, having been badly beaten by a hammer in Kidbrooke Lane, Eltham, and had died five days later from her injuries. Her murder gripped the public's attention, and particularly those living in south-east London.

Clouson had lived in No. 12 Ashburnham Road, very close to where Dick had been born, so it was natural that he would take an interest in the case, and he and Willie set out to try to solve the mystery. Margaret Lane records:

While the hue and cry was on they went up on the Heath [Blackheath] after dark nearly every night, pretending to discover clues and hunt for the murderer, and taking care to keep prudently close to each other until it was time to go home to the Freemans' kitchen and the solid comforts of strong tea and a bloater.[4]

Although they didn't succeed in bringing the killer of Jane Maria Clouson to justice,[5] they did have plenty more adventures as they explored the back ways and dark alleys of London's docklands by night in search of excitement. Once, they pulled an old lady out of the water – *they* didn't know that she had wanted to commit suicide. They saw adventure and excitement in even the smallest incidents, even fights in bars, and Dick got into the habit of writing their adventures down in his exercise book. 'If I ever get the chance, I'm going to publish this,' he told Willie. If the two boys' night-time explorations didn't lead to real-life adventure, they would just use their imagination to add in the drama. 'The boys would concoct blood-curdling stories between them, and tramp across London Bridge as satisfied as though they had encountered Jack the Ripper,' writes Margaret Lane.[6]

Dick Freeman craved excitement, and his life can be seen as one big search for it. It was this desire to avoid a life of boredom and repetition which drove him on, more than a desire for money, or even fame, even though he knew that money and fame would enable him to lead a more interesting life. It was more or less inevitable, given Dick's love of adventure, that he would one day end up going off to sea, and it all started when he met a seaman in the gallery of a theatre.

Dick shared his toffee with the friendly sailor and, it seems, told him that he was bored with his lot, going from one dead-end job to another. If Dick wanted to make a clean break, then why not run off to sea, the sailor suggested? He could get him a job on a Grimsby trawler. The only snag was that one of Dick's parents would have to give written permission, since he was only 15. Consent was unlikely to be given, and Dick knew that if he told his parents of his plans they would forbid him to go. The problem, though, was not insurmountable. Dick simply forged his foster father's signature, told his foster mother that he'd got a new job 'out of London' and set off to meet his sailor friend.

He had signed on for a year as a ship's cook and captain's boy on the biggest trawler of the fleet of the Hewitt Fishing Company, in Grimsby. His excitement about his new life soon evaporated as the boat set sail. It was December, and the weather was bitterly cold. 'A gale blew us out and a gale blew us home, and in between whiles it blew an intermittent blizzard. The yards were frozen stiff. The fish were solid as they shovelled them into the hold,' Wallace later remembered. His cooking efforts were not greatly appreciated: 'I was cuffed by the captain and the mate for my deficiencies as a chef.' He also was cuffed by the rest of the superstitious crew for bringing a paper of pins on board – 'an unpardonable crime on a fishing boat.' On top of it all, he was seasick for much of the time.

One can imagine his relief, therefore, when the vessel finally returned to Grimsby on 7 February 1891 and, although he was still bound legally to serve for another ten months, Dick couldn't wait to do a runner. He stole a shilling from the captain's cabin, and a pair of sea boots that were two sizes too big for him, and set off to walk back to London. It is 143 miles from Grimsby to London as the crow flies, but Dick, so relieved to be back on *terra firma*, was undaunted by the journey which lay ahead. He did odd jobs on his way and stole bread from baker's vans. He slept in barns and outhouses: 'Literally my diet was bread and water,' he recalled. It took him the best part of three weeks to get home, but fortunately he was able to ditch his sea boots on the way down for something more comfortable. 'I reached home wearing the shoes of a trustful but wealthy gentleman of St Albans. His servant had cleaned them and put them on his window-sill. There I found them when I came prowling round in search of food.'

Many of Edgar Wallace's novels involve characters tramping long distances across the country, and to modern readers such feats will seem far-fetched, but walking – as a way of getting from one town to another – was more common in the nineteenth century, and indeed well into the twentieth, since for people without money there was no other way to travel. His time spent on a fishing trawler in the North Sea and his long hike from Humberside to London may have been arduous, but they were just two more experiences that Dick would put to good use when he embarked on his writing career.

Our hero returned home looking like a tramp. His foster mother was pleased to see him, but, after Dick had told her his story, she warned him not to say anything about what had happened to 'any of the others' – a course of action which George Freeman agreed with. The problem was that Dick had deserted, and desertion carried with it the threat of imprisonment. Mr and Mrs Freeman then held a conference over what Dick should do next. They were keen, after all his gallivanting, for him to find a job that he would stick at. 'You'd better go into milk' was George Freeman's conclusion. Clara Freeman, the Freeman sibling whom Dick was closest to, had married a milkman called Harry Hanford. How about Dick going to live with Clara and Harry at No. 67 Tanner's Hill, and helping Harry on his morning delivery round? Dick would be paid half a crown a week and his keep – and Clara would be there to keep him out of trouble. And so it was that Dick went off to Tanner's Hill to start yet another new job.

Harry Hanford was a 'character' to say the least. A bit of a rogue – he had been in trouble once for embezzlement – he was also an incorrigible woman-iser. He was a man of great contradictions – a prominent member of various temperance societies, who also had a fondness for drink. He got away with it all because he possessed enormous charm – he loved to pay compliments to the ladies. Indeed, Clara had met him when she was working as a servant in a house to which Harry delivered. 'He had a way with housemaids which left them with dreams, and when he was not "on the drunk" he was the most passionate abstainer. Harry the Milkman was known far and wide: even today Deptford recalls his name and remembers his doings,' Wallace wrote.

For the most part, Harry and Dick got on well – though there was friction. Dick, loyal as ever to Clara, didn't much like Harry's flirting with female customers. 'He's a married man … as a matter of fact he's my sister's husband,' he would tell ladies who seemed likely to fall for handsome Harry's attractions. Dick's job involved accompanying Harry on his rounds, carrying the milk cans from door to door, and washing them at night. It was this part of the job which he detested. 'The milk round itself was well enough, but scouring the cans was too much like drudgery to appeal to him,' records Margaret Lane. She tells how Dick would dawdle about in the scullery in the evening, hoping that Clara would help him which, 'in the cause of peace', she usually did. Not that it always worked out. 'Dick was often found out and abused by Hanford for his laziness. The milk-cans were a source of frequent quarrelling.'[7]

Dick didn't like Harry's drinking, or his womanising, but there was one thing the two did have in common – a love of reading – and in particular a love of mysteries and adventure stories, with Sherlock Holmes and Deadwood Dick particular favourites. 'Often and often on chilly mornings we sat in front of the fire together, each with our slim volume, devouring every line – enthralled by hairbreadth escape, by haughty defiance, by daredevil rescue of innocent maidenhood,' Wallace recalled. Sometimes Harry Hanford would read out aloud, 'his voice quivering with excitement'.

It was Harry who induced Dick to take the pledge of abstinence when he was 15. Despite his bouts of drinking, Harry was a member of the Rose of Crown Temperance Lodge, the local branch of a temperance society known as 'The Sons of the Phoenix', and was elected its 'chief noble'. Dick enjoyed his role, 'As an officer of the lodge I wore a large scarlet velvet sash, embellished with a tinsel eye of God which should have appeared over my heart, but, owing to my lack of inches, invariably glared on the world from the region of my stomach,' he recalled.

He also liked the other lodge members, 'The members were working men – good fellows doing good work. I have nothing but respect and affection for them. The old lodge still stands – I saw its new banner go past the window of my flat in a hospital parade, and I would have gone on to my balcony and saluted it – only I was in my pyjamas,' he recorded in his autobiography, many years later.

As with almost everything he experienced, Dick was able to put his time as lodge secretary to good use when he came to writing his crime novels. Many of his books feature secret societies, organised along the lines of temperance societies or Masonic lodges, and although 'The Sons of the Phoenix' was far from being a clandestine criminal conspiracy, Wallace, with his fertile imagination, was able to see how such societies could be transformed into organisations with sinister intentions, such as the notorious 'Fellowship of the Frog', in his 1925 novel of the same name; or the 'The Proud Sons of Ragusa', in his 1927 work *The Hand of Power*, a benevolent organisation which is infiltrated and subverted by a criminal mastermind. In the latter, Wallace even has a policeman talking about his membership of 'Sons of the Phoenix'.

In Wallace's own account, his career as an assistant milkman ended when he and Harry Hanford fell out over the cleaning of milk cans. 'He said I was a bad cleaner and I told him loftily that my hands were never intended for the cleaning of milk cans. We parted.' However, in Margaret Lane's biography, there is a different version of events, which understandably Wallace did not want to publicise. It all started with Dick falling in love. Lane describes the object of his affections:

> Edie Cockle was not more than seventeen, and pretty with a pathetic, wistful prettiness. Her gentle blue eyes, full mouth and tip-tilted nose made her seem prettier than anyone he had ever known; they became engaged, more or less secretly, and he saved up and bought a ring for her … whenever they could they went for long walks together, and to temperance outings when these were available.

Lane says that there was a private understanding between Dick and Edie to marry when he was 'in a sufficiently good position', but that seemed a long way off when he was only earning half a crown a week.[8]

Then occurred 'the incident'. Dick slept every night on a camp bed in the front parlour of the Hanford's. It was in that same room that Clara and Harry kept their savings, locked up in a small drawer. Clara kept the key to the drawer pinned into the pocket of her heavy serget skirt, and – according to Lane – never allowed it out of her possession. Except, that is, one very cold night when she added her skirt to the layer of thin blankets under which Dick slept. The next morning, Clara went to the drawer for money, she found it locked, but the savings – around £7 or £8 in gold and silver – had gone.

She told her husband, who sent for the police. On investigation, the policeman declared that the robbery was the work of someone living in the house. There were no obvious signs of a break-in and, moreover, small packages of the money wrapped up in newspaper were discovered in the house.

A furious Harry Hanford accused Dick of taking the money. According to Lane's account, he did not deny the charge and stayed silent but confided, in tears, to Clara that he had not stolen the money but 'borrowed it'. Lane doesn't tell us any more about Dick's motives, but the fact that he was courting Edie Cockle at the time is surely too much of a coincidence. The likeliest explanation for this totally out-of-character action is that Dick, a young man very much in love, wanted the money to impress Edie.

While Clara was prepared to let things go after Dick's confession, her husband was far less charitable, and had Dick marched to the police station. Lane relates that when the charge was read out, the magistrate looked over to Harry Hanford and asked, 'Do you really wish to make a charge against this boy?' Before Hanford had time to reply, Clara shouted 'no!' The magistrate dismissed the case, and Dick went home with Mrs Freeman.[9]

There's an interesting postscript to the story. Several years later, Harry Hanford, who had been so indignant over Dick's actions, himself 'borrowed' Clara's savings in order to travel to Liverpool and sail to South Africa with a mule convoy at the start of the Boer War. Clara never saw him or her money again, and believed that her husband had run off with another woman.

5

'I'LL BE A GREAT MAN ONE DAY!'

'I tried to buy an old builder's cart and a wheelbarrow today,' said Mr Jones to a workman. 'I'll probably get it tomorrow at my own price, and it wouldn't be a bad idea to get a few sacks of lime and a couple of cartloads of sand and bricks in, also a few road pitchers to give it a finishing touch.'

Edgar Wallace, *Angel Esquire*, 1908

What next for young Dick Freeman? He was now 17, and had gone through almost as many jobs. Fortunately, once again, he landed on his feet. 'There was a worthy brother of the [Son of the Phoenix] lodge who was also a worthy plasterer. Also a worthy foreman to a road-making firm. He offered me a job,' Wallace recalled.

Dick was appointed a timekeeper and a mason's labourer:

My duties were various. I kept some sort of accounts, I can't remember what, and I carried huge pails of water from a distant standard to the place where the concrete was mixed. I also held the tap when the job was measured up. I relieved the night watchman whilst he had his tea. I helped him trim the red lamps that hung on the scaffold poles.

It was hard work, but the pay – 15*s* a week – was the highest he had ever earned. There was one person, however, who subsequently was to become very famous, who didn't think that even 15*s* was enough. 'One day when I was helping to hang the lamps on the poles a man came up to me and asked me how much I was earning,' Wallace recalled:

I told him, with conscious pride, that I robbed the firm to the extent of fifteen shillings a week. 'Pah!' He said. He was a man with a beard and talked with an accent. He wore a deer-stalker cap and he had the manner of authority. 'You're doing a man's work,' he said, 'ask for more.' I was astonished.

I never dreamt that I was worth as much. Here I was – I who had been glad
of five shillings a week, and now I was earning fifteen shillings.

Wallace recorded that 'the seed of revolt' did not take root, and he asked the
night-watchman who the 'old bloke' was. 'That's Keir Hardie[1] and he's standing for this district,' was the reply.

Young Dick Wallace wouldn't have known that the man who urged him
to stand up for his rights would go down in history as the founder of the
modern Labour Party, and Keir Hardie would never have imagined that the
young man he saw hanging the lamps on the poles would one day go on to
become one of the most famous writers in the world. Margaret Lane records
that 'beyond a feeling of mild astonishment' Dick's brief meeting with the
great Socialist 'left no impression', but although the encounter didn't turn
Dick into a revolutionary, it couldn't have done Dick's self-confidence much
harm to be told that he was worth more than he was getting.

Keir Hardie was elected as Independent Labour MP for West Ham South,
while Dick was sent by his employer to Silvertown wharf to check the
weights of granite that were loaded from barges to crates. It was there that he
came across a rather eccentric French inventor who was experimenting with
a new kind of brick. 'He was a green-eyed, pimply-faced man, terribly thin
and full of admiration for Motley the historian,' Wallace recalled. 'He brought
me a copy of *The Rise and Fall of the Dutch Republic*, which though I tried
hard, I could not read. It was terribly dry after Deadwood Dick.' The inventor
was a convinced atheist – 'He told me there was no God, which was a great
relief to me,' Wallace later wrote. The green-eyed Frenchman also believed in
reincarnation and that he had been a cat in a previous life.

When his job was over, Dick once again had to decide what to do. He
elected to join the 3rd Battalion of the West Kent Militia, describing himself
as a 'clerk' on the enrolment papers. The militia was a voluntary part-time
defence force, a mix between the modern Territorials and the Home Guard.
Militia regiments for all counties of England and Wales had been established
by the 1757 Militia Act. One can see why enrolling in the militia would
have appealed to him. There was the fact that for three months at least, he'd
receive pay, and board and shelter. There was also the chance that he could
be drafted into the regular army. But, after his three months' training was up,
Dick didn't do what some of his acquaintances did – change his name to join
another militia to get another three months' payment – but returned to the
labour market.

McKay, the 'worthy brother of the Phoenix' plasterer for whom he had
worked earlier that year, had got a contract to plaster some new villas which
were being built in Clacton-on-Sea in Essex, and he asked Dick to help him

out on the job. It was to prove an unhappy experience. For a start, it meant leaving Edie, who saw him off tearfully at New Cross Station. Then there was the nature of the work, 'it was the depth of winter' he later wrote:

> Timekeeper, I was, but usually when the other work was done. From dawn to sunset I lorried lime with a long-handled hoe and filled hods and carried them up steep ladders. The lime worked into my hands till I could not bear water on them. I testify to the health-giving qualities of Clacton air – I was hungry all the time.

Dick bought a penny exercise book at Clacton which he used as a diary. 'Work as usual,' he wrote in October, 'went out along cliff, mile or so. Plenty of girls about. Not having any. None like E …' 'Feel a bit homesick and a bit Ediesick,' he recorded on another occasion.

Dick didn't much like his new base. 'First impressions of Clacton-on-Sea not very favourable,' he wrote. But there was one good thing about the town – it had a lending library. 'I have been down here for three weeks,' he wrote to Mrs Anstee, his book-loving mentor, 'and am still alive. But thank God there is circulating library (bob down security which is returned and 2*d*. a book) out of which I have had *Colonel Quaritch, V.C.*, *She* (2nd time), *Witch's Head* by Haggard, *Novel Notes* (good) by J.K. Jerome, and *The Naulahka*, an up-to-date Hindoo-Yankee tale by Rudyard Kipling and Wolcott Balestier …'

Apart from doing lots of reading at Clacton, Dick also liked to write in his spare time, composing rhymed epitaphs in his penny notebook while crouched over the fire in his landlady Mrs Grown's kitchen. 'You know Ma,' the young plasterer told her, 'I'll be a great man one day.' Some would have believed the prophecy to have been wild and supremely overoptimistic, but not Mrs Grown who, like others who came into contact with Dick, could sense that there was something very special about the young working-class man who recited Shakespeare.

As evidence of her belief, Lane points out that Mrs Grown preserved Dick's notebook, pen and imitation leather writing case, all of which he left behind when he left Clacton, for more than forty years – 'an extraordinary gesture of faith towards a young plasterer's labourer.'

6

THE NEW RECRUIT

The army is not a profession for which a man makes careful preparation, except in a very few instances. A man enlists, as a bankrupt commits suicide, because under the circumstances it seems the easiest course to follow.

Edgar Wallace, letter to *The Regiment* magazine, 16 December 1905

Dick was in very low spirits. On 31 October 1893 he wrote, 'Good-bye, October. You've been a long while going, but thank goodness you've almost gone. If ever a fellow got tired of waiting for his friends to write to him, I'm that fellow … Edie! Edie! Edie!!! What *does* this mean, no letter for ten days … Beginning to damn everybody and everything.' It is easy to understand why he felt so unhappy. His job was exhausting him, he was away from his friends and family, and his boss was a tyrant. 'His employer was frequently drunk, found fault with him on every possible occasion, and paid him only when he felt like it; he was so constantly hungry that hardly a day passed but he entered his meals in the diary with anxious detail,' records Margaret Lane.[1]

Dick had been at a low ebb before, but this time the situation really was desperate. For all the confidence he had in his own abilities, he was now 18 and his prospects looked bleak. A lifetime of physical labour, working long and hard for low wages, for tyrannical bosses like McKay, stretched out in front of him, but the one thing that Dick always had was the courage to make a clean break. He decided to run away from his employer and join the army. From the perspective of a put-upon plasterer's assistant with hunger pains in Clacton, the army seemed like heaven. 'In the militia at least he had not been forced to work long hours with lime and water for an employer who was hard to please and a pittance which was rarely forthcoming; there had been enough to eat, and congenial company in the barrack room,' writes Lane.

Just before Christmas, Dick wrote a letter to his step-parents and the Hanfords to explain why he had to leave his job:

MY DEAR FATHER AND MOTHER, CLARA AND HARRY,
AND TO WHOM IT MAY CONCERN, –

I am writing this … to tell you that I have left McKay and struck for myself.
I did not think it would last long. The work that I hitherto have not spoken
about is of the hardest description, and you know that my love of this kind
of work (Harry especially) will know what a struggle I have had to keep
at it for 8 weeks … With regards to McKay. The only thing I can say about
him is that he is slightly hot-headed … He was as much opposite me as
Harry is like me. He hates books and novels and such trash and loves to talk
about building, plastering, Keene's cement as much as I adore literature and
detest talking 'shop'. He is neat and fastidious whilst I am careless and easy.
I expect Clara to be rather down on me for leaving, but … I have the future
before me.

Dick didn't ask McKay for the pay he was owed, but he did accept a shilling from Mrs Grown as he bid her farewell. He walked to Colchester, about
16 miles away, and on the way pawned his overcoat for 6s. En route to London,
he had a long talk with himself:

'Here you are!' I asked.
    'Where are you?' said I. 'You're earning fifteen shillings a week, you have
    no education, no prospects. Your handwriting is rotten – you're not strong
    enough for a navvy and you're not clever enough for a clerk. You're in a rut
    – how are you going to get out of it?'

No one could ever accuse Dick of not having a gift for vigorous self-appraisal.
    It was Christmas 1893, and on Boxing Day, Dick spent his last shilling
on going to see *Cinderella*. The next morning, he bid farewell to a tearful
Mrs Freeman, who tried to persuade him to change his mind, and then took
the tram to Woolwich, to enlist for seven years as a private in the Royal West
Kent Regiment of the British Army.
    The Royal West Kent Regiment, or to give it its full name, The Queen's
Own Royal West Kent Regiment, was an infantry regiment which had
been formed in 1881.[2] Its headquarters were at Maidstone, and so it was
there that Dick Wallace was sent by train after he had enlisted. Army records
show Private R.E. Wallace to have been small and undeveloped, like so many
working-class army recruits of the time. His height was given as 5ft 4¾in, his
weight as 115lb and his chest measurement as 33in.
    Wallace described his train journey to Maidstone as 'desolate'. 'I occupied
the same carriage as two convicts being transferred to Maidstone Prison, and
on the whole they were more cheerful than I. They had been there before and

canvassed the possibility of returning to their old jobs, discussing the advantage of one "ward" to another.' Wallace lamented that while the two 'agreeable and experienced adventurers' had only 'got' five years, he was in the army for seven, with no remission for good conduct.

When he arrived in the barrack room at Maidstone, the Christmas decorations were still hanging. 'There was only one other man in the long bare room when I came in,' he recalled; 'he sat on the edge of his bed and he was polishing his buttons. The bed was laced with snowy white belts and straps, a tiny knapsack no bigger than a lady's white handbag glistened blackly at the foot of the bed. "Don't touch them straps or I'll gallop your guts out" he said, in a mild, almost friendly, way.'

The man, Nobby Clark, 'the first of the many Nobby Clarks I met in the army,' soon filled in the new recruit with important information. 'All "quarter blokes" made enormous sums out of cheating the troops and bought rows of houses; the sergeant-major wasn't a bad feller, but the colour bloke was a reg'lar barstid.'

The first question Wallace asked Nobby was where the library was. 'Lib'ry?' the astonished old soldier replied, 'Libr'y. You mean the canteen, don't you?' Wallace was firm about seeing the library, but it proved to be a huge disappointment to our keen bibliophile. 'The library was chiefly distinguished by its innocence of anything that looked like a book. There were two large volumes on a shelf, but investigation revealed these as draught or chess boards camouflaged as literature.'

Wallace soon settled down to army life. Despite his description of the accommodation being 'inferior to the average workhouse, and very much below the standard maintained at Dartmoor Prison', he enjoyed his new surroundings. 'Army life suited him,' records Margaret Lane; 'he was well-fed and regularly employed for the first time in his life'.[3]

The kindness of his fellow soldiers towards him, coming after the way he had been treated by McKay at Clacton, was another important factor in making him feel contented. 'The men were most kind to the new recruit; but then, Tommy is the everlasting flower of chivalry,' he wrote, many years later:

> … There are some people who think that there is a magic atmosphere in the army which translates wasters and blackguards into good fellows – but of course that is rubbish. They were good fellows before they came in. They belong to the cheerfully suffering class … The Tommy is the salt of the earth because the working poor of the Anglo Saxon race is the salt of the earth.

The work itself was monotonous. The first parade every day was at 7.30 a.m., the last at 2.30 p.m. Whenever he got any leave, he headed straight back to

London to visit the Freemans and other old friends. 'From time to time he used to come down on leave and he would always come into my shop and have a talk with me,' recalled Aaron Campbell, the umbrella-maker of Tanner's Hill.[4] 'When it was time to leave, he used to say "It's time to go, Aaron" and I always used to accompany him to New Cross Station to see him off to Maidstone.'

After three months in the infantry, Wallace got a lucky break which saw him move on to an army job which was more interesting – and less physically demanding. There was a pub near the barracks called 'The Phoenix'. One night there was a ruckus there, and Wallace and another soldier on picket duty were ordered to go and throw out a militiaman who was drunk and causing trouble. On seeing the size of the militiaman, Wallace decided that diplomacy was the best policy, and told him that the corporal of the picket wanted him to come out and fight. The militiaman swung a punch at Wallace and knocked out one of his teeth.

Wallace, showing admirable sangfroid, carried out his duty and helped frog-march the man to the guardroom. 'Twice we had to drop him heavily,' he recalled, 'He was a sick man the next morning, but bore no malice and was a good fellow really.' As it turned out, Wallace would have cause to be grateful to the drunk. He had to go to hospital to have his tooth attended and there he saw the comfortable quarters of the Medical Staff Corps. 'Nice beds, cosy sitting-room, better pay,' he reflected. He was also impressed by the dark blue uniforms of MSC privates, and the fact that they had a title – that of 'orderly'. Working in the MSC had to better than being a foot soldier. He made up his mind to ask for a transfer.

Nobby Clark was not impressed when he told him. 'What you want to go an' mix poultices for? And you a teetotaller! You'll be dead in a month!' But Wallace's request for a transfer was granted and so, on 17 March 1894, just two weeks short of his 19th birthday, the young soldier began another new chapter in his life.

Becoming a medical orderly had several plus points for Dick. Firstly, it meant a transfer to the MSC depot at Aldershot, which had the great advantage of being nearer to London. That meant he could visit his beloved Edie when he had a day's leave, and go to the music hall in the afternoon. Secondly, there was the nature of the work. Dick enjoyed the anatomy classes he had to attend, and found the subject matter fascinating. 'Classes of anatomy brought me to a new acquaintance with human beings,' he recorded, 'They were no longer men, but bits of flesh with bones stuck inside them and certain organs which had the trick of going wonky on the slightest excuse.' Dick relished the fact that he was no longer just an ordinary foot soldier. 'We class men grew terribly important as we progressed from knowledge to knowledge. We ceased to be entirely military – we became scientists.'

He passed his exams, and was sent off to hospital duty at North Camp. His first job was to be put in charge of a ward which contained twenty-four cases of syphilis. 'I was sick at the thought of it. In those days, the disease was viewed as leprosy was once regarded,' he later recalled. 'A sick man was regarded as a criminal. He was told that his case was hopeless – but not by doctors of the Army Medical Corps.'

Wallace fulfilled his duties well. As Margaret Lane has noted, his cleanliness, tidiness and reserve made him an excellent medical orderly. For the first time in his life, he had been given real responsibility and he proved himself up to the task. 'When I had got over my repugnance to handling the sheets and bed linen, and no longer picked them up with my carbolised fingertips, when I had taken a few dead men to the mortuary and had learnt to dissect them for post-mortem purposes without the hollow sensation in the pit of my stomach, I enjoyed the work. And what good chaps they were in No. 2 detachment!'

All infectious cases came to North Camp. 'I slept in wards or tents with men suffering from every disease from itch to smallpox. In such cases the orderly was isolated as much as the patient, and none could approach him,' he recorded.

He began to write little verses for his comrades. For a canteen concert he composed a verse about the sinking of the HMS *Victoria* off Tripoli.[5] He then wrote a verse on the Battle of Albuera,[6] which went down so well that, after its performance, he was shouldered round the canteen by his enthusiastic admirers. Further success came when he contributed a poem, about the north-west frontier, to the North Camp Music Hall, where the men would go on Saturdays.

By now, he was writing his work down in exercise books, with the wording 'R.E. Wallace, Compositions' on the covers. His life as a serious writer had begun.

It was one thing, though, to get his work performed at army canteens and the North Camp music hall, but quite another to get a verse accepted by a London music hall. How many 19-year-olds would have dared to aim so high? Dick Wallace did. He wrote a song for his great music hall idol, Arthur Roberts, entitled 'A Sort of a Kind of a –', and sent it off to him at the Prince of Wales' Theatre. It was a witty number:

You've a sort of a kind of a sort of a don't know where you are sort of feeling,
A no size at all feeling, dreadfully small, quite a crushed and choked-off sort of feeling:
　　You grin for a while in a curious style, but you feel like a thief that's caught stealing,

It's a kind of a sort of a wish the ground opened and swallowed you up
sort of feeling …

To his great joy, he received a letter from Roberts to say that the song had
been accepted.[7] Wallace wouldn't have missed seeing his song performed by
Arthur Roberts for the world. However, rather ungenerously, he was refused
leave by his superiors. Unabashed, he simply walked out of camp and headed
to the railway station, taking leave for a whole five days to enjoy himself in
London, on the principle that he might as well be hanged for a sheep as for
a lamb.

Wallace saw Roberts perform his song several times. How proud he must
have felt to see his hero perform it in front of a delighted, applauding audience. Afterwards, he went to introduce himself as the author of 'A Sort of a
Kind of a –' to the theatre manager, Mr Robert Lowenthal, who gave him
£5 and 'a lot of good advice'. Wallace left the meeting on a real high. Here
was surely the start of a grand career, writing for the theatre and the music
hall. His act of grand daring in sending a song to Roberts had paid off, and he
never forgot the lesson – that fortune really does favour the brave.

While his head must have been full of the exciting possibilities which lay in
front of him, he was soon to come down to earth with a bang on his return
to barracks. He was picked up by the military police on arrival, and charged
with breaking out of barracks and remaining absent without leave. He was
taken to see 'Old Colonel Cleary', who sentenced the young music hall songwriter to ninety-six hours hard labour.

Dick was marched off to the military prison by a Sergeant Ben Hannan.
Thirty-six years later, Hannan and Wallace's paths would meet again in very
different circumstances. In 1931, Hannan would be superintendent of police
at Blackpool where Wallace, one of the biggest celebrities of the age, would
be standing in the Lancashire seaside town as an Independent Liberal candidate in the general election. But in 1895 he was just a humble medical orderly
being led off by Hannan to a ninety-six hour ordeal.

The term 'glasshouse' became used to describe all military prisons. But the
original 'glasshouse' was at Aldershot, so called because of its large glass lan-
tern roof. The military prisoner sentenced to hard labour was arguably treated
far worse than any convict in a civilian prison. By the late nineteenth century,
reformers had already done much to make prisons more humane, but military
prisons, which were first established in 1844, were a different case all together.
Wallace described his arrival thus:

The glass house … was like every prison I have seen. A wide hall surrounded
by galleries, the walls punctured at intervals with small, black doors. I was

given a bath and changed into convict attire, ornamented by the conventional broad arrows, and marched up to a cell. It was a bare apartment, with a board bed and a ridiculously inadequate supply of blankets. There was a Bible and a set of rules to read, a window of frosted glass (behind bars) to admit daylight and share of a dim light at night. An hour after I arrived a warder came and cut off my hair.

For the first day Wallace was given no work to do, and practised doing headstands against the wall. He was given 'skilly' and potatoes for tea 'unsalted, unsugared oatmeal at which my proud stomach revolted' and this delightful meal was repeated the following morning for breakfast. On his second day, he was put to work. A warder came in, threw him a piece of rope and taught him how to turn the rope into oakum. That was boring, but it was on the third day that the worst punishment was inflicted. 'Shot drill' was abolished by the army in 1904, nine years too late to save poor Dick from experiencing this 'damned and heartbreaking punishment' as he himself described it.

'Shot drill' involved prisoners being assembled in four lines. Each man had a heavy iron cannonball at his feet. When the command was given, the prisoner had to lift the ball, or shot, up to his breast, carry it four paces to the left and put it down. On going back to his original position the prisoner was to find the ball that the man on his right had deposited. He then lifted this to his breast, and carried it four paces to the left. Then, the balls were carried to the right. And so it continued. Lifting cannon balls all day. And the next day too.

The punishment served no useful purpose except to humiliate the prisoners and to push them to the brink of physical and nervous exhaustion. Two days of 'shot drill' broke Wallace physically. Only the intervention of the army chaplain, the Rev. Hordern, ended his nightmare. The exhausted 20-year-old was told to go back to his cell and pick oakum. After 'shot drill' it must have seemed like paradise. When his ninety-six hours of purgatory were finally up, Wallace had learnt one thing – 'I took a good look at the Glass House as I marched away, and decided that the Lord had never designed me for a callous criminal.'

7

OFF TO SOUTH AFRICA

A man who travels picks up information.

Edgar Wallace, *Angel Esquire*, 1908

Wallace was never one to brood on his setbacks and he got back into the swing of things very quickly after his punishment. Old Colonel Cleary, the man who had sentenced him, recommended him as a second-class orderly, which meant an extra tuppence a day. Dick carried on writing songs without any success and his enthusiasm began to wane.

A few months later he was in the mortuary room, dealing with the corpse of a 'poor boy' who had died in the night. Dick's room corporal came in and had some exciting news, 'Wallace – you're marked for Foreign Service – you go to the depot on Saturday!'

Dick's mind immediately got to work. Where might he be going? The British Army was involved all over the world in 1896, protecting the biggest empire the world had ever seen. There were drafts to Singapore, Malta, Egypt, Gibraltar, Hong Kong, Jamaica, Bermuda, Nova Scotia, South Africa, even to Mauritius. Several days later Dick learnt his destination: he was being sent to the Cape in South Africa.

He was excited about the prospect – remember, he had never before been out of England – and South Africa, so far away and in an entirely different continent, appealed as a particularly adventurous destination. However, there was a downside. It meant saying goodbyes to his family, to Edie and his other friends from home, like Mrs Anstee. 'Edie, prettier than ever in her fresh white blouse and gored skirt, with a hard straw boater pinned on her fair hair and a nosegay of flowers tucked in her filigree belt, was the hardest to leave, and they exchanged fervent promises to write every week and to marry as soon as Dick's army career made it possible,' Margaret Lane records.[1]

Dick bade farewell to the Freemans, little knowing that it would be the last time he would ever see Mrs Freeman, the woman to whom he owed so much. 'I never saw "mother" again,' he wrote, many years later, 'I have only one satisfaction, that I was able to make her life a little more easy before the end. She forgot her own children at the last and remembered me.' On 18 July 1896 Dick, now 21, headed to the port of Southampton to sail on the transport ship *Scot*, bound for South Africa. Another adventure was just beginning and, when he next returned to England four years later, he would already be on his way towards fame and fortune. The journey to South Africa was uneventful. The weather was generally good and Wallace recorded that he arrived in Cape Town 'without discomfort'.

South Africa in 1896 was a place of tension and political intrigue. The second Boer War was only three years away. The Boers, the hardy descendants of seventeenth-century Dutch settlers, had set up the South African Republic in 1852, and had regained their independence from the British after the First Boer War in 1881. The British maintained their presence in Cape Colony, in the south. From 1890 to 1896, the prime minister of Cape Colony was the aggressive imperialist Cecil Rhodes, keen to expand British domination of the region.

This wasn't just about patriotism, but profits too. In 1886, gold had been discovered in Transvaal[2] and, by 1896, two-thirds of the Transvaal's population were British immigrants, or 'Uitlanders'. The Boers denied the newcomers voting rights, knowing they were outnumbered, and the British weren't happy. In December 1895 there was an attempt at 'regime change' in the Transvaal, with the so-called 'Jameson Raid'. Backed by Rhodes, it was a daring plan to trigger an uprising against the Boer leader, Paul Kruger. It failed, and Rhodes resigned as prime minister of the Cape. Understandably, it didn't go down too well with the Boers, and the relations between them and the British became even more poisoned.

You could say that the blue touchpaper for the second and deadliest Boer War had already been lit by Cecil Rhodes and his co-conspirators when Dick Wallace arrived in Cape Colony at the end of the South African winter. When he landed at the Cape, its beauty made an immediate impression on him. 'From the sea, standing at the foot of Table Mountain, the town is a beautiful sight. There is no spot on earth quite like it,' he later wrote.

Wallace hoped he would be sent to Natal, the principal British garrison, but found his destination was Simonstown, on the shores of False Bay, on the eastern side of the Cape peninsula, and about 20 miles from Cape Town. 'You lucky devil!' one of the crowd at the Cape cried out to him, and when he got there he understood why:

Simons Town was in those days the greatest 'loaf' known to orderlies the world over. It was the ideal station – a non-dieted hospital, with four beds and a staff of four, a surgeon, a sergeant, an orderly and a cook. All bad cases that required nursing were transferred at once to Wynberg. The only cases I remember being detained were a lunatic and an unfortunate sergeant who fractured his skull by a fall from a bicycle. And he died.

There was a 'compact little surgery' at Simonstown and Wallace made good use of it. When he was alone in the dispensary, he experimented with the drugs that were in store. 'I took opium, morphia, cocaine (which made me laugh hysterically), ether and Indian hemp. The morphia nearly killed me, but I suffered nothing from the others. And I had no desire to repeat the experiments.'

Simonstown was not the most exciting place on earth, but Margaret Lane notes that Wallace was 'dazed and enchanted by the brilliant strangeness' of his new surroundings.[3] With its lush gardens full of lovely tropical flowers, its sunlit bay and exotic atmosphere, how different it must have all seemed from Clacton-on-Sea in winter. The hospital itself was situated at the end of a long avenue of eucalyptus trees, and at night-time Wallace could hear the sound of baboons barking and a nearby waterfall. 'There were gardens everywhere,' he wrote; 'Gardens where narcissus and freesia, heliotrope and roses, grew in their seasons. Geraniums ran wild in thick bushes, and there were traces with great pink blossoms.'

There were some drawbacks, however. As the summer advanced, Wallace found the high temperatures uncomfortable. Hot temperatures didn't just mean beautiful flora, but some nasty creepy crawlies too – Lane notes that Wallace was deprived of the comfort of going barefoot because of the number of red ants which overran the hospital, the kitchen and dispensary in the summer.

Dick's tasks were not particularly onerous; his main duty was doing the daily shopping in the mornings. In the afternoons, there was little else to do but read, rest and smoke, and, in Dick's case, do some writing too. Perhaps it was the hot weather, but he never really hit his stride with his written work at this time. Margaret Lane records how he would start to write a play, but never got further than the first scene before scribbling over it 'another blooming failure'. He wrote verses, which, according to Lane, his colleague Sergeant Pinder listened to 'with the gravity of an examining professor,' but which other members of the hospital staff got tired of.[4] All the time, however, Dick was learning. He'd go up to Zigzag Hill behind Simonstown, taking with him his copy of *Collins' Large Type Pronouncing Dictionary* determined to learn new words.

Outside of the many brothels and bars, there weren't too many recreational opportunities for British soldiers stationed at Simonstown – that is, until a Wesleyan chaplain called the Reverend William Shaw Caldecott settled there, with the plan of building a Soldiers' and Sailors' Home. While that was under construction he established a temporary reading room, with a small lending library. This was great news for Dick the bibliophile and he began to spend his evenings there, poring over the books. There was tea and lemonade served and, as Margaret Lane notes,[5] Dick would have been reassured by the atmosphere which must have reminded him of his beloved temperance societies back home.

The Reverend Caldecott was, to use Dick's own words, 'a bearded giant of a man, an autocrat of autocrats, a brilliant scholar and the author of several books on the Temples of Ezekiel and Solomon.' A photograph reveals a man who would have made a good double of the (then) Prince of Wales, who a few years later would become King Edward VII. The Reverend, although a rather dour man was, at least at the beginning, kind to Dick, but it was his much more charismatic wife, Marion Caldecott, who was to prove the greatest influence on the young Tommy.

Wallace found himself instantly attracted to Mrs Caldecott's magnetic personality, and the Reverend's wife took to Dick straight away too. Despite coming from very different backgrounds, they had much in common. Like Dick, Marion loved books – she was a keen reader, and had even written articles. Marion talked to Dick about books and authors, and read his own work and encouraged him as much as she could with his writing. She quickly became a kind of literary mentor to Dick, fulfilling the role that Mrs Anstee had played a few years earlier. Dick referred to Marion as his 'literary fairy godmother'.

He was soon a regular visitor at the Caldecotts' home. The Reverend and his wife had four delightful daughters. Florence, aged 21, was already engaged to be married and Ivy, the next oldest at 18, was pretty and fair-haired. Shy and sensitive, she listened attentively to Dick and, according to Lane, 'followed him with her eyes'. Gladys and Nellie were in their mid-teens, and their relationship with Dick was more playful. The only member of the household whom Dick felt uncomfortable with was the rather stiff and overly formal Reverend Caldecott, the least friendly member of a charming family.

Revealingly, in his letters home to Mrs Anstee and Edie, Dick did not mention the Caldecott girls. Was it because he was already coming under their spell, or more particularly under the spell of Ivy Caldecott? By the time she met Dick, Ivy had already had her young heart broken. Shortly before Dick entered her life, she had suffered a health breakdown after the tragic death, following an accident, of an older man she had been in love with since she was 12 years old. Mr William Rowley Thomson had been a friend of her father's, who had died from cancer after having been struck in the stomach when he heroically prevented a wagon carrying the Caldecotts from falling over a precipice.

It's not hard to understand why, with all the heartache behind her, she would have been attracted by the enthusiastic and cheerful army private who became such a regular visitor to her home. Her romance with Edgar Wallace, as he was now calling himself, developed slowly but surely, to the consternation of the Reverend Caldecott. On her 19th birthday, Edgar penned Ivy a poem:

Twixt Dawn and Eve', our little day
The sands of joy and sorrow run;
Guide Thou this woman on her way–
And let her stand at Thy right hand–
Almighty God! Thy will be done.

In a letter to his sweetheart, Edgar wrote that he knew:

… Of no bad habit that requires overcoming to make you a perfect woman – to me you are all that, and the only text I can think of is 'Blessed are the meek! …'. You are good and sweet and thoroughly domesticated – all this you know, and you are something else, which you probably don't, and which shyness and bashfulness … prevents my telling you.

Margaret Lane records how Ivy and Edgar made 'a secret sign' which resembled a sharp (music) in their respective journals against certain dates. 'The only clue to this curious little hieroglyphic is that it appears only against those days when he briefly records that he has seen Ivy, and so is perhaps significant of brief moments alone together, or even of kisses.'[6]

'There was plenty happening to relieve the monotony of life – if there had been monotony,' Wallace later wrote of this period of his life. In 1897, British forces, under Admiral Rawson, launched a 'Punitive Expedition' to Benin, on the west coast of Africa, after an earlier British invasion party had been massacred. The wounded from Rawson's campaign were landed at Simonstown, and Wallace was commended by the admiral himself for his care of the patients. As usual Wallace used the experience to great effect. He talked to the patients about their time in Benin. 'In the details of that little war, most of which I learnt at second-hand, was born the germ of an idea which later was to fructify in my series of "Sanders" stories,' he wrote, in his autobiography.

In 1897 though, Wallace had no ambitions to be a novelist. Poetry was his speciality. Mrs Caldecott had bought and published one of his poems for the Methodist magazine which she wrote and edited. He also had his work published in a weekly Cape Town review called *Owl*. In his 1940 book of reminiscences[7] the journalist and newspaper editor G.H. Wilson explained the part he played in the inexorable rise of Edgar Wallace:

One afternoon a young private walked into the *Cape Times* office, where George Green and I used to produce the *Owl* and asked me whether the

Owl ever printed poems. I told him that it depended on the poems, and he then produced a short poem which was quite attractive in the Kipling vein. I told him we would use it, and gave him half a guinea. He was delighted, and said almost with tears in his eyes that this would be the first time anything he had written would have found its way into print. I told him that we would always be glad to have verses as good a character as this, and Wallace for some time became a fairly regular contributor of light verses, generally modelled on the style of Rudyard Kipling, to the columns of the *Owl*.

An even bigger breakthrough was to come when Wallace's poem 'Welcome to Kipling' was published in the *Cape Times*, the first daily newspaper in South Africa, which had started publication in 1876. There are differing versions as to how the poem came to be written; Wallace says that he was reading the *Cape Times* one morning and saw that his great literary idol was coming to visit South Africa. In 1898 Kipling was in his early forties, and firmly established as the British Empire's foremost man of letters. The short-story writer, poet and novelist had already published the novel *The Man Who Would Be King*, and his most famous work of all, *The Jungle Book*, had appeared in 1894. Wallace 'soaked' himself in Kipling's work.

Kipling was a particular favourite among ordinary soldiers, on account of his *Barrack-Room Ballads*, a collection of songs and poems, mainly written in the vernacular, that he had published under the title *Barrack-Room Ballads and Other Verses* in 1892. The collection included two of his most famous poems, *Mandalay* and *Gunga Din*. Lane records Wallace's 'painstaking attempts at the *Barrack-Room Ballads* style', and how he tried to weave 'neat rhymes and Kipling meters into the racy cockney that came naturally to him'.

In his autobiography, Wallace records how he sat down and wrote a 'Welcome' to his hero 'in the Kipling manner', and sent his work off to the *Cape Times*. He heard no more about it, until the poem was printed in the *Cape Times* on the day that Kipling was due to arrive, and he was summoned to meet the newspaper's editor, Edmund Garrett.

According to G.H. Wilson, however, Wallace's poem wasn't sent in 'on spec'. but had already been commissioned. Wilson said that Edmund Garrett had read Wallace's work in the *Owl* and had asked where the verses came from. Wilson explained that a very shy and modest private in the Medical Corps was the author. '"Well," said Garrett, "Rudyard Kipling is arriving in South Africa in a fortnight's time. Ask Wallace if he thinks he could write an ode of welcome to him in Kipling's own vein, which we could publish on the day that Kipling lands", Wallace was delighted to have the opportunity.'[8]

Which version of events should we believe? For Wallace, it was of course a better story that he wrote his 'Welcome' to Kipling unsolicited and it was accepted by the paper. But equally, for G.H. Wilson, writing in the 1940s when Wallace was one of the most widely read authors in the world, it would have been a feather in his cap to be regarded as the man who played such a big part in Wallace's rise.

Like all writers about to make their big breakthrough in print, Wallace waited nervously to see how his work would be presented. 'I have got an idea that my "Welcome" won't be the feature that I thought it would be,' he wrote in his diary. In fact, Wallace had nothing to worry about, the *Cape Times* did him proud. His poem was prominently displayed, and an editorial note declared: 'Mr Rudyard Kipling, who is expected to arrive by the *Dunvegan Castle* today, will be interested to know that the following lines are contributed to the *Cape Times* by a private in the Medical Staff Corps stationed at Simon's Town.' The poem began:

O, good mornin', Mister Kipling! You are welcome to our shores:
To the land of millionaires and potted meat:
To the country of the 'fonteins' (we 'ave got no 'bads' or 'pores'),
To the place where di'monds lay about the street
At your feet;
To the 'unting ground of raiders indiscreet ...

Lane records that Wallace read his verses over 'in a kind of ecstasy'. Little wonder as, for our budding writer, this was a major turning point.

'I hear that the "Welcome" has made me quite a celebrity,' he wrote in his journal, 'I returned from town today bringing very encouraging opinions concerning my thing ... Received cheque for £1.1.0 from *Cape Times* for poem. This day's *Owl* contains a very nice notice of my thing ... What a happy life this is ...'

Wallace, whose self-confidence was never lacking even at the worst of times, was now on a roll. Six weeks later there was more excitement as he learnt that he had been invited to a dinner held in honour of Kipling at Cape Town's City Club. There 'the celebrated poet who had dared to address Kipling in his own vein', would get the chance to meet the great man himself.

According to G.H. Wilson, it was Rudyard Kipling who expressed his 'anxiety' to meet Edgar Wallace, and not the other way round. So, to bring the men together, Wilson and Edmund Garrett decided to 'arrange a little lunch' at Cape Town's City Club.

'Received invitation to dine with Garrett and Kipling,' Wallace recorded. 'Whoop!' This invitation was more important than we can at first imagine, for it was sign that the young soldier poet was breaking through the glass ceiling which seemed to hold back the talented people of his class. Yes, he could get his work in print, yes, his poems could be celebrated, but it was still another thing altogether for someone from his background, however gifted, to be treated as a social equal. Even at the Caldecotts', he was put in his place whenever officers came to tea. When higher-ranked soldiers played tennis with the girls, he was not invited to play, but had to act as a ball-boy.

Now, after enduring such humiliations, Edgar Wallace, the working-class private, was being invited to dinner with Rudyard Kipling! He accepted the invitation, but not without misgivings: 'Should I know which were the right knives to use and the right forks? How many wine glasses were there, and which wine went into which?' He consulted Mrs Caldecott, who gave him a practical demonstration. 'She was rather hazy about wine glasses, but put me right over such problems as knives and forks. I had had the same trouble when I dined with her family, but there the courses were few.'

G.H. Wilson records that, at the lunch, Wallace 'was almost overwhelmed by such minor difficulties as whether to use a knife or fork for the cheese.'[9] But cutlery aside, the main thing was that the meeting with Kipling went well. Edgar asked his hero for his autograph, and Kipling responded by writing out a verse from the 'Song of the Banjo' on club notepaper and inscribing it 'For Edgar Wallace' at the top.

'He [Kipling] seems to have been genuinely touched by the admiration of the young soldier, who, spruce and rigid in his private's uniform in a crowd of boiled shirts and condescending faces, concealed his nervousness under a show of poker-faced assurance which Kipling probably understood well enough,' wrote Lane. Kipling, according to Wilson, advised Wallace to write as much as he could, but to stay as a 'soldier poet', as the fact that he was a private in the ranks 'added greatly to the distinction of his verse'.[10]

A day after meeting at the dinner, Wallace received a letter from his hero, complimenting him on his poem 'London Calls', which had been published in the previous day's *Cape Times*. Kipling gave the young soldier his London address, adding that he would be glad to give him any advice that lay in his power. Ironically, given what Wallace was later to achieve, Kipling advised him 'For God's sake, don't take to literature as a profession. Literature is a splendid mistress, but a bad wife!'

Wallace, understandably, was on cloud nine after his meeting with Kipling: 'My writings have given me a certain amount of "tone" and I am received in the best houses, in fact I have asserted myself, and overcome the social barrier that debars "Tommy" from getting a good many privilidges [sic] that he would obtain, were it not for his "cloth",' he enthused in a letter to the Freemans and Mrs Anstee.

Although he had no immediate plans to quit the army, he was now convinced that his best chance of a rewarding career lay as a writer. Meeting

Kipling, seeing his work in print and hearing the praise heaped upon it was confirmation that he could make it. Energised by his success, he redoubled his efforts to get work published, but despite his great enthusiasm he still faced considerable barriers. Edmund Garrett told him he would accept more verses.

However, breaking into journalism was another matter, 'I was just a cockney soldier, half illiterate, gauche and awkward. Between me and this product of Oxford was a gulf wider than Table Bay,' Wallace later recalled. He asked Garrett if it would help if he learnt shorthand. 'For God's sake don't do that – you'll become an automaton,' was the reply. Wallace sent verses off, not just to the *Cape Times* and the *Owl*, but also to publications back home in England, such as *Pearson's Weekly*, *Little Folks* and the *Daily Chronicle*. He was prepared to write anything for anybody, so long as they paid him.

The assistant editor of the *Cape Times* suggested that he could write reports of Simonstown municipal meetings and Wallace jumped at the chance. He also wrote to the editor of a new local newspaper in Simonstown offering to supply news reports, and his offer was accepted. The man who would become world-renowned for his prodigious output was already pumping out the words at a ferocious rate on a wide range of topics, and still fulfilling his army duties at the same time.

His relationship with Ivy was getting ever closer. Ivy had always believed in him, and his run of success only convinced her that her boyfriend was a genius. She was no admiring bystander though, but sat up at night typing up his work on the parsonage typewriter.

Wallace's writing occasionally got him into trouble with his army superiors. After he wrote a newspaper editorial denouncing the Boer leader, Paul Kruger, he was sent a sharp note from his colonel.

Wallace was never frightened to ask anyone anything, a trait which served him well throughout his life and was particularly useful for a journalist after a story. He wrote to Cecil Rhodes asking for an interview (he did not get one). He had the audacity to write to the naval secretary at Simonstown, asking for advance information of the movements of British warships for the *Cape Times*. The secretary forwarded the request to the military chief staff officer at Cape Town, who wrote on the margin of the correspondence 'Who is this whippersnapper? Have him called into Headquarters and give him a lesson in military discipline.'

Wallace was duly summoned to Cape Town within forty-eight hours, but Lane records that he 'received the rebuke with the same irritating calm that had masked his nervousness at the Kipling dinner.' The young medical orderly was told to knuckle down. He was transferred to Cape Town Military Hospital. 'I had discovered a limitation of journalism,' he wrote, 'my colonel talked to me very seriously, pointing out certain paragraphs of Queen's

Regulations. I was given a ward to look after – thirty medical cases. The *dolce far niente* of Simons Town became a delightfully remembered dream.'

Our hero had, unsurprisingly, fallen out of love with being in the army. Previously, he had thought that promotion within the army was his best career route. In 1897 he had taken, and passed, examinations for promotion – obtaining a first-class certificate of education for corporal's rank and a second-class qualification equivalent for sergeant. Unfortunately though, there was more to promotion than the passing of exams, one also had to serve a number of years in the ranks before reaching qualifying service. Wallace decided to ask for a transfer to the Reserve, where he would be able to focus more on his writing, but his request was refused.

His determination to make his name in journalism only intensified. 'I considered the matter one night as I was taking my turn to sit by the bedside of a dying sergeant, and decided upon a new plan,' he recalled. His 'new plan' involved writing to the editor of another Cape newspaper, the *East London Daily Dispatch*, introducing himself as 'the famous Edgar Wallace who wrote such wonderful poetry in the *Cape Times*' and offering to write him a weekly humorous column. 'I told him it would be light and frivolous and possibly witty. I didn't call it a "causerie" because I hadn't met the word then, and I shouldn't have been able to spell it if I had,' he recalled. To Wallace's joy, the editor accepted his offer.

He was to start straight away at 30s an article. The editor told Wallace that he had no objection to him syndicating his pieces. What was syndication, Wallace wondered? He learnt it meant sending the same article to other newspapers. So, instead of receiving just the one fee for an article, he could, if he was lucky, receive several. The money started to roll in. 'After I had been writing for a month or two I received an order from the *Midland News* in Cradock, and *Grocott's Penny Mail* in Grahamstown. From these sources I received £3 12s a week.'

Wallace wrote his weekly article when he was on night duty in the waiting room. Often, his creative flow was disturbed. 'Many a bright paragraph, scintillating with calf humour, was interrupted by the arrival of casualties,' he wrote. 'Once I turned out to resuscitate a half-drowned civilian who had tried to commit suicide on the beach.' But the writing got done, and Wallace never missed a deadline.

He was not only producing work to order, but the quality of his output was improving as he honed his craft. One has to admire his diligence and determination to get things right. 'I would spend half an hour in search of the right word – even delved down to the very roots to secure one which expressed the exact shade of meaning,' he later wrote. Mrs Caldecott gave the budding writer a copy of *The Study of Words* by Richard Chevenix Trench, and it proved a valuable guide.

The problem was that his vocabulary was still very small, 'I discovered this when I found that in the leading article of the *Cape Times*, consisting of 700 words, there were twenty words I did not understand and eleven sentences which conveyed nothing to me.' So what did Wallace do? For six months, he rewrote the *Cape Times* leaders, reducing them to 'understandable terms'. At the same time, he practised condensing them to forty words – no more, no less. Both exercises were to be of enormous practical benefit to him.

A large part of his future success as a novelist came because his work was so readable, and so fast-moving. It was readable because he set out to make his work as understandable as possible, and it was fast-moving because he never used twenty words to describe something when ten would do. Wallace made writing look incredibly easy, but it was the hard work he put in during this period that was the foundation of his later success.

No matter how long it took, Wallace kept to his task. 'One article in the *Quarterly* took me three weeks to understand, and involved the reading of some thirty articles in an old encyclopaedia which Mr Caldecott had in his study. At the end of that time I could have written a *Quarterly* article on economics, for, incidentally, I had unearthed a flaw in the writer's argument and a gross error in the basis of his calculations.' Another article in the *Atlantic Monthly* brought him to a study of the Chinese dynasties. But, all the information he collected would be stored in his wonderful memory and be used at a later date in his work. As we have seen, nothing with Edgar Wallace was ever wasted.

His list of outlets was growing all the time. He wrote a weekly verse for the *Owl* and the *South African Review* gave him a standing order for 36in of political poetry. He wrote poems about Kruger, and again got a ticking off, with Sir William Butler, commander-in-chief, privately sending word that it was 'not seemly' that a solider should interest himself in politics.

He was getting more work placed in England, with his cockney poems published in the *Pall Mall Gazette*, *Evening News* and the *Daily Chronicle*. He also had his first stories published. The first was called 'Richard Bruce-Burglar', and appeared in the *Cape Illustrated Magazine* in April 1898.[11]

In addition to his journalism, Wallace was now preparing his first book: a collection of his published verses from the *Owl* and other newspapers. Mrs Penstone, the editor of the *Owl*, seems to have suggested the idea and helped Wallace with its compilation. A Cape Town bookseller agreed to put up the money. In homage to his great hero Rudyard Kipling, Wallace called the collection of twenty-two poems *The Mission that Failed*. It was brought out as a small fifty-two page paperback volume, and sold for a shilling. On its cover – designed by Mrs Penstone – was a picture of a soldier slumped against a telegraph pole with a bottle in his hand and a pair of wire cutters on the ground. Above the letter 'N' on the word 'Mission' perched a small owl. It was a modest start, and no one who bought a copy could possibly have thought that its author would go on to become the publishing sensation of the first half of the twentieth century.

The Mission that Failed was not a huge success, but at least Wallace could now truthfully call himself a published author. Reviews were mixed: the newspapers and journals that Wallace regularly wrote for, and from which the verses had been reprinted, praised it while rival publications were less kind. Here's the view of the *Cape Mercury*: 'Mr Edgar Wallace is doubtless an amiable and inoffensive member of the Medical Staff Corps at Cape Town, but why he should have gone to the expense of printing "The Mission That Failed" and other poems in book form is difficult to understand.'

Good, or bad, Wallace cut out all the reviews of the book and pasted them into his journal. 'At present I hardly realise the importance of these notices, but I cannot fail to see that they will be of immense advantage to me in my future literary life', he wrote in his diary.

By now, he had decided it was time for him to leave the army. He discovered that it was possible to buy himself out, provided that war had not actually been declared, for the sum of £18. He didn't have such a sum of money, so he asked Mrs Caldecott for assistance. She wrote to her son, Arthur Caldecott, who was a successful metallurgist in the Rand mines and he generously lent Wallace £20. Wallace applied for a purchased discharge, and began to count down the months to when he would become a free man and could devote all his energies to writing.

In the meantime, he carried on combining his army duties with his poetry and journalism. Although he was disappointed that his 'Ode' on the Grahamstown Exhibition was not selected as the anthem for the opening ceremony, he went to the exhibition instead as a reporter for the *Cape Times*. He arrived in private's uniform and stayed, not at a hotel with the other correspondents, but at the barracks of the Middlesex Regiment. Margaret Lane records that, when the press pack were enjoying their champagne and biscuits after the opening ceremony, Wallace strode up and down the room 'to tell them that he would soon be free of the army, and one of themselves.' 'It's money I want, lots of money' he declared, and when they asked him what kind of writing he had in mind, he replied 'Anything and everything that will bring in money.'[12]

At the very height of his success, thirty years later, Wallace was still keen to point out that he wrote, first and foremost, for money. Even then, he was prepared to write 'anything' and 'everything' that would bring in money. One has to admire his lack of pretentiousness. Others might claim that they were writing for the sake of 'art' or had loftier ideals, but for Wallace, there was never any hiding the fact that he wrote in order to make a living.

In May 1899 he finally got his army discharge papers. He received a gold-headed cane as a goodbye present from his comrades at the Cape Town Military Hospital, and there was a riotous farewell party. The night after his release, he walked about Cape Town until three in the morning for the satisfaction of using his own latchkey. After the years of having to be back at a certain time, to wake up at a certain hour and to go to bed at a certain hour, Wallace could now do exactly as he pleased. He found lodgings in Wynberg, a suburb of Cape Town.

Another new chapter had begun in his life – the most important one of all. 'There I was in my own room, with a window looking out upon the mountains, and a large, smooth table and pen and ink and paper, a big dictionary, Roget's *Thesaurus*, and a volume of familiar quotations. I had all the necessary equipment for a successful writer.' Not even Wallace, with his enormous self-belief, could have imagined just how successful he would become.

8

EDGAR WALLACE:
WAR REPORTER

The South African war came inevitably – one saw the black cloud rising,
and there was warning enough before the storm broke.

Edgar Wallace, People, 1926

Wallace could now devote all his energies to writing. He'd already got into
the habit of rising early to write – a habit which he maintained throughout
his professional life. Although he was continuing to write poems, the lion's
share of his time at this stage of his career was spent reporting.

He reported on council meetings in Cape Town, detailing debates on such
scintillating topics such as whether Little Cloof Road was to have another
lamp post. More interestingly, he covered parliamentary proceedings too,
summarising debates in longhand from the gallery.

In his role as a reporter, he was able to meet some of the top political figures in late nineteenth-century South Africa, including Jan Hoffman, 'the big
power behind the Dutch', and Cecil Rhodes, whose power at that time was
admittedly on the decline. His meeting with Rhodes took place at the latter's
Groote Shuur estate. Wallace wrote of the famous imperialist:

> Possibly Kipling had spoken of me to him, for he was very kindly, took
> me round his terraced garden, but refused to talk any kind of politics …
> His voice alternated between a squeak and a rumble; he himself thought
> quicker than he could speak and sometimes he would leave you with the
> wreckage of a sentence to disentangle as best you could, whilst he went off
> at a tangent to talk about something altogether different, again to leave it in
> the middle of an uncompleted sentence.

It was while he was reporting at the South Africa Exhibition at Grahamstown
that Wallace recorded his first journalistic 'beat' – a report of a pro-peace
speech made by the British acting high commissioner, Sir William Butler.

It seemed to many that the British and the Dutch states were sliding inexorably towards war. The dispute was ostensibly about the rights of the 'Uitlanders' – the British immigrants who constituted a majority in the Transvaal but who were denied full rights by the Boers. However, if the British had really only been concerned over Uitlander rights, they would have accepted an offer from the Boer leader, Paul Kruger, to grant the immigrants full civil rights, within a period of time, in return for the British relinquishing their claim to Transvaal. It's not hard to understand why Transvaal was so eagerly coveted by the British. In 1899, the gold mines of Transvaal were producing around £20 million worth of gold a year. Reserves were conservatively estimated at £700 million. Transvaal was described by a British minister as 'the richest spot on earth' and he probably wasn't wrong. We've heard a lot in recent years about wars for oil – the Boer War was effectively a war for gold.

The British high commissioner, Sir Alfred Milner, the man who rejected Kruger's offer, shared the 'radical imperialist' mindset of Britain's colonial secretary, Joseph Chamberlain. However, at the time of the South Africa Exhibition, Milner was back in Britain on leave, and so Sir William Butler addressed the audience at Grahamstown. He clearly hadn't read the official script. 'South Africa wants peace,' the acting high commissioner declared, and Wallace duly reported the statement. 'I heard the speech and by some queer instinct recognised its significance. It was almost a gesture of challenge to Milner,' he recorded. Sir William saw Wallace later that day and beckoned him. 'You're the writing soldier, aren't you, Mr Wallace? Well, what do you think of my speech?' he asked.

'I think, sir, there will be an awful fuss at home about it,' Wallace replied.

'I think so too,' Sir William nodded. For deviating from the 'party line', Sir William was recalled to London and Milner returned.

Joseph Chamberlain gave the Boers an ultimatum – give the Uitlanders immediate full citizenship, or face war. Milner had earlier sent London a telegram saying that 'the Boers are still bluffing and will yield if the pressure is kept up.' But the Boers, far from caving in to Chamberlain's threat, merely responded with one of their own. On 9 October 1899, they demanded that no more British troops be landed in any part of South Africa and that an answer be given within forty-eight hours. The great imperial power was outraged at the Boers' impertinence. The ultimatum passed, and for the next three years South Africa was to face all the horrors of warfare.

However, for one young reporter based in Cape Town, the outbreak of hostilities meant another opportunity to further his career. Edgar Wallace was in the right place at the right time, at the heart of the biggest story going on in the world at that time. Another exciting chapter in his life was about to begin.

At the time the second Boer War started, on 11 October 1899, Wallace had been out of the army for one day short of five months. His work was going well not only was he established as a reporter, he was also contributing verses for publication in British newspapers and magazines. Looking ahead, he knew that if the fighting did start, there'd be a big demand for war correspondents, so he had already contacted H.A. Gwynne, the chief correspondent of Reuter's news agency, and bureau manager in Cape Town, about a job as a war reporter. Gwynne gave no firm commitment, but 'half-promised' a job if indeed war broke out.

As soon as the Boer ultimatum passed, Cape Town geared up for the coming fight. The town was overcome with war fever. Troop reinforcements arrived from Britain. Wallace himself had no doubts as to the rights of the British cause. 'On the one hand you had the psalm-singing, coffee-drinking Dutch; on the other hand the true-born Englishman with his inalienable right to do as he damn pleased in any country at any time. Could there be the slightest doubt in what directions my sentiments leant?' he wrote.

For Wallace, these early days of the war were a time of great frustration. He longed to be part of the action, along with his former comrades, doing his bit for the empire, but instead sat in the office of the *Midland News* and *Karoo Farmer*, churning out patriotic war poems. Had he done the wrong thing in leaving the army? He decided to re-enlist. Fortunately, before he had time to do so, a telegram arrived from H.M. Gwynne offering him the job of Reuter's second correspondent with the Western Division. Even then, Wallace had his doubts that he would be involved in the action. 'If Reuter doesn't send me up to the front, what in God's name shall I do?' he wrote. He didn't have much to worry about. Gwynne asked him if he'd like to go to the front, and Wallace jumped at the offer. He was given a correspondent's pass, 100 hundred golden sovereigns for expenses and left Cape Town on a night train en route for De Aar, an important railway junction on the Cape Town–Kimberley line, almost 400 miles away. His Boer War adventures could now begin.

How proud he must have felt as he travelled on the train up through the Hex River Mountains and across the semi-desert of the Karoo, 'a place of silence and desolation', towards the Orange River. He, Edgar Wallace, the illegitimate son of a travelling actress, was working for Reuter's – reporting on an event that the whole world, or at least a large part of it, was following closely. The hundred gold sovereigns in his pocket – equivalent to almost six years' soldiers pay – made him feel like a millionaire. 'A hundred pounds! It was all the money in the world. No Rothschild was richer than I,' he later reminisced. 'I shall never forget his look of astonishment when he received the money,' wrote H.A. Gwynne in a tribute to Wallace after his death, 'He said to me "I have never seen so much money in my life".'

Travelling up with him in the same railway compartment on the train to De Aar was another war correspondent, Cecil J. Sibbett. Years later he wrote of the impression the young Reuter's man had made on him. 'When I first met Wallace he had nothing to show to justify his faith in himself except a number of Kiplingesque parodies, yet he felt assured that he was a "great man".'[1]

Wallace, however, still had doubts as to what lay in store for him. 'I was going into the blue, to an unknown and ominous beyond, where there was fighting and death and the confusion of war. I sat through that moonlight night as the train crawled up through the Hex River Mountains, wondering whether this was an opening, or whether I was slipping into a dead end,' he wrote.

In a literal sense, he had arrived at a dead end – the railway line from De Aar and Newport was impassable, so he had to stay at the junction until daylight.

It was taken as a given that the war would not last long and would result in an easy victory for the British. The rag-tag 'army' of Boer farmers would be routed and the Union Jack would be raised in Bloemfontein and Pretoria, establishing British control over the whole of South Africa. Lloyd George, a Liberal critic of the war, said it was like 'the British Army against Caernarvonshire'.

However the Boers, although clearly the underdogs, did have some important advantages. They had superior knowledge of the terrain. The Boer soldiers were much more mobile, and moved around the country more freely than the British counterparts with all their equipment. The Boers were also well-armed, having received up-to-date armaments from Europe for the past three years, including Krupp guns from Germany. By contrast, British mounted troops were still using swords and lances. In addition, it could also be argued the Boers were better led.

The British Army was commanded by General Sir Redvers Buller, who had won a Victoria Cross for bravery in the Zulu War twenty years earlier, but who seems to have developed too much of a fondness for alcohol. 'His contemporaries very seldom speak of him without mentioning champagne,' noted C.E. Vulliamy in his book *Outlanders*.[2] He also came with too much baggage – literally. 'Unfortunately Buller did only move with enormous transport, full of superfluous furniture for the camp, large tents and luxurious provisions from Piccadilly for the senior messes.'[3]

The first few weeks of the war were to prove a shock to those who believed that defeating the Boers would be a cake-walk. Although the British chalked up some very early victories, the Boers soon took the upper hand, laying siege to three towns, Ladysmith, Mafeking, and Kimberley, the diamond capital, to where Cecil Rhodes had rushed on the outbreak of war.

When Wallace arrived at Naawport, 'a ghastly hole of a place', he went up in an armoured train and heard for the first time the boom of the guns. At

Colesberg, he met two men who would go on, in turn, to lead the British Army in France in the First World War – Douglas Haig, then a chief staff officer and major of cavalry, and Sir John French, then a general. Wallace found Haig, whose reputation took a battering after the First World War, 'very charming' and 'a very courteous man'. 'I'm afraid there is very little news for you here,' Haig told the cub reporter, before helpfully adding, 'Would you like to see the general?'

'It was curious experience to have met the two men who in turn commanded the army in France, within five minutes of each one another,' Wallace later recorded. He noted the differences between the two men: 'French, a whisky and soda in his hand, a little talkative; Haig, debonair, very silent and thoughtful; and somewhere in the distance the intermittent "klik-klok" of rifles.'

Wallace arrived at the Orange River Station in late November, the day that forces led by General Lord Methuen had left to push northwards with the aim of relieving Kimberley. While Methuen was accompanied by eight newspaper correspondents, Wallace, Reuter's 'second correspondent' had his instructions to stay in Orange Station and await further orders. He was disappointed to be left behind but there was a pleasant surprise in store for him when he came across his old army comrades from the RAMC working at the small hospital. He cancelled a previously arranged appointment to be with them:

> I had had an invitation to dine that night with a swell I had met on the train – I think it was the Earl de la Warr, who was corresponding for some newspaper or other – and I sent a message over telling him that I had been unavoidably detained, and squatted down with the gang around the black-ened camp kettle to an over-rich dinner of boiled rabbit, chicken and bully beef. It was a gorgeous evening, somewhat spoilt by a raging thunderstorm which came up by the Orange River.

As we have seen, Wallace was given £100 in expenses – and now it was time for him to spend some of it. The first thing that had to be sorted was transport. He spent £20 on a pony, but he lacked the necessary riding skills, and later decided that he would be better off with a bicycle. Although H.A. Gwynne had told him to stay at Orange River, Wallace's insatiable curiosity – a great asset for a reporter – saw him cycling across the veld and exploring the front. He witnessed Lord Methuen's first victory, at the battle of Belmont, from a *kopje* – a small isolated hill.

But Methuen's mission – along with others – was soon to go terribly wrong. In December 1899 came 'Black Week', a period during which the Boers inflicted three military defeats on the British. The 1800s – the century of great imperial expansion for Britain – was ending with some humiliating setbacks.

Back at Orange Station, Wallace combined his reporting with helping out, unofficially, at the field hospital where casualties were sent to. The experience of being with the soldiers as they lay dying made a big impression on him. 'The courage of the dying Tommy is beyond belief,' he wrote, 'I never saw a tear, never heard one regret from these men who were taking farewell of life and all that life held. They fill me with wonder and awe, even to-day, when I remember those death beds.'

Whenever he could, Wallace would get on his bicycle to explore the surrounding countryside. He frequently got lost in no-man's-land. On one occasion, he encountered the enemy. A small group of Boer soldiers were riding eastward to join the forces of the Boer commander, Kronje, when they came across Wallace. The leader of the party questioned Reuter's second correspondent and allowed him to go on his way. The soldiers seemed to have been quite a laid-back bunch. Wallace noted that the Boers not only made no attempt to blow up or destroy the line of rails which provided the one slender line of communication with Methuen's force, but that they even stopped to remove an obstruction which had accidentally washed upon the rails.

It didn't take long for Wallace to have his first tussle with the military censor. After the Battle of Modder, he wrote up a story he had got from a wounded officer. He mentioned that a certain officer had been killed but spelt the officer's name wrongly. General Wauchope, 'a nice little man with a quiet, gentle manner', sent for him and gave him some sound advice: 'Be awfully careful about names.' The story has a sad postscript. Only a week or so later, Wallace learnt that the 'quiet, gentle' General Wauchope had been killed while leading the Highland Brigade. Wallace got the news before the other correspondents, but was determined not to make another mistake and so waited until the news was officially confirmed before cabling it. It is understandable why he should be so cautious after his previous error, but he lost a great chance to get one-up over the more experienced correspondents.

Wallace was still writing poetry in his spare time, and showing the skill for which he was to become world famous – being able to rattle off work at a lightning pace. 'One morning he came up to me at Modder River and, while at breakfast, he wrote a parody on "The Road to Mandalay",' remembered Cecil J. Sibbett.[4] 'I can still remember two of the verses:

On the Road to Kimberley,
With the giddy RHA [the Royal Horse Artillery]
Oh, what funny pranks they play,
With Boers across the way
Place me west of Fleet Street,
With a Modder River thirst,

Where the barmaids are so lusty,
And I'll drink until I burst.

'He [Wallace] passed this to me with the remark, "When I'm a great man you can say that this was written at your breakfast table."' Sibbett also recalled that, when a writer in the *South African News* described Wallace as 'a great man but a minor poet,' Wallace took it 'seriously and literally' and said to him 'Well, he could not deny that I am a great man.' A further boost to Wallace's already high self-confidence came when he learnt that the British publishers, Methuen, had agreed to publish a new collection of his Kiplingesque verses.

Meanwhile, Ivy Caldecott was putting her thoughts down on paper, on a year that had brought her 'the greatest joy as well as more trouble and worry' than she had ever experienced:

> The truth is, my life is not my own any more – in fact I am in love! Dick is at present at the front – O. River ... I am having a really hard time with regard to my love affair. None of my sisters approve – Father says if I marry Edgar he will disown me ... It is only Dick's love and mine for him that sustains me. May the New Year be a brighter one. This terrible war that is being carried on casts a cloud over everyone and everything.

As the 1900s began, the biggest empire the world had ever seen was determined to avenge the defeats of December 1899 and finish off the Boers. 'We are not interested in the possibilities of defeat; they do not exist,' Queen Victoria told Arthur Balfour. There was change at the top of the military command, with General Redvers Buller being replaced as commander-in-chief by Lord Roberts, a hero of the Crimean War and the Afghan Campaign of 1879, and Lord Kitchener – who in 1898 had become an Imperial hero for winning the Battle of Omdurman and securing control of the Sudan – appointed Roberts' chief of staff.

The appointment of Roberts and Kitchener was a sign that Britain meant business, and gave an immediate boost to morale. Imperial forces were also strengthened with contingents arriving from Australia and Canada. The British army now had nearly 250,000 men in South Africa, compared to the Boers' 30,000.

However, before the superior numbers began to tell, there was another setback. At the Battle of Spion Kop, fought on 23–24 January, forces under General Buller suffered another crushing defeat, with around 1,500 British soldiers killed or wounded.

Meanwhile, Edgar Wallace, Reuter's second correspondent, had been getting to meet some of the 'elephants of the newspaper world', having been sent up to Orange River. These 'elephants' don't appear to have overwhelmed the young cockney reporter with their friendliness. Wallace wrote of the 'gratuitous snubs' he received from the *Daily Telegraph*'s Burnett Burleigh, the man dubbed 'the greatest of all war correspondents' and who covered twenty-four campaigns over a fifty-year period. He found George Steevens of the *Daily Mail*, 'difficult to know.' One journalist Wallace unfortunately missed out on meeting was a certain Winston Churchill, who had already made the headlines himself on account of his daring escape from Boer imprisonment and his 200-mile journey to safety – his escapades were dramatised in the 1972 feature film *Young Winston*.

'Winston, I only saw,' Wallace wrote. 'I had an opportunity of meeting him, but was rather shy about meeting celebrities.' He described Churchill as 'a sturdy, red young man, brimming over with life and confidence.' In the light of the role Churchill was to play in the Second World War, it's interesting to note that Wallace also wrote:

> I am one of the people who believe that he has a large quantity of the military genius of the first Duke of Marlborough, his ancestor. All his life he has comported himself in the field with an absolute disregard for his own safety – whether you like his politics or not, you have to acknowledge his personal bravery; he is a man without fear.

Wallace found less snobbery towards him from upper-class military types than he did from the press corps. 'Throughout the war I thanked God when my work brought me into contact with officers of the Brigade of Guards. They never made me conscious of my social limitations, and that is the highest compliment I can pay to their breeding,' he recorded.

Wallace's work in the main was sending off short, shilling-a-word cables back to Reuters. He felt frustrated by the necessary brevity of his communications, but again, it was all very good training for when he came to write crime novels, as it further entrenched in him the skill of making every word count.

In addition to his cables, which he had to send off if and when he heard anything worth reporting, he also worked on longer, descriptive 'mail stories', which he had more time to write. These 'mail stories' would be forwarded to Reuter's head offices in London and distributed to newspapers which subscribed to Reuter's service. Because of his 'shocking calligraphy and curious spelling' Wallace 'took the precaution' of sending these stories first to a typist in Cape Town, who would check for any errors in spelling or punctuation. When the *Daily News* published one of his stories back in England, Wallace, with great pride, sent copies of the newspaper to everyone he knew, even though the only by-line was 'by Reuter's Special Correspondent'.

He sent three copies to the typist in Cape Town, and that single action was to have a great long-term consequence for his future career. The typist, confused as to who Wallace really worked for, began to send his articles directly to the *Daily News*, but also sent one to the *Daily Mail*. It was only when he returned to London, later in 1900, that he realised just how much he owed to the girl typing away his articles in Cape Town.

For the moment, though, there was a war to be won. The British set out to end the sieges of Kimberley, Ladysmith and Mafeking. Kimberley was relieved on 15 February, and Ladysmith two weeks later. Wallace received his instructions to join Sir Frederick Carrington's mixed forces of Australian, Canadian and New Zealand troops at the port of Beira, in Portuguese East Africa (now Mozambique). The plan was to cut off any possible northward movement of the Boers into Rhodesia – the country named after Cecil Rhodes – and also to arrive at Mafeking from the north in time to support the relieving forces under Plumer. Wallace went by train to Cape Town and then embarked on a tiny, overcrowded troopship which sailed up the tropical coast to Beira.

He described it as a 'painful' experience. There was even worse to come. After arriving at Beira, the next stage of the journey involved travelling about 60 miles by a narrow gauge railway to a place named 'Bamboo Creek' (now Nhamatanda). There, troops were transferred to a broad gauge railway, on a journey which took them through jungle and swamp to Marandellas (now Marondera, in Zimbabwe). They were then herded onto overland mule-driven coaches, conveyances which reminded Wallace of the old 'Deadwood Dick' stories he used to read, for another 285 miles to Bulawayo, and then from Bulawayo to Ootsi (now in Botswana), a distance of 460 miles, they again were transported by a slow train. As if that was not enough, the troops were then faced with a forced 70-mile march to Mafeking.

It was no surprise, seeing the journey that they had to make, that nearly all of Carrington's forces arrived too late to help with the relief of the town. Mafeking was relieved on 17 May, and the news led to wild rejoicing back in London. Wallace arrived on the outskirts of the town soon after it had been relieved and, to use his own words, 'when the powder of Plumer's attack still hung in the air.' Robert Baden-Powell, the garrison commander at Mafeking, became an imperial hero, and a few years later set up the Scout movement. Wallace missed meeting him, as Baden-Powell was already preparing to go home when the Reuter's second correspondent arrived.

Wallace spent two days in Mafeking, interviewing the inhabitants, and picking up as many stories about the 217-day siege as he could, before sending his cables back to London. On his tour of the town he was surprised to bump into an old acquaintance – a soldier who had left the medical corps at the same time as he had. The man had grown tired of army life and said he was going to find a nice, quiet office job somewhere up country. 'There's going to be a war, and when you fellows are slogging across the veld, you can think of me sitting in civvies outside my hut, with a pint of beer and a big cigar,' he had told Wallace. Sadly, it hadn't turned out like that. As Wallace was walking down the main street in Mafeking, he saw a man who looked like a scarecrow eating a banana, and recognised him as 'The Man Who Wanted a Quiet Time'.

The tide of the war had turned heavily in Britain's favour. A few days later Lord Roberts announced the annexation of the Orange Free State. At the end of May, the Union Jack was hoisted in Johannesburg. The Boer capital, Pretoria, fell on 5 June. The British then proclaimed the annexation of Transvaal. The war appeared to be over, and once again there were wild scenes of rejoicing in London, the imperial capital.

What next for Reuter's second correspondent? Wallace was given orders to head back north to Bulawayo, and from there on to Salisbury, where there was talk of a native rising against the British. He spent several weeks there, waiting for a rising that never came, before heading back to Bulawayo by train and then back to Cape Town. As the second Boer War appeared to be over, he was given three months' leave. Having been four years away from home, Wallace didn't have to think too long and hard about what to do with his leave. He took the first ship back to Britain.

Wallace had last set foot in Britain in July 1896. Politically, little had changed when he arrived home in the summer of 1900. Lord Salisbury was still prime minister, in charge of a Conservative/Liberal Unionist administration, and Queen Victoria was still on the throne. However, personally, things were very different for Wallace. While in South Africa he had received the sad news that Mrs Freeman had died and it had caused him great distress. On arrival in London, he went round to see Mr Freeman and his family in their new home in Lewisham, but without his warm-hearted foster mother there, it was simply not the same. Mr Freeman told Wallace that the money he had faithfully sent to his wife throughout the last four years had scarcely been touched. Mrs Freeman, always thinking of others before herself, had been saving it for Dick's return. The money was used to help give Mrs Freeman a decent funeral, so at least there was some comfort for Wallace in that.

Clara Freeman was there to meet her foster brother too. She was obviously delighted to see him, but Lane records that she was not in the best of spirits either, for not only had her beloved mother died, but her husband, the Romeo milkman Harry Hanford, had run off with her savings.

Always the optimist, Wallace had tried to arrange a meeting with Edie Cockle, the girl he had deserted while in South Africa. He wrote to her suggesting that they meet, but Edie was now married and refused to see him.

While on a personal level Wallace's return to London was depressing, in regards to his journalistic career there was better news, thanks in no small part to the lady typist in Cape Town to whom he had sent his articles. A man called Douglas Sladen told Wallace that he had seen a piece of his in the *Daily Mail*, the newspaper set up by Alfred Harmsworth in 1896, and which was already achieving daily sales of around 1 million. Wallace was intrigued and the very next morning went to the *Mail* offices in Carmelite House to see if he could trace the article. And there it was, an article published in June entitled 'With Carrington in Rhodesia' by Edgar Wallace.

He realised that the piece must have been sent to the *Mail* by his typist in Cape Town. Now, if one article of his was deemed good enough to be published in the *Daily Mail*, why not more? As we've seen, Wallace was never frightened of asking for things when he really wanted them. He sent his name up to the *Mail*'s editor, Thomas Marlowe. 'And there began my acquaintance with a man who, more than any other, founded my journalistic fortune,' he later wrote. Marlowe invited the Reuters man to his office. He told Wallace that he remembered his article, and that he had liked it. He said that it was clear that Wallace could write, and that he knew what he was talking about on South Africa. Wallace, for his part, told Marlowe that he was going back to the Cape and that, in his opinion, the Boer War would last for at least another year. He said that his talents were better suited to writing longer articles, like 'With Carrington in Rhodesia', than short cablegrams for Reuters. It was a brave attempt to persuade Marlowe to appoint him a *Daily Mail* correspondent in South Africa. There was certainly an opening, as George Steevens, sent by the *Mail* to cover the Boer War in 1899, had died of typhoid during the siege of Ladysmith.

Marlowe didn't offer Wallace a job, but he did commission him to write a few more pieces for the paper from South Africa when he returned, and said that they would then take it from there. It may not have been exactly what Wallace wanted, but it was another important breakthrough all the same.

Wallace had been keen to be back in London for the publication of his second book, a new collection of his Kiplingesque army verses. However, there was still some time before the publication so he decided to travel up to Ravensthorpe in Yorkshire to renew his acquaintance with the Frisbys. It was to be a thoroughly enjoyable week. Not only did he did he enjoy the company of the delightful Frisby girls, Emily and Julia, but he was also charmed by the Hirsts, the equally jolly and high-spirited sisters who were nearby neighbours.

He was also pleased to see that, as far as the local media were concerned, he was already something of a celebrity. In the *Dewsbury District News*, Wallace was described as 'a gentleman who knows a good deal about what has taken place in South Africa' and someone who had 'an amount of literary talent' and had 'travelled well on the road to success'. Another local paper reported that he had advocated annexation of the Boer republics as the best way of settling the conflict in South Africa once and for all, and that he was 'sanguine that after two or three years under British rule the burghers will find our regime better for them than the corrupt Boer Oligarchy'.

After a week in which he had been lionised more than at any time in his life, Wallace left Yorkshire on a high. Back in London, however, he soon came down to earth. He had called his new collection of verse *Writ in Barracks*. He dedicated the book 'to the rank and file of the Royal Army Medical Corps amongst whom I spent six happy years of my life.' He was optimistic about the book's chances of success, and had good reason to be – in the summer of 1900, Britain was gripped with patriotic fervour over what appeared to be the 'victory' in the Boer War.

But *Writ in Barracks* did nowhere near as well as Wallace had hoped. The publisher ordered an initial print run of 2,000, and in the end 977 were sold and 926 remaindered. Reviews were mixed. Ironically, given the newspaper's encouragement to him as a journalist, the harshest appeared in the *Daily Mail*. 'We can only regard Mr Wallace's *When in Barracks* as a book which had better not have been published,' the review said, and it even managed to get the name of the book wrong.

Many up-and-coming writers would have been destroyed by such unkind notices, but while Wallace was obviously disappointed by negative reviews of his book, he characteristically didn't allow his despondency to linger. As usual, he cut out all the reviews for his album, and took encouragement from the better ones. 'Some of the pieces are as good as any of Mr Kipling's,' enthused *Outlook*. *Country Life*, meanwhile, prophesied that 'if Edgar Wallace does not allow the literary agents to get hold of him and persuade him into over-production he will go far.' It was an ironic prediction, as Wallace did go far, and arguably it was because he allied his genuine writing skills with the most effective production system any writer had yet devised.

It was now August 1900, and Wallace still had one month of leave left. There was an easy way to revive his spirits – head back up to Yorkshire. This time, he found himself spending more time with the three Hirst sisters than he did with his hosts, the Frisbys. From the Hirsts' perspective, it's not hard to see why they would have taken such a shine to Wallace. He not only shared their love of books, but he was a published author and celebrated war correspondent. He possessed great charm and was handsome too. 'The figure he cut in Ravensthorpe was both dashing and romantic,' writes Lane, 'at twenty-five he had become a handsome young man, with fine eyes, clear-cut features and a baffling expression.'[5]

For her 22nd birthday in August 1900, Jeannie Hirst had received an 'Opinion Book' from the Frisby sisters. On the left-hand pages of the book were printed various questions, and on the right hand side were spaces for friends to fill in their answers. Wallace wrote down his answers in the book on 22 August 1900.[6] It's interesting to reflect on his views at the age of 25.

It was no surprise to see him name Joseph Chamberlain, the radical imperialist and colonial secretary, who was then at the height of his popularity, as the 'greatest living statesman'. Nor was it a shock that this patriotic Englishman, living at the time when the British Empire was at its zenith, and fourteen years before the horrors of the First World War, named '*Dulce et decorum est pro patria mori*' (It is sweet and right to die for your country) as his favourite quotation.

His favourite prose, poetical and all-round writer was, naturally, Rudyard Kipling. He listed Mulvaney (one of Kipling's soldiers), Sherlock Holmes and Becky Sharp from Thackeray's *Vanity Fair*, as his three favourite fictional characters. 'The South Africa problem' was, understandably the political question he was chiefly interested in. Although no radical revolutionary, both 'The wrong he would like addressed' and the political reform he advocated were 'overworked shop girls'.

He gave his favourite composer as Sir Arthur Sullivan, and his favourite artist as G.F. Watts, the father of British Symbolism. Wallace's favourite flowers, beasts and birds were, respectively, 'Violets, dogs and laying hens'. His preferred season was spring, the season in which he was born, and the scenery he most admired was 'peaceful, rustic'. He defined love as 'the desire for the unobtainable'. His greatest wonders of the world were 'the phonograph and a woman'. His idea of happiness was 'hot day, shady verandah, iced drink, cigarette and Kipling's latest'. Perhaps the most telling of his answers in the light of what he was to achieve was the one he gave to the question 'The noblest aim in life?' – 'to give others pleasure'.

Before he left Yorkshire, Wallace inscribed a copy of *Writ in Barracks* to Jeannie Hirst. His dedication read:

When reading these in years to come,
When years have fled – and with them youth;
Midst thoughts inane there may be some
That speak above their fellows dumb
Of life and love and truth.
And as you scan each measured line
Each rounded thought, each laboured jest,
And add, if truthfully you can,
I like his poems best!

Wallace must have travelled back in London heavy in heart at having to leave behind his female fan club in West Yorkshire.

However, there were exciting prospects for him to reflect on as he sailed back to South Africa – professionally, as well as personally – but there's no doubting that he felt pangs of regret as he left home shores once again. He wrote the following letter to one of the Hirst sisters while on the boat to Cape Town:

> Dear little girl, sometimes I want somebody to whom I can confide my little troubles, and it is so difficult to find one whom I can look for sympathy … I am rather worried just now – partly because I am leaving England, and partly because I have had some heavy losses on the Stock Exchange … I am starting on my voyage with a gloom which the knowledge that I am leaving some of the sweetest girls in the world in Ravensthorpe, but intensifies. If you get letters full of trouble, and gloomy views, you will only have yourself to blame for offering to befriend so wretched a creature as Yours affectionately Dick.

Edgar Wallace arrived back in Cape Town in October 1900. That month in Britain a general election, dubbed the 'Khaki election' was being held, with the Conservative/Liberal Unionist government, led by Lord Salisbury, keen to cash in on the patriotic – some would say jingoistic – national mood. 'A seat lost to the government is a seat won by the Boers,' Joseph Chamberlain declared, and the government duly increased their majority. Perhaps if the election had been held a few months later, it would have been a different story. For it soon became clear that the Boer War was a long way from over, and that the British had been guilty of celebrating a great victory far too soon.

In fact, the war was about to enter its most vicious stage and was to drag on for another year and a half. Although their provinces had been formally annexed, the Boers fought back by waging a tenacious guerrilla campaign. The British responded with measures of extreme ruthlessness, which included the herding of Boer women and children into concentration camps and Boer farms being burnt or blown up. The man in charge of this 'scorched earth' policy was Lord Kitchener, who took over as commander-in-chief from Lord Roberts in November.

For Wallace, the continuation of the war meant increased professional opportunities. He had only sent a handful of dispatches to Thomas Marlowe at the *Daily Mail* before the newspaper made him their official correspondent giving him 'the freest of hands'. Wallace now had the opportunity to write regular, longer and more discursive articles from South Africa, and moreover, had plenty of time in which to write them. He was now not only a war reporter, but a war commentator too.

He hadn't been in Cape Town long before he headed to the front, attaching himself to a column that was leaving Magersfontein to search for the Boer commando leader, Hertzog, who had been giving the British plenty of trouble. In his autobiography, Wallace claimed that he may have 'brought down' Hertzog while accompanying an unofficial sniping expedition:

> My shot killed the horse, and probably I should have killed the rider, but a loud-mouthed officer demanded what in something we were doing at the moment I was drawing on my prey. I am pretty certain, from what we subsequently learnt, that the gentleman I brought down was Hertzog himself.

If true, then it was indeed a lucky escape for Hertzog, who went on not only to survive the war but to serve as prime minister of South Africa from 1924–1939, and who died at the ripe old age of 76 in 1942.

With the enthusiasm for the war waning in Britain, the imperial propaganda was stepped up. The Boers, it was said, weren't playing fair – they fired on Red Cross outfits, murdered wounded British soldiers and hoisted the white flag under false pretences. Britain's war correspondents played their part in pushing the imperial line, but considering that he was writing for a strongly pro-war newspaper, Wallace's reports to the *Daily Mail* – with one or two exceptions – weren't particularly outrageous in their anti-Boer sentiment, compared to others.

His dispatches, which were lively, engaging and well-written, soon built up a keen following. They not only appeared in the *Daily Mail*, but were syndicated to a wide range of local and colonial newspapers. They were praised by the *Spectator* as showing an 'excellent temper.'[7] His reports started with factual descriptions and morphed into sketches in which soldiers would have their say. Because of his own experiences, he was in a class of his own when it came to reporting the views of 'Tommy Atkins'.

A dispatch of 4 May 1901 introduced the character of 'Smithy' to *Daily Mail* readers:

> P'haps your'e telling this yarn, and p'raps I aint; any 'ow, whether it makes no difference about bein' a lord or sir or not, that's wot Kitchener told Buller – 't any rate, Kitchener's the bloke to end this war … why 'e''s got more sense in 'is little finger than – than – (lamely) twenty Bothas, and he'd no more think twice about shooting you or me than I would about killin' a fly.

From January–March 1901, Wallace was attached, as the *Daily Mail* correspondent, to Lt-Col Henniker's column in the 'Great De Wet Hunt'. Like

Hertzog, Christiaan De Wet was a Boer general who was causing considerable problems to the British with his daring raids. Around 14,000 troops set out to try and capture the rebel leader. Wallace's articles brought home to British readers the excitement of the hunt for De Wet, but the Boer managed to successfully evade capture until the end of the war in 1902.

Things were going well for Wallace but, in June 1901, his reporting brought himself into conflict not just with Lord Kitchener, but with the War Office and the British government too. It was the first major controversy of his career. Wallace was in Pietersburg, in northern Transvaal, when he heard that there had been a military engagement between the British and the Boers at Vlakfontein, about 200 miles away. He travelled by train to Krugersdorp, about 20 miles from the action, and to where the wounded soldiers had been taken. He spoke to the wounded and came upon what he believed was a sensational story. Namely, that the Boers had been guilty of the wholesale shooting of wounded men.

Perhaps mindful of how he had missed scooping the news of the death of General Wauchope, due to his caution in waiting for official confirmation, Wallace quickly sent off a cable with the news. It was 'censored out of existence' by the British authorities. However, Wallace had also sent a long written dispatch to the *Daily Mail*, which did get through and which caused a huge scandal when it appeared in print. It was incendiary stuff:

> The Boers murder wounded men. Yes, the gentle, bucolic Boer, who was forced to take up the rifle, purchased for him a dozen years before by a paternal Government, to guard the independence of his country, may be placed in the same category as the Matabele, the Mashona, the Dervish, the Afridi, and with every savage race with which Britain has waged war. And the soldier who is stricken down on the field is no more certain that his life will be spared by brother Boer than he was that brother Fuzzy would pass him by.

The modern reader would be appalled – quite rightly – at the casual racism which underpins the article, with its talk of 'every savage race' and its assertion that every group or tribe that the colonial power had waged war with was as bad as each other.

Britain's war secretary contacted Kitchener, who replied that the report was 'unfounded'. However, he had to modify his statement a few days later after a Lieutenant Hern had said that he had indeed seen Boer men shooting wounded soldiers at Vlakfontein. Wallace found himself at the middle of a heated quarrel between the government and the *Daily Mail*. While the British authorities had been happy for anti–Boer propaganda to circulate a few months earlier, the line had now changed. 'K [Kitchener] was getting very weary of the war, most anxious to bring about its end, still more anxious that the feeling at home should not be further inflamed against the enemy. He was prepared, as I know, to grant the Boers a measure of self-government immediately on the signing of peace,' Wallace later explained.

Wallace's allegations – and also the issue of censorship by the authorities in relation to charges he had made earlier in the year – were discussed in the House of Commons.[8] The exchanges included a question asked by Winston Churchill, now back from the war, and at the start of his political career as the MP for Oldham.

Lord Stanley, the under-secretary of state for war, threatened that if Wallace's report were proved to be incorrect he would be severely punished. The *Mail* stood by their man, and accused the War Office of lying. The War Office responded by accusing the *Mail* of obtaining secret information through the bribing of officials. The *Mail* challenged the war secretary to repeat the accusation 'on a public platform'. Kitchener, meanwhile, had Wallace sent down from Johannesburg to Cape Town with a military escort. Wallace, to his credit, refused to be intimidated, and after a few days, travelled back to Johannesburg.

He struck back at Kitchener with a new article entitled 'The Corruption of the Censorship', getting in plenty of digs at the head of the British forces. 'There is much that Lord Kitchener does not think important enough to cable to Downing Street that I think is sufficiently interesting to send to Carmelite House ... I think the time is close at hand when I shall want to wire something that Lord Kitchener will not want to send or the Government to receive,' he wrote. It was all very plucky stuff from a journalist at the start of his career.

His bravery, though, did bring him reward as it helped to raise his journalistic profile. The magazine *MAP* (*Mainly about People*) published a highly laudatory 'A Pen Picture of Edgar Wallace', written by its editor T.P. O'Connor:

> Mr Edgar Wallace, the *Daily Mail's* daring war correspondent, is another illustration of the rapid making of reputations that has gone on since the beginning of the war in South Africa. Mr Wallace has formed a wider circle of readers, and for the present he remains one of the most talked-of personalities in South Africa. The tone of Mr Wallace's vivid complaint against the military censorship is largely characteristic of the man. Absolute fearlessness is the keynote of his character, with a tendency to free, alert, hard-hitting ...
> He is an excellent type of the pushful Anglo-Saxon.

Meanwhile, Kitchener had fired his own salvo at Wallace by claiming that the Boers received all their information from British newspapers – later adding that the only newspaper the rebels got was the one Wallace wrote for.

On 16 September 1901, Wallace shared his thoughts on developments in South Africa in a letter to a friend, Mr Waugh. 'There is however the chance that the unexpected may happen, but personally I believe that the darkest days, and the most hopeless stage of the war is to come.'

In December, a selection of Wallace's *Daily Mail* articles on the Boer War was published by Hutchinson for 6s under the title *Unofficial Despatches*. 'His *Unofficial Despatches* is for the most part attractive reading, especially in the chapters in which he champions the cause of the private soldier' said a review in the newly launched *Times Literary Supplement* on 24 January 1902. The reviewer, though, was less generous towards the six sketches which went under the title 'Has Kitchener failed?' 'Few will read Mr Wallace's criticisms and agree in his final judgment. Few will fail to read between the lines a bitterness of expression more deep and subtle than the justifiable sarcasm of an impartial essayist.'

In the spring of 1902 Wallace heard that peace talks were to begin between the Boers and the British at Vereeniging, and tried to convey this news by telegram to London. Once again, the censor intervened and handed the correspondent his message back. He was told it was on Lord Kitchener's orders. The *Daily Mail*'s correspondent hit upon an ingenious scheme to beat the censor. He had become friends with a wealthy financier, called Harry Freeman-Cohen. The financier had an office in London which was run by his brother, Caesar. Wallace, with Freeman-Cohen's approval, sent a wire to the brother, saying 'Any message that comes to you, take to Carmelite House.' The message passed the censor. Wallace then designed a code by which he could send messages about developments in South Africa to his newspaper, without them being intercepted by the authorities.

Wallace's first message was a tester. It said that he had 'bought 1,000 Rand collieries' at a certain price. As expected, he was hauled before the military censor. He came well prepared, with a broker's note which confirmed that he had indeed purchased the shares. The censor was satisfied, and so the scheme could begin in earnest. The message, 'With reference Paxfontein Mines, all parties necessary to contract are now in Pretoria, whither Alfred has gone, get bottom price', seemed to be about share dealing. In fact it meant: 'Peace negotiations begun. Boer representatives are in Pretoria. Milner gone there to secure basis negotiations.'

'In this obscure way I was able to send home from day to day the progress of the peace negotiations,' Wallace later explained. The negotiations had barely started when Wallace was summoned by Kitchener for breakfast. Had the code been discovered? Wallace arrived too late for breakfast, and his interview with Kitchener took place in the latter's study. 'Your newspaper has a large influence in England, hasn't it?' Kitchener asked him. Wallace replied that it did indeed have a tremendous influence. 'Well, I'll tell you what I wish you would do, Wallace,' he said, 'can't you persuade your people to take this line in regard to concessions to the Boers?'

So Edgar Wallace, the war correspondent who had caused a major controversy with his reporting of the Boers shooting of injured prisoners, whose cables had often fallen foul of the censor, and who had annoyed Kitchener probably more than any other journalist in South Africa, was now being asked to help persuade the British public to support a generous peace deal with the Boers. It was quite a turnaround.

Kitchener outlined the 'concessions' he had in mind. Wallace said that he couldn't send them as a new message, and consequently both men agreed that it would take the form of a leader column. 'So between us we sat down and constructed a *Daily Mail* leader (which, I believe, never went into the newspaper) urging the necessity of dealing gently with the Boer,' Wallace wrote. The leader was sent, and two days later the two men wrote another one – but, according to Wallace, the news that the first one had not appeared in the newspaper 'inhibited any further confidence' and he was not summoned by Kitchener again.

Meanwhile, peace negotiations were continuing. The British camp and the town of Vereeniging were heavily fortified, with Lord Kitchener determined that no news of the negotiations would be leaked to the press. At the same time, Wallace was determined to find out what was going on and scoop any important news for the *Daily Mail*, sent by code via the London office of Caesar Freeman-Cohen. But how? 'To find one's way into the guarded peace camp was of course impossible. One elderly correspondent tried it, but his disguise would not have deceived an amateur detective, and he was unceremoniously booted forth into the cold world,' Wallace wrote. Nevertheless, Wallace was able to keep his newspaper and its readers in Britain fully up to date with what was going on behind firmly closed doors at Vereeniging.

It was a truly brilliant scheme. An old soldier friend of his was one of the guards at the camp. Wallace arranged with his accomplice a code of signals. The guard would have three handkerchiefs – a red one meant 'nothing doing', a blue signalled 'making progress' and a white handkerchief meant that a peace treaty had been signed. Every morning Wallace would take the Vaal River train, which passed the camp, and look out for his friend's signal. He would then take the next train back. 'I don't know how many journeys I made on that infernal railway,' he recalled.

To try and avert suspicion from what he was doing, he occasionally travelled further down the railway line – even as far as Cape Town. Once at Beaufort West, in the Western Cape, he sent a wire with the latest news, but his language was 'unguarded' and he was overheard by another man waiting to send a telegram. The eavesdropper happened to be none other than the Boer commander, General Smuts, and he notified Kitchener. Wallace denied any wrongdoing.'One of Lord Kitchener's staff subsequently stated that I had given him my word that I would not break the censorship regulations; but the truth is, I had made no promise.'

Meanwhile, he continued with his regular railway rides past the camp at Vereeniging.'Then one morning when rumour was rife that negotiations had fallen through, I saw my friend standing at the end of the tent lines, and he was displaying a white handkerchief conspicuously. I did not wait to get back to Pretoria. Instead I sent a wire from Germiston:"Contract signed".'

Thanks to Wallace's ingenuity, the *Daily Mail* was able to steal a massive march on its rivals. Throughout the negotiations it had been the newspaper which had made the most confident predictions of how the talks were going. Now its staff excitedly readied the front page, which announced the news that Britain and the Boers were now at peace. It was important that none of the *Mail*'s Fleet Street rivals got wind of their great exclusive.'The printers, compositors and entire editorial staff of the *Daily Mail* were locked into Carmelite House throughout the night, to prevent the scoop leaking to other newspapers,' records Margaret Lane.[9]

Wallace's breaking of the news of the peace treaty was undoubtedly one of the most ingenious journalistic scoops of all time. When the *Daily Mail*, which had been accused of obtaining their story by bribery and corruption, revealed how their reporter had got his information, Lord Kitchener was livid. It was the very last time that he would allow Wallace to cock a snook at the authorities. In July 1902, Wallace received a letter from the Censor's Office in Johannesburg informing him, 'that in consequence of your having evaded the rules of censorship subsequent to the warning you received, you will not in future be allowed to act as a war correspondent: and further, that you will not be recommended for the medal.'

Wallace's days as a war correspondent were over. However, he had no regrets over what he had done:'I had been warned of the dire consequences to me should I continue sending uncensored messages; but a correspondent's first duty, within the bounds of honour and decency is to his newspaper. It is the ship for which he is prepared to make any sacrifices.'

Wallace's sacrifices were to be richly rewarded. The *Daily Mail* was to show its gratitude to its star reporter in a most generous way when he returned to London, while in South Africa, Wallace's wealthy friend Harry Freeman-Cohen had an exciting venture in store for him. Professionally, Wallace's ingenuity and bravery as a war correspondent opened up new vistas for him. Personally too, the Boer War had seen great changes in his life, as we will now discover.

9

A HUSBAND, A FATHER AND A NEWSPAPER EDITOR

The cleverest detective in the world can rarely discover the woman's man!
Ever stand in a window of a hotel or an office and watch the crowds going
up and down, and try to place the professions of the passers-by? That's easy
compared with knowing what your most intimate friend looks like from
the point of view of his wife!

Edgar Wallace, *The Terrible People*, 1926

In order to appease the Reverend Caldecott, Ivy and Edgar had reluctantly
agreed to separate in September 1899 and not see each other for two years.
In April 1901, Wallace decided that he had waited long enough. He went to
Cape Town and married Ivy. The Reverend Caldecott was no longer around
to voice his objections – the old misery had left his family and his wife of
thirty years' standing and moved back to Britain. Edgar and Ivy had a short
honeymoon at Gordon's Bay, before he returned to his war reporting. Lane
informs us that the new bride was 'established alone in a small furnished bungalow in a suburb of Cape Town'.[1]

In their first year of married life, Ivy saw precious little of her new husband, but they relished the limited amount of time that they could spend
together. May 1902, the month that the Boer War officially ended, also saw
the birth of Ivy and Edgar's first child, a daughter whom they christened
Eleanore Clare Hellier Wallace. The baby was born while Wallace was making
his daily journeys past the peace camp at Vereeniging. 'It had been intoler-
able to be torn between two anxieties, and only the knowledge that Ivy had
had Mrs Caldecott, capable and reassuring, constantly beside her, had enabled
him to concentrate on the important business of eluding the censor,' says
Margaret Lane.[2]

Wallace was now a married man and a father. But the end of the Boer
War and the birth of his first child were not the only things that he had to
celebrate. Let us allow Edgar to tell us himself the story of the next exciting
development in his life:

On the day peace was officially proclaimed, and while the church bells were still ringing, the churches were filled with the thankful citizens of the Transvaal, Freeman-Cohen walked into my room at Heath's Hotel, a large cigar between his white teeth and a twinkle in his eyes. He had been riding all morning and his horse was at the door of the hotel. 'I have bought the *Standard and Diggers' News*,' he said. This was the most important paper in the Transvaal, and had in pre-war days been subsidised by the Kruger government. 'I want you to edit it,' he went on. 'I'll give you fifteen hundred and year and a share of the profits.'[3]

Could things get any better? Here was Edgar Wallace, at the age of 27, a man who, by his own admission, had never been in a newspaper office in his life save to hand in 'deathless prose' about municipal councils, being offered the editorship of a newspaper – on a generous salary and with a share of the profits. The *Daily Mail* had been paying him around £28 a month – now he was being offered around £2,000 a year.

The decision on whether or not to accept Freeman-Cohen's offer, was, to use a contemporary expression, a 'no-brainer'. Yes, it would be a pity to end his association with the *Daily Mail*, but here in Transvaal, he would be a newspaper editor, and not just a mere reporter. He discussed the news with Ivy. Taking on the job would mean moving to Johannesburg, and beginning a new life there as soon as Ivy was strong enough. It was all tremendously exciting.

Before he began his new job, Wallace had something else to look forward to – a trip back to England to attend the ceremonial dinner which Alfred Harmsworth and the *Daily Mail* had arranged for him. On his return to London, Wallace found that he was the man of the moment in Fleet Street. Perhaps he felt a pang of regret that he had accepted Freeman-Cohen's offer so quickly, and had not instead decided to return home and continue his association with the *Daily Mail*. The *Mail* did Wallace proud, giving him a lavish banquet at the Savoy Hotel on the night of the coronation of Edward VII.

He was presented with a small silver casket 'in recognition of his services during the South Africa War'. Flattering speeches were made, and Margaret Lane informs that the toastmaster had to hammer for silence when Edgar rose to reply to 'a few well-chosen words from the chairman's table'. Alfred Harmsworth parted with his star reporter with a shake of the hand. It had been a profitable association for both men, and one that was later to be renewed. As he set sail for South Africa once again, Wallace probably had no doubts that his editorship in Johannesburg would be a great success. It was not to work out like that, but fortunately, in his relationship with the *Daily Mail* and Alfred Harmsworth he possessed a good insurance policy.

The *Standard and Diggers' News* had been an important newspaper before the war, but when Freeman-Cohen bought it, it was moribund. The entrepreneur's idea was not to try and resuscitate it, but to build a new paper from its shell. And so it was that on 22 September 1902, the first issue of the *Rand Daily Mail*, with Edgar Wallace as its editor, hit the newsstands. Working conditions at the newspaper offices were far from luxurious. 'The room was too small to admit more furniture than a battered desk, a chair and an old-fashioned bookcase; the only telephone hung on the outside of the partition, and was answered by whoever happened to be near it,' writes Margaret Lane, about Wallace's office.[4]

Not that Wallace minded much. 'I had now a position: I was editor of what promised to be – and the promise was well kept – the most important newspaper in Johannesburg. My salary was roughly £2,000 a year; I had the entrée to whatever society there was – it was the most tremendous period of my life,' he later wrote. Although he retrospectively enthused over Johannesburg in his autobiography, it's worth pointing out he didn't always have a high opinion of the city, having described it as a 'heartless godless place' in one of his earlier poems.

However, now he was a newspaper editor, and part of the 'Jo'burg elite', Wallace saw things from a different angle. Wallace was responsible for setting, admittedly within limits, the editorial policy of the *Rand Daily Mail*, and in charge of a small staff and a large number of foreign correspondents, which he appointed. It was all a far cry from working in a paper bag factory, or being a foot soldier at Aldershot.

As we shall see throughout his career, any success Wallace achieved had to be celebrated on a grand scale. It was during his time as editor of the *Rand Daily Mail* that we first witness the extravagance that he was to become famous for. Yes, Wallace was being paid well to work for Freeman-Cohen, but his expenditure soon outstripped his salary. Unlike his wealthy employer, he was not a millionaire yet; nevertheless he started to live like one.

He rented, at the considerable sum of £50 a month, a large bungalow, which he furnished with expensive items from the Paris Exhibition. He took on a staff of native servants. He generously entertained celebrity visitors to Johannesburg at Heath's Hotel, before bringing them to his home to ply them with brandy and cigars. On one occasion he brought home – and invited to lunch – the entire cast of a touring theatre company. Wallace's most endearing quality was his open-handed generosity: whether it was taking his staff out to meals or for a drink, or entertaining dignitaries, he was always the one who picked up the bill.

The racecourse and the stock exchange were two other arenas where he would like to splash out. He became a director of the Auckland Trotting Club.

He bet on horses, entertained lavishly at the racetrack and speculated on mining shares at the stock market. 'I plunged into the market with the best of them, made £12,000 in one week and lost £20,000 between eleven in the morning and one o'clock in the afternoon,' he recalled.

A Johannesburg newspaper editor not only had to live well, he also had to dress well. Margaret Lane describes how Wallace changed his appearance:

> He indulged his taste for large, pale-coloured hats with rolling brims, and strolled to the office in high-buttoned suits of a sporting and opulent character. The gold-headed cane, the solid watch-chain festooned across his waistcoat, the ring on his little finger, bespoke him a man of consequence in Johannesburg, and if fulfilling that pleasant position were costing a little more than the £2,000 a year which Freeman-Cohen was paying him, what did it matter?[5]

What did it matter indeed? I believe there are three main reasons why Wallace was so extravagant and so relaxed about living beyond his means. Firstly, he loved spending money – not just on himself, but on others. He was a man who was incapable of a mean act – his high-spending, open-hearted generosity sprang from his open-hearted, expansive character.

Secondly, there was his enormous self-confidence and innate optimism. If he got into debt, then he had absolutely no doubt that he'd be able to get himself out of it. If he lost money on the horses, then next day he'd not only win it back, but win a lot more. So far, nothing in his life had really occurred to dent his innate optimism and the belief in his ability to get out of scrapes. Let's also not forget that he was living in a place, Johannesburg, where great fortunes could be won overnight.

Thirdly, there was the sense of celebrating just how far he had come. Wallace had known extraordinary poverty. Yet here he was, earning a princely sum as the editor of a newspaper when he was still only 27. What was the point of money, if he couldn't enjoy it? What was the point of scrimping and saving when he didn't have to? That said, the aspect of his editor's job which Wallace probably most enjoyed was not the money, but the way it enabled him to rekindle his love of the theatre. He was a frequent visitor to the Johannesburg Gaiety. Tickets were no problem to arrange, given his position, and he occasionally doubled up as the *Rand Daily Mail's* theatre critic.

Leonard Rayne, a famous actor-manager, who was nicknamed 'The Guv'nor', became a close friend, and the two men would sit and analyse plays together. Wallace's mixing with Johannesburg's theatrical set[6] not only brought him great pleasure, it also gave him a new idea. He had already seen his work performed on stage – so why not now write a play? His idea was for a drama about the extraordinary life of Cecil Rhodes. A play on Rhodes, who had died in 1900, would surely be a huge success, not just in South Africa, but across the empire, he reasoned. He started to work on it, whenever his other work commitments allowed him a breathing space.

Wallace's editorship of the *Rand Daily Mail* proved to be a rollercoaster ride, not just for himself, but for the paper's owner and its staff. His 'send off the cable and be damned' philosophy as a reporter had got him into trouble with the authorities, and so too did his 'publish and be damned' philosophy as an editor.

The first major scrape came with Lord Milner, the former high commissioner for South Africa, who was now the first governor of the Transvaal and River Colony. One of Wallace's correspondents reported a rumour that the British government were planning to buy the town of Lorenco Marques from Portugal, as an *entrepôt* to the Transvaal. Without waiting for official confirmation, Wallace decided to 'go big' on what appeared to be a sensational story, and splashed it on the front page of his newspaper in heavily headed type.

Milner was furious, and instantly – and vehemently – denied the claim. He sent in an official denial for the paper to print. Wallace came up with another of his ingenious ideas to make sure that 'the smack in the eye' that his paper had received didn't leave a mark. He had the whole of his correspondent's column translated into Portuguese. Milner's denial was duly printed, but with the following addendum: 'Whilst of course we accept His Excellency's statement that the British Government contemplate no such purchase, we can only reprint our correspondent's message as we received it, and ask our readers to judge for themselves.' Wallace was confident that 'not one reader in twenty thousand' would be able to understand the message, and would assume that because the paper had been bold enough to print it, that it must confirm their story.

The year 1902 was something of an *annus mirabilis* for Wallace, but in 1903 his winning streak came disastrously to an end. In March, he endured a family tragedy when his baby daughter Clare, just 10 months old, died suddenly from meningitis. Wallace was stunned, but for Ivy, who lacked the solace of meaningful and engrossing work, the blow was even greater.

Meanwhile, the debts were piling up after six months of reckless spending. With tradesman starting to knock on the door for their money, Wallace realised that he had to somehow cut his cloth and start to live within his means. By the summer, he had lost his job and his financial position became even more precarious. In his own version of events, Wallace recorded that he had a row with Harry Freeman-Cohen on a 'purely personal matter' and resigned his editorship.

Margaret Lane fills in a few more details.[7] Freeman-Cohen had personally guaranteed £250,000 – a sizeable enough sum today but a huge one in 1903

– towards a government loan for the development of certain goldmines in Transvaal. Because of the loan, Freeman-Cohen had a direct financial interest in the profitability of the project, and expected the paper to toe the right line in its coverage of the story. Wallace, as we've seen, was never one to bow automatically to a superior authority, and his natural inclination when someone put pressure on him to do something was to do the opposite.

He dug his heels in, and there ensued a huge row – held behind closed doors – between him and his proprietor. Wallace emerged from the room 'pale to the point of phosphorescence', 'stalked into the office' and wrote 'Edgar Wallace: Finis!' on his blotting pad. His nine-month spell as editor of the *Rand Daily Mail* was at an end.

Years later, Wallace conceded that the fault had been his. 'He [Freeman-Cohen] was in the right and I was in the wrong, but I was just a little bit swollen headed and rather too satisfied with my own infallibility.' We can, though, surely admire Wallace's courage in standing up to his proprietor who, after all, had been attempting to get Wallace to push an editorial line conducive to his business interests. It was, in many ways, a stupid thing to try and hold his ground against Freeman-Cohen, but it was brave nonetheless.

Lane records that Wallace made 'a melancholy round of the building, saying goodbye'. She claims that he hinted at suicide as he bade his farewells and, as a consequence, his colleagues refused to let him leave the office alone. They accompanied him to the Heath's Hotel, and there was a 'last lugubrious round of farewell drinks'. Wallace had been kind to his staff and now they were repaying that kindness to him. 'Half a dozen of them still clung to him on the way home, and left him with confidence only on his own doorstep, when the thought of breaking the news to Ivy had apparently sobered him, and he had reluctantly promised not to lay his revengeful death at the door of Freeman-Cohen,' records Lane.[8]

We can imagine just how low Wallace must have felt. He had been a newspaper editor at the age of 27, and he had blown it. He was out of work and in debt. His baby daughter had died. His world, which had appeared so rosy twelve months earlier, had been turned on its head. There was nothing else for him and Ivy to do than to pack their bags and head to Britain, leaving behind their unpaid bills. South Africa had been the making of Edgar Wallace, but it also came very close to being the ruin of him too.

10

THE SPECIAL CORRESPONDENT

Mine disasters, royal processions, important funerals, religious troubles, riots in France, murders, mysterious disappearances, a procession of trouble ... The special correspondent's job is a wonderful school for the budding novelist.

Edgar Wallace, *People*, 1926

Edgar and Ivy embarked on the ship at Cape Town with just £80 in their possession. When they arrived in London, the sum had been reduced to 6s. Edgar, showing once again his innate optimism, had tried to win back some of the money he had lost in South Africa by playing poker on the ship, but his opponents were far more experienced than he was and they took him to the cleaners. After all his successes in South Africa, Wallace had come back home with less money to his name than when he had sailed on the *Scot* six years before. He was broke, unemployed and had a young wife to support.

Things, though, were not as black as they appeared. He was still, thankfully, in the good books of Alfred Harmsworth and the *Daily Mail*. While he had been an editor in Johannesburg, he had kept his association with the newspaper going, sending them occasional articles, including a critical piece on Lord Milner which the over-sensitive governor had attacked in public. The first thing Wallace did when he arrived back in London was to pawn his gold watch and chain for £12, the money enabling him and Ivy to rent rooms in a boarding house in Lordship Lane, Dulwich. Then, as Ivy did the unpacking, he headed to Carmelite House to ask for a job. Thomas Marlowe, the editor, was delighted to see him again. Wallace told him what had happened in South Africa, and that he was out of work. Marlowe sent him to John Cowley, the *Mail*'s manager, who offered him a reporter's job on £15 a week.

Wallace accepted it without hesitation, and with characteristic chutzpah, asked for the immediate advance of his first month's salary. With £60 in his pocket, Wallace left the building and reflected on his wonderful good fortune. Yes, he had lost his editorship in Johannesburg, but wasn't this much better? The money was lower, but he was now a proper Fleet Street journalist, working for the most widely read newspaper of the day. Seventeen years earlier he had stood, frozen to the bone, selling newspapers at Ludgate Circus. Now, he was on his way to joining the other Fleet Street legends. 'Now Edgar Wallace could call himself a colleague of the great names of the times, Charlie Hands, Philip Gibbs, Tom Marlowe,' observed James Cameron.

He was in the right profession at the right time. It wasn't just the *Daily Mail* which was thriving, but the newspaper industry as a whole. The early years of the twentieth century were the golden age of print journalism in the UK. The number of daily newspaper readers is estimated to have doubled between 1896 and 1906, and to have doubled again by 1914. Spending on newspapers increased from less than £8 million in 1901 to over £13 million in 1913.[1] Newspaper and magazines were being launched all the time. Between 1901 and 1914, ten evening papers were available at one time or another in London alone. It was a great time to be working for a newspaper and particularly for one as popular as the *Daily Mail*.

That Saturday night an amazing coincidence occurred. Wallace, no doubt keen to celebrate his success in landing a job with the *Daily Mail*, went to one of his old haunts, the Gaiety Theatre. During the interval he was sitting in the vestibule, along with the other smokers. Suddenly, the theatregoers rose to their feet. Wallace turned round to see what all the fuss was about and, lo and behold, Lord Kitchener, his old adversary from South Africa, had entered.

Wallace's first inclination was to rise to his feet like the others. Then he thought better of it. Why should he get up for the man who had banned him from working as a war correspondent? Kitchener's eyes looked round the room and rested on the solitary fellow who remained sitting down. To Wallace's amazement, he walked over to him. Wallace got up and the two men shook hands. Kitchener had clearly respected his courage. 'Had I stood with the others, he would have treated me like dirt,' he later wrote.

Wallace settled quickly into his new job, despite his lack of experience. 'Here was I, dropped down in Fleet Street, a tyro amongst experts, expected to deal authoritatively and efficiently with every phrase of trouble.' He had never learnt shorthand, and as an interviewer his technique left much to be desired. The trouble was that he was a much better talker than he was a listener. 'I possessed the fatal faculty of interesting conversation, and usually after half an hour with a victim I had not given him an opportunity of expressing single view, whilst I, on the other hand, had expressed many!' he was honest enough to admit later. Once, he was sent to interview Ray Lankester, a very distinguished scientist. At the end of 'about an hour's animated talk' Lankester turned to his interviewer and said, 'Very interesting indeed – now, shall I talk?'

Wallace had a wide variety of assignments from the *Daily Mail*, some he greatly enjoyed, others less so. In the latter category we can place a series of statistical articles he was asked to compile on unemployment. Having escaped poverty – and unemployment – he had no great desire to return to the topic. Unfortunately, the *Mail* soon came to regard him as their 'go to' man on unemployment, and would send him to carry out research in the East End of London. 'I have had two years of this kind of work and I do not want any more of it. However, they are so keen on it and I cannot afford to lose any sort of advertisement just now so off I go,' he complained in a letter to Ivy.

Crime reporting was much more to his liking. There was a wide variety of cases and trials to report and it also provided him with a rich source of material which he would be able to use when he came to writing his detective novels. 'My experience of crime reporting taught me a great deal about humanity that has been very useful to me, and alas! I have seen that indignant prisoner in many guises, for vanity is behind four-fifths of the murders I have reported,' he wrote.

Wallace claimed to have been the first reporter to notice that when a jury came into court to return a verdict of guilty against a murderer, they never looked at the person in the dock. These were, of course, the days when being found guilty of murder meant the death penalty. Covering executions was one way newspapers could boost sales. Edwardian newspaper buyers loved reading about crime and the fate of criminals and newspapers were happy to meet the demand.[2]

Wallace witnessed many executions as a *Daily Mail* crime reporter. At one hanging in the east of England, Wallace was in for a surprise when he saw the prisoner. A couple of years earlier, when he had been covering the 'Hunt for de Wet' in South Africa, he had been shot at by a British soldier firing from a small hill. He rode towards his would-be assassin. Only when Wallace got closer did the soldier stop firing. Wallace asked why he had been shooting at him. 'I thought you were a Boer', the man replied, 'Why do you want to wear a hat like that?' 'If you shoot people because you don't like their hats, you'll end up being hanged', Wallace had replied. His words were to prove prophetic, for the man who had tried to kill him two years earlier, was the 'weed of a man' being led forth by the hangman to his death.

Wallace's work brought him into contact with Britain's hangmen. As a keen student of psychology, he was interested in what sort of men did this job, and how their work affected them. He asked a young executioner named Billington if his job gave him nightmares. He said it kept him awake but that, no, he didn't have nightmares. Billington's father was a hangman too. One day, friend of his father's was tried for murder, found guilty and sentenced to death. Billington senior was taken very ill, but the rumour-mongers claimed that he was feigning illness to avoid hanging his friend. 'It needed only this to stimulate the sick man,' Wallace wrote, 'he rose from his bed, went to Strangeways Jail, hanged his sometime friend, and came home to die.'

Amid all the tales of human misery that he covered, there was occasionally some humour too. In a pub at Chelmsford, where he had travelled on the morning of a hanging, he was mistaken for the executioner. Another time, he was sent up to Newcastle Assizes to cover what he described as 'the most horrible story of assault that has ever been told in a court of law'. The prisoner, 'a red-faced brute' stood in 'a studied attitude of nonchalance' in the dock while his victim described her ordeal. She twice fainted while giving evidence. Even when the jury returned their verdict of 'guilty' and the judge said that he was sending the prisoner to seven years' penal servitude, the 'red-faced brute' still smiled. It seemed nothing could shake the man from his callous indifference. But then, as Wallace recorded, a woman, 'her face wet with tears', turned to the dock and wailed, 'Oh Bill! Oh Bill!' 'It was the prisoner's wife, and the effect of this interruption was electrical. His face went purple, his neck was swollen with fury and, shaking his fist at his unfortunate wife, he hissed: 'What do you mean by coming here – AND SHOWING ME UP!'

Wallace formed an unsentimental view of the criminal fraternity, which was demonstrated in his novels. He regarded the idea that hardened, habitual criminals could be reformed as wishful thinking – theories put forward by people who didn't really know too many hardened, habitual criminals. 'Once a wrong 'un, always a wrong 'un,' was the way he saw it.

His crime reporting made him increasingly interested in psychology. 'I began to take a real and intelligent interest in the human race,' he recalled. Once more, he had a grand idea. He would write a book, 'a monumental work' which would be entitled 'Motives and Expressions'. Sadly, it was one book which he did not get round to writing, but he did, over the years, collect 'an immense amount of data' and translate the significance of over 500 human attitudes. He found that the language of expression and gesture was universal. He noticed how an English baby of 2 or 3 years employed exactly the same gestures as a child of the same age 'in the most primitive part of Africa'. He discovered that 'a man who is telling another that he has been badly treated, and will not endure such injustice, moves his hands, his feet, and inclines his body at a similar angle, whether he is a member of the London Stock Exchange or a Ngombe warrior'. In his 1926 autobiography, he modestly hoped that 'a much cleverer man' than he would one day write the definitive work on this subject.

By now, he and Ivy had moved from their guest house in Dulwich to a sizable furnished Victorian villa in Flanders Road, Bedford Park in west London. Money was coming in again, but it was going out just as fast. Even with debts from South Africa still outstanding, Wallace was back to his high spending, extravagant ways. Margaret Lane records how, on his way to Carmelite House, he would routinely stop off at the Press Club for a game of cards with his fellow journalists, 'impressing the other members with the expensiveness of his cigarettes and the flamboyance of his hats'.[3]

Wallace was very popular with his fellow journalists. 'As a friend in Fleet Street he was always kindly, and generous, and good humoured, though very quiet and unboisterous,' wrote Philip Gibbs.[4] Gibbs was once with Wallace in an old inn in Doncaster, and joined the 'born gambler' in a game of poker:

> He had a Royal Flush – the rarest thing – and scooped the pool. Our land-lord who had been watching the game thought it looked good and offered to take a hand. Wallace bid him for high stakes. The landlord thought he was bluffing. But, incredible as it seems, Wallace put down his cards and revealed another Royal Flush! The landlord departed, a sadder and a wiser man, and we laughed at the sham incredulity at this run of luck. But nobody would have accused Wallace of manipulating his cards. He was as straight as a yardstick.[5]

According to Lane, Wallace had only been back in London for a few weeks when he had a surprise visitor – his mother Polly Richards, who travelled down from Bradford to see him. In what Graham Greene later described as 'the one repulsive moment in the biography',[6] Lane has Wallace turning away his sick, poor and elderly mother after a short and painful interview. Such behaviour, as even Lane conceded in 1938, was totally out of character for Wallace, who was generous to a fault and the most open-hearted and friendly of men. Lane surmised that Wallace's 'unrelenting hostility' to his mother was due to the fact that he still felt betrayed by the woman who had abandoned him when he was only a few days old.[7] The story undoubtedly did Wallace's posthumous reputation much harm.

How could he have been so heartless and so cruel towards his mother in her hour of need? The answer is – he wasn't. In 1987, almost fifty years after her book was published, Lane conceded that the story was untrue.[8] Polly Richards was a dying woman in 1903 – suffering from senile phthisis and haemoptysis – and it's inconceivable that she would have been physically capable of making the long journey from Bradford to London. Moreover, the wonderful kindness that Wallace showed towards his niece (the daughter of Polly's daughter, Joey) when he learnt of her existence, seven years later, proved again that he wasn't one to bear grudges. 'I am convinced I view all of the evidence that the story of his turning his mother away in her last days was a scrap of malicious gossip, a fabrication,' Lane concluded, though she did not reveal from whom she had heard the story.

As well as his domestic reporting, Wallace was also sent abroad from time to time by his newspaper. His first foreign assignment, in 1903, was to Canada. Canada then had Dominion status – meaning that it was self-governing, but that its foreign policy was still controlled by Britain. There were two big news stories involving the Dominion which Alfred Harmsworth was keen for his new reporter to cover. The first concerned the Alaska–Canada border dispute. The Alaskan Boundary Commission had recently met in London, and the casting vote of Lord Alverstone had controversially ceded the disputed strip of Alaskan coastline to the United States and not Canada, thereby denying the latter an all-Canadian route from the Yukon goldfields to the sea. Canadians were incensed at what they saw as a great imperial betrayal, and the country saw a widespread eruption of anti-British sentiment. It was Wallace's job to report on this tide of resentment.

The other big story was tariff reform, which had become the burning political issue of the day. Joseph Chamberlain, Wallace's great political hero, was advocating a system of Imperial Preference – arguing that Britain should drop its traditional policy of free trade and instead impose tariffs on goods imported from outside the empire, with reciprocal tariffs being agreed with countries inside the empire, such as Canada. In September 1903, Chamberlain resigned from the government in order to be free to pursue his campaign for tariff reform. The *Daily Mail* initially opposed his scheme, labelling it the 'Stomach Tax', and argued that it would increase the price of food.

Wallace spent six weeks travelling around Canada, reporting on the local view, but his newspaper's line on tariff reform changed while he was in the country, and so Wallace's line had to change too. Fortunately for him, the articles he sent back were well received at Carmelite House.

Wallace journeyed back to Britain by boat from New York, and on the voyage home he met another celebrity of the day who made a big impression on him, William Jennings Bryan. Bryan was a leading American politician, a charismatic left-wing Democrat, nicknamed 'The Great Commoner', who had already stood twice unsuccessfully for the Presidency, in 1896 and 1900. In 1903 he was still hopeful that his dream would be fulfilled. 'I shall one day be President of the United States and on that day wars will cease,' he told the *Daily Mail*'s reporter. Wallace told the pacifist politician that his wife was expecting their second child and that if it was a boy, they would like to call him Bryan and that they would consider it a great honour if William would consent to be the child's godfather. Ivy and Edgar's next child was indeed a boy, and they did christen him Bryan, but alas William Jennings Bryan never got to be the president of the United States, and world peace remained as elusive as ever.

In 1904, Wallace was sent to warmer climes – to Morocco – and plunged into an extraordinary adventure.

A rebel leader, called Raisuli, had kidnapped a rich Greek-American and his English stepson, and was holding them to ransom in the Rif Mountains, asking for a sum of £14,000 for their release.

Wallace had to overcome one major problem when he arrived in North Africa – his nervousness when it came to riding a horse. He had had a bad fall in South Africa and had opted there to hang up his reins and go around the veld by bicycle. There was no such option open to him in Morocco but, to his credit, he overcame his fears and rode out to meet Raisuli. However, as he rode through a souk, his horse slipped and he fell between the animal and an old wall, spraining his ankle. 'An aged Jew ran out of the bazaar and gave me help,' he recalled, 'incidentally he paid me a real left-handed compliment. "You fell off because of the saddle," he explained soothingly. "I will send a saddle to your hotel from which you cannot fall". Thinking it was something new in Moor inventions, I gave him an order for this prince of saddles, and that afternoon there arrived at my hotel – a pair of boots!'

The *Daily Mail* wanted their star reporter to try and obtain an interview with the rebel leader, but there were significant difficulties lying in the way – not just the horse-riding problem and Wallace's sprained ankle. The British Legation had a policy of non-intervention in Moroccan affairs and weren't going to offer any help. Moreover, Wallace spoke no Arabic. Yet, once again, he achieved what many would have thought was impossible – and acquired for his newspaper a letter from Raisuli, addressed to the *Daily Mail*'s Own Correspondent in Tangier, Edgar Wallace, which was published on 20 June 1904.

Was the letter genuine? Margaret Lane wrote that the letter was 'curiously familiar in style, but with just enough pious reference to Allah to convince the suspicious'.[9] But would Wallace have dared to write it himself and pass it off as Raisuli's work? Surely, if he had done so, the rebel leader would have publicly denounced him, and his journalistic reputation would have been in tatters. Lane theorises that Wallace might have received a letter from Raisuli in response to a 'we should like you to put your case before the public' request, but that he 'resourcefully' padded out the message to fill a full column. A third explanation, equally credible, is that the letter was indeed the sole work of Raisuli. We shall never know for sure, but it went down as another scoop for Wallace, and once again he had left his rivals trailing in his wake.

Wallace's most dramatic experience as a special correspondent came in Spain. He had come to know the country well, having made a least half a dozen trips to Madrid, and had grown to love the Spanish way of life and the Spanish people. Once, he was having a meal in a restaurant in Madrid and the head waiter brought a young English waiter over to his table to help him with the menu. He discovered to his great delight that the waiter had also attended Reddin's Road Board School. 'Now, listen here, my lad,' Wallace said to him, 'bring up a bottle of the best this house can produce and bring two glasses.'

In May 1906 he was sent to Madrid to report on the wedding of the young King Alfonso XIII and Victoria Eugenie of Battenberg. The date of

31 May 1902 had proved a memorable one for Wallace, as it was the day he had scooped the signing of the Boer War peace treaty. The same day in 1906 was to prove even more memorable.

In order to speed up the sending of his report, he had gone the day before the wedding to San Jeronimo, the church where it was to take place. He made a brief sketch of the architecture, examined the service and then wrote an account of the ceremony, leaving blanks in which he could insert 'unforeseen details'. On the big day itself, he enlisted the help of a local correspondent to watch the ceremony from inside the church, and then when it was over the two men, standing in the street outside, checked over the account which Wallace had already written and added in the extra details. Wallace then rushed off to send his cable.

A few years later, in an article entitled 'Condensation in Despatches' he discussed the art of sending cables and getting as much information into a message in as few words as possible: 'Be brief. Don't "have the honour to report" ... If you want help, say "Help". Don't explain why you want it – you can do that at a court-martial. Never mind about grammar; write sense.' Wallace was a brilliant condenser and I am quite sure that if he was around today he'd have no problem with the 140 character limitation on Twitter!

His cable sent, he set off to follow the royal procession. 'I was not exactly "dressed for the party",' he wrote, twenty years later. 'My kit consisted of a white shirt, a pair of grey flannel trousers, nondescript shoes and a broad sombrero, for it was a poisonously hot day; but Spain is essentially a democratic country, perhaps the most democratic country in the world except our own.' Wallace followed the royal coach along the Calle Mayor. Then, according to the account published in his 1926 autobiography, something made him look up. From an upper window in one of the buildings which lined the street, Wallace said he saw a bunch of flowers hurtling down towards the ground. He also thought he saw a glimpse of a man's bare head. 'The moment I saw those flowers, my heart nearly stopped beating. They were dropping at such a rate that there could be no question that they concealed something heavy, something sinister ...'

As the flowers hit the ground there was a huge explosion. 'In a second I was in the middle of a confused, screaming throng of people, mad with fear.' Dying horses lay on the ground and Wallace saw the half-fainting Queen Victoria Eugenie being assisted from her carriage, with her white dress splashed with blood. He saw the King of Spain, standing up and calmly waving encouragement to the crowd – or so he said ...

Wallace, good newspaper man as he was, knew he had to get to the telegraph office as quickly as he could to report the sensational news. But when he arrived, the lines were already closed. Madrid was imposing a media blackout. Wallace not only had to find a way to get the news back to Britain, but he also needed to get some money. He had spent his last peseta on his wedding cable. 'There began the queerest search that any correspondent has ever made – a search in a strange city for money on a holiday when all the banks were closed and Cook's was barricaded!'

Wallace borrowed some money from a hotel by leaving his watch with the hall party, and also got a small amount from a group of British Lancer officers who had come to the wedding. But it was 'a philanthropic American of a trustful disposition' who saved his bacon and who gave him 200 pesetas.

Wallace got to the telegraph office but found that nothing about the assassination attempt would be allowed to pass the censor. He wrote out a series of cables describing what had happened, and mentioning the most plausible of the explanations that he had heard. But how was he to transmit the news to Britain? When he had arrived in Madrid, he had had the foresight to make friends with 'certain important telegraph operators' and had invited them to a dinner at the luxurious Café Fornos. He knew that a special correspondent must keep on very good terms with those who helped him to dispatch his copy to his newspaper. His friends told him that there was unfortunately no way around the censorship, and that even the Prince of Wales' message to King Edward VII had been held up. However, they did tell him that when the wires were open again, he could send a few short ones at 'urgent rates' – i.e. three times the ordinary cost per word. One of the clerks gave him a handful of little red labels, which denoted that the message was urgent and had precedence over ordinary telegrams.

Wallace told his friend that he had insufficient money to send a long wire at urgent rates. He had in his hand a sheaf of telegrams, ready to send. His friend then shrugged his shoulders and turned his back on him. Wallace thought that he was being rude, but he soon understood that the man was trying to help him, for close by was a special basket reserved for the most important telegrams of ambassadors and ministers to their governments. 'Rapidly I stuck on every one the magic red labels and placed them in the basket!' Wallace's wires got through to London, and the next morning's *Daily Mail* contained a series of messages about the dramatic events in Madrid, which Wallace was delighted to record had been conveyed free of charge courtesy of the Spanish government! The brilliant condenser was able to convey all the most important facts about the assassination attempt in just twelve words. 'Royal lovers bombarded returning palace miraculously escaped spectators shambled assassin escaped confusion.'

As we have seen, in his recollection of the assassination attempt published in 1926, Wallace claimed to have seen the actual bomb-throwing. Yet a message he sent to his newspaper from Madrid contradicts this, 'I was writing the last words of a dispatch, when from a distant street came what sounded like a solitary explosion. Some ten minutes later a courier came galloping past and brought the terrible news that a diabolical attempt had been made on the lives of the King and Queen.' It seems that in order to add more romance to the story, Wallace decided to claim in his autobiography that he had witnessed the assassination attempt. If he had been there, then surely he would have said so in his *Daily Mail* cable. Perhaps it's understandable that Wallace should seek to add even more colour to one of his biggest journalistic scoops.

His meal invite to the Spanish telegraph operators had paid rich dividends. Once again he had proved that there was no journalist better at beating the censor and getting an important story out to his editor. This man of working-class origins, who had left school at the age of 12, was showing that he could run rings round his better-educated press colleagues. He took pleasure in the fact that he was outscoring unfriendly upper-middle class journalists who looked down their noses at him.

In his autobiography, Wallace describes how after he had got rid of his cables in Madrid, he went to the house 'of a most important person' who 'was writing for a most important newspaper' which was, at the time, affiliated to the *Daily Mail*. The man was wearing court dress and slippers. He was writing up his account of the wedding. He looked up at Wallace's intrusion 'with no friendly eye'. Wallace told the man about the assassination attempt. The eminent journalist 'closed his eyes wearily' and his hand gesticulated towards the door, 'my dear fellow,' he said, 'I am in the middle of the wedding. Please don't bother me now.' Wallace noted that the man's newspaper did contain a three-lined reference to the bomb-throwing, but added proudly, and with great justification, that 'it owed its origin to the indefatigable Reuter.'

Wallace's adventures were far from over for that day. Most journalists would have thought that they had already earned their stipend. Not Edgar Wallace! That same evening he called on the Royal Palace. The odds of him being allowed in were probably as big as 100–1, especially as the Spanish newspapers were reporting that the assassin was an Englishman – on the basis of a straw hat with the label 'Made in England' being found in the room from which the bomb was thrown. But Wallace, as we have seen many times before, didn't allow wildly improbable odds deter him from a course of action.

To his amazement, he not only got through the military cordon but gained admission to the palace itself. He worked his charm on someone who was either a grandee or a court servant, and was rewarded with a glimpse of the king and queen of Spain on their wedding night. He saw the couple walking slowly down the picture gallery, and he overheard the king amusing his bride with stories of his ancestors. What a day it had been, not just for the royal couple, but for the *Daily Mail* reporter who had been following them around

– 31 May 1906 was certainly a date which neither King Alfonso, Queen Victoria Eugenie nor Edgar Wallace would ever forget.

Wallace had only been working for the *Daily Mail* for a few months when he received a surprise promotion. Walter J. Evans, the editor of the *Evening News*, Alfred Harmsworth's popular London newspaper, was sent north to reorganise the northern office, meaning that the *Evening News* was in need of a temporary editor. Alfred Harmsworth was already impressed with Wallace's work as a reporter and this, together with his experience of editing the *Rand Daily Mail* in South Africa, made him the obvious choice. There would be no pay rise, but for Wallace it represented a stunning come-back. Just a year ago he had been unceremoniously sacked as an editor; now he was in charge of London's best-selling evening newspaper, albeit on a temporary basis.

He had already worked with the London newspaper, on the advertising side. It had been his grand idea to bring out a special Saturday 'Shopper's Edition' of the paper, sponsored by the big department stores. Journalist Bernard Falk, writing in 1951,[10] remembered the impression that Wallace had made on him at the time:

> I would notice a dark, handsome man with nicely-shaped features, an attrac-tive moustache and firmly-rounded chin. Helping to rivet my attention was a glimpse of immaculate white spats over shining boots which looked as if an enormous amount of time and labour had been spent on them. In my memory, too, there is the suggestion of a leather watch-chain, then fash-ionable, strapped to a waistcoat button-hole. My colleagues told me I was gazing at the great Edgar Wallace, who far from nourishing a literary ambi-tion was now set on making money on the advertising side.

Alas, Wallace's 'Shoppers Edition' had not been a success, and only ran to three editions. Now, though, the man with the 'immaculate white spats over shining boots' was back in charge of the whole newspaper.

One of Wallace's many endearing characteristics was his lack of side – he was the same person to underlings as he was to his superiors. He was never one to give himself airs or graces, or lord it over employees when he was in a position of authority. A young sub-editor on the *Evening News* remembered, many years later, how for two nights running, the paper's acting editor came down to sit with him. While he was there, a friend called Wallace to ask if he was free, 'I shall be here until ten o'clock. I'm stopping with the junior sub-editor,' Wallace said. 'You don't mind being called the junior sub-editor?' he asked his companion. 'Well, I am the junior sub-editor,' was the man's answer. Wallace then sent for two jugs of beer. 'Rather admiringly I watched him puff smoke from his amber cigarette holder, which was extended by an inordinately long quill mouthpiece,' the sub-editor recorded.

Although he was very popular with the staff, Wallace did not enjoy the job as much as he thought he would. He was tied to the office far more than he had been in Johannesburg. 'It was a deadly sort of job, involving, as it did office work, and I am not sure I was a born Delane,'[11] he commented. Wallace was in his element as a reporter, wining and dining with contacts, popping off to the races when he had the chance, and using his great charm to coax stories and information from those who didn't really want to say anything, but he was clearly not in his element as a deskbound editor of a London newspaper, with the pressure of overseeing the production of two editions a day.

Personally, as well as professionally, it was a busy time for him. In April 1904 his first son, Bryan, was born. Wallace fetched his American politician friend William Jennings Bryan from his hotel and brought him along to the christening. Bryan received a volume of Tolstoy from his pacifist godfather. Ivy had been ill before and after the birth, and her frail health gave her husband cause for concern. Before the birth, he had paid for Ivy's sister to come over from South Africa to look after her. That was a welcome arrival from the South Africa, but much less welcome were the letters Wallace was receiving on a regular basis from his creditors. It was clear that his debts could not be cleared unless he had a big boost to his income.

Wallace pinned his hopes on the play he had written, based on the life of Cecil Rhodes. He called it *An African Millionaire*. He had sent the finished work to Leonard Rayne, and Rayne had accepted it for production at the Cape Town Opera House. Wallace believed that *An African Millionaire* would make himself a millionaire. It would be a smash hit in South Africa, and then be performed before packed audiences in London and across the empire! What could possibly go wrong?

Alas, quite a lot. The play was mauled by the critics, and ran for just six nights. Rayne quickly dropped it from his repertoire. For Wallace it was a crushing blow, not just because he had hoped that it would help him make his name as a playwright, but because of the financial bonanza he had expected of it. Characteristically, he didn't allow the depression to linger. *An African Millionaire* had been an abject failure, but he would learn from it and move on. In the short term, though, there were still creditors to evade and an urgent need to cut living costs, so Edgar and Ivy moved from Bedford Square to the more affordable Notting Hill Gate where, as Margaret Lane notes, he was not known to the tradesmen.

At No. 37 Elgin Crescent they made a comfortable home for themselves and their baby child as best they could. Edgar was a model father, and for him children were never a distraction from his work. His great ability to be able to do more than one thing at the same time meant that he could sit at his desk composing his newspaper articles, while gently rocking Bryan's pram as he worked. Although he couldn't really afford it, Wallace also employed a general servant, called Susan, to help with Ivy and the baby and with household duties.

In November 1904 Wallace was off again on his travels to cover another important international story. War between Russia and Japan had broken out in February, when the Japanese had launched a surprise attack on the Russian Far Eastern fleet in Port Arthur. On 21 October there was a major international incident when Russian ships, sailing down the North Sea from the Baltic on their way to the Far East, mistakenly fired on and sank some British trawlers. Three British fishermen were killed, as were a sailor and a priest on a Russian cruiser which was caught in the crossfire. There were angry diplomatic exchanges between Britain and Russia and for a time it looked like the so-called 'Dogger Bank incident' could even lead to war.

The *Daily Mail* dispatched their star correspondent to Vigo in Spain, where the Russian battleships were due to stop for coaling, to find out exactly what had happened. Wallace got to the port before the fleet arrived and used the time to good effect to employ a couple of locals to act as interpreters and scouts. He was informed that two petty officers, one of whom spoke English, had secretly come ashore and were spending the evening in a brothel, so Edgar went off to join them. It was a profitable evening for the British reporter, but not for the two sailors. Wallace learnt from the men that the admiral of the fleet, Rozhdestvensky, had panicked. In dense fog, he had believed the trawlers were Japanese torpedo boats. Wallace sent his cable and was told to make his way to Tangiers, the fleet's next port of call. There he learnt some shocking news – his two informants had been detected and had been hanged from the yardarm and buried at sea. They had paid the ultimate price for talking to a British journalist.

11

THE FOUR JUST MEN

> I am going to start a middle course and give them crime and blood and three murders to the chapter; such is the insanity of the age that I do not doubt for one moment the success of my venture.
>
> Edgar Wallace, letter to Ivy, 1905

It was the summer of 1905, and Edgar Wallace could look back with satisfaction at the events of the past two years. Still only 30, he had become established as a well-respected special correspondent. He was in the good books of the most powerful media baron of the day. Millions of people read the daily newspaper in which his work appeared. He had certainly come a long way from his days as a plasterer's assistant in Clacton-on-Sea.

Wallace though, being the man he was, was always looking ahead to the next challenge. He had a steady and reliable income at the *Daily Mail*, but in order to clear his debts and to live in the grand style to which he aspired, he would need to up his game still further. His dream of being a successful playwright had taken a battering with the flop of *An African Millionaire*. But what about trying to make his fortune as a best-selling novelist?

He already had one book on the go in 1905 – a collection of the Smithy army stories he had written for the *Daily Mail*. He tried to get a publisher for the work, but no one was interested, so 'in a moment of magnificent optimism' he decided to set up his own publishing firm. He took a room at No. 11 Temple Chambers and called his business 'The Tallis Press'. Billed as 'The 1905 Holiday Book', copies of *Smithy* went on sale for 1s and The Tallis Press sold around 30,000 copies.

Wallace now conceived of writing a sensational thriller, but one with a difference – the solution to the mystery would be left blank and the public would be invited to solve it, for a cash reward. The plot would involve four highly principled vigilantes – the Four Just Men.

The men's mission is to punish those 'to whom justice could not touch'. The man in their sights is Sir Philip Ramon, the British foreign secretary who plans to introduce an Aliens Extradition (Political Offences) Bill, which would put in danger the brave leader of a Spanish Carlist movement who was based in England. The four threaten to execute Sir Philip at a certain date and time unless the bill is withdrawn, but the home secretary stays firm.

Wallace failed to interest a publisher in his idea, but was not taken aback – if no one else wanted to publish what was sure to be a bestseller, then he would publish the book himself at the Tallis Press. He settled down to writing his thriller, with all his usual energy and enthusiasm. Ivy and his baby son, together with Susan, were away in South Africa, visiting Ivy's family, so at least he had no distractions on the personal front. To help him with his work he employed a young assistant called Mr Wood. 'Mr Wood was neither a rapid shorthand writer nor an infallible typist, but he was industrious and willing, and with his help Edgar first discovered a talent for dictation,' informs Margaret Lane.[1] He also employed a man-servant called Tombs to help with household duties.

To promote his book, Wallace planned a massive advertising campaign. His first thought was to pledge a huge prize of £1,000 for the reader who came up with the correct solution for how the Four Just Men had managed to kill the foreign secretary in a room guarded by police and into which no one had entered. He was persuaded to change his mind by his colleagues at Carmelite House. He told Ivy:

> At the earnest representation of people in the office who know I have made a sweeping change in my prize award. It has been pointed out that £1,000 would probably scare everybody and I have reluctantly reduced it to £500 and split it up into a first prize of £250, a second of £100, a third of £50, a fourth of £25 and fifty prizes of £1. I think this will be much better and will not alarm those people who think there is a swindle in all big prizes.

As for the advertising, Wallace decided to spend £1,000 buying space in the *Daily Mail*, the *Evening News* and the *News of the World*. But that was only the start of it. He arranged for the printing of over 1,000 huge sixteen-sheet posters – each depicting the death of a new character which he had introduced but planned to slay – to appear on 1,250 hoardings across London. 'If that does not sell the book, plus £1,000 worth of advertising, may I be damned!' he wrote to Ivy. He then ordered a further 1,200 eight-sheet posters to be posted 'throughout the best residential suburbs of London and the city' and 2,000 miniature posters to be displayed in shop windows. Wallace was determined that no one in England would be unaware of *The Four Just Men*. Wallace also had grand plans to set up 'establishing book agencies in all the principal towns in England at all the principal stores with the object of forcing a circulation on the public as in the American method'.

Left: Where it all began.

Below left: Polly Richards (Edgar's mother).

Below: Mrs Clara Freeman, 'the gentlest mother that ever lived'.

The young Edgar (Dick Freeman) doing the milk round with 'Handsome' Harry Hanford.

Edgar Wallace, *Reuters* South Africa war correspondent.

As a medical orderly in Simonstown, South Africa. Edgar (right, standing) with his friend, Sergeant Pinder (seated).

Left: Edgar as editor of the *Rand Daily Mail*, 1902–03.

Below left: Edgar at home with Ivy and son Bryan, at Tressilian Crescent, *c.* 1910.

Below: The classic pose.

Edgar and family
at Chalklands
(left to right:
Jim, Edgar, sons
Michael and
Bryan).

Edgar with his
daughter Penny,
c. 1931.

Edgar (sitting,
second left),
formally adopted
Independent
Lloyd George
candidate for
Blackpool,
General Election
1931.

Left: Electioneering with baby.

Below: With Pat and Jim in Blackpool.

Bottom: Edgar (left) working in Hollywood with Robert Curtis, shortly before his death.

Left: Final resting place, in the graveyard at Little Marlow, Buckinghamshire.

Below: Chalklands today, now the Ramakrishna Vedanta Centre.

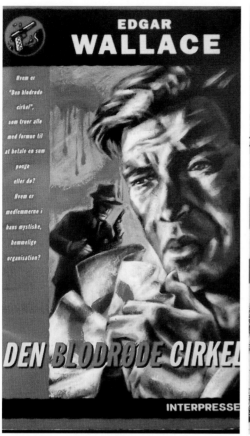

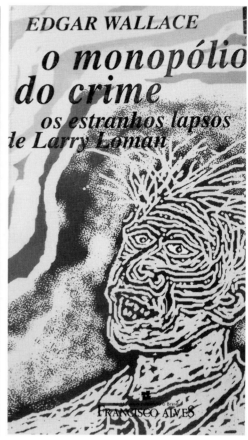

Edgar's international appeal: translated books in Danish, Portuguese, German, Hungarian and Italian (see overleaf).

E. WALLACE

**A
kék kéz**

detektívregény

WALLACE

207 N61

UNA MENTE DIABOLICA

Garden GE Editoriale

He was spending an enormous sum of money to promote the book, but he was fully confident that he'd be able to meet his bills through the profits that would be generated by the book sales. Reckless as it no doubt was, one can only admire his extraordinary optimism. 'The nearer the day comes the less doubt have I to the success of the book. I believe I shall not have an ordinary success but a phenomenal one,' he enthused in a letter to Ivy.

The trouble was that the bills for printing – and for bill-posting – had to be paid before the book brought in any money. He asked Alfred Harmsworth for some financial help, but his employer refused to invest in the project. A friend called Florence Thornton-Smith, a journalist who Wallace had first met on the *Evening News*, proved more helpful. She wired to a friend and borrowed the money to allow Wallace to meet his debts – at least for the time being.

The author and publisher of *The Four Just Men* left no stone unturned in his attempts to make the book a success. It's doubtful if there is any book in history where so much effort had gone into its promotion by just one man. Wallace sent his assistant, Mr Wood, and his man-servant, Tombs, to make a tour of bookshops to request *The Four Just Men*. He posted a copy of the book to Joseph Chamberlain, saying that he would 'everlastingly be obliged to him' if the great man 'could find some way of dragging the FJM into a political speech'. It was wonderfully cheeky, and a typical example of Wallace's chutzpah, but alas, there's no evidence that Chamberlain ever did make a speech mentioning *The Four Just Men*.

The book was sold for 3s 6d and sales were excellent. It deserved to succeed, not just because of the extraordinary effort put into its production and promotion but because it was a rattling good thriller, which engages the reader from the first page to the last. Wallace gets everything in the book right – not a word is wasted, and although he is describing some sensational events, the matter-of-fact style of writing makes it all wonderfully believable. '*The Four Just Men* is a story of anarchists in England, much above the average … Though patently it relates what never occurred, the reader is almost deluded into the idea that it might,' enthused the *Hereford Times*.[2]

Here, for example, is Wallace's description of the preparations made by the authorities to protect the foreign secretary on the day he was due to die:

And within an hour there was witnessed in London a scene that has no parallel in the history of the Metropolis. From every district there came a small army of policemen. They arrived by train, by tramway car, by motorbus, by every vehicle and method of traction that could be requisitioned or seized. They streamed through the stations, they poured through the thoroughfares, till London stood aghast at the realisation of the strength of its civil defences. Whitehall was soon packed from end to end; St James' Park was

black with them. Automatically Whitehall, Charles Street, Birdcage Walk,
and the eastern end of the Mall were barred to all traffic by solid phalanxes
of mounted constables. St George's Street was in the hands of the force,
the roof of every house that overlooked in the slightest degree the Foreign
Secretary's residence was subjected to a rigorous search. It was as though
martial law had been proclaimed, and indeed two regiments of Guards were
under arms the whole day ready for any emergency.

Today we are used to such security operations in our major cities, but to the
reader of *The Four Just Men* in 1905 it would have all seemed terribly fresh
and exciting.

Wallace struck a chord with his idea of four men acting outside the law, in
order to right blatant injustices. Principled vigilantism is an eternal theme, and
works because we all know that some people, whether through their wealth
or connections, or through legal technicalities, are able to evade answering for
their crimes in a court of law. We don't regard the Four Just Men as murderers for killing the likes of the evil embezzler Jacques Ellerman, or Madame
Despard, a notorious 'dealer in lost souls', but as executioners, and we applaud
them for their courage. We also marvel at their ingenuity. In one scene, one of
the Just Men, Leon Gonsalez, disguises himself as an elderly parliamentarian
to leave a dummy bomb in the MPs' smoking room, just to show the government what they are capable of.

The book deserved to make Wallace a very rich man, yet it almost bank-
rupted him. The problem was not just the high advertising costs, but the prize
money which he had offered to readers who came up with the right solution. Foolishly, he had failed to insert a limitation clause when promoting
the book, to stipulate that there could only be one winner for each category.
Correct solutions to the mystery were piling in. Legally he was bound to
pay the money to everyone who had got it right. One man wrote to him
to ask if Wallace would have any objection to him advertising in the *Daily
Mail* and other newspapers that the 'true solution' to the mystery would be
furnished for 6d. Wallace said he had no objection, but the man then proposed
that the author give him the real solution so that he would not give it away.
'I addressed a few words to him which must have left little or no doubt in his
mind as to the view I held of the proposal,' Wallace wrote.

Three months after the book was published Wallace calculated that he still
needed another £2,000 if he was to break even. By now, thousands of readers'
solutions had arrived at the office of the Tallis Press. With no one yet declared
the winner, suspicions were beginning to grow among the public that the
whole thing had been one big swindle. Letters questioning the competition
were sent to the *Daily Mail*. There was even a very funny parody of Wallace's

story and the difficulties he had got into over the reward, called 'Just Four Men in the Same Boat':[3]

> In the foregoing pages I have told a story of absorbing interest, in a style which, I submit, at once places me in the foremost rank of living writers – of this sort of thing. So far I have done well. Now I am non-plussed. This is where you can help. To anybody furnishing me with the best solution to this mystery I will immediately forward a cheque for £500, crossed 'Not Presentable'.

Among the 'instructions' listed at the end of the spoof piece were:

> Solutions may be accompanied by Postal Orders addressed to the 'Lunacy Department, C/o 'Printers Pie'; The reader who sends the greatest number of Postal Orders will have the greatest chance of winning the prize. ... In order that all competitors, their children and grandchildren, may have a fair chance, no date will be fixed for the closing of the competition.

Wallace was under real pressure. He couldn't possibly pay everyone who had got the correct solution. What was he to do?

Work provided a temporary respite from his concerns. Edgar Wallace the novelist was in a pickle, but Edgar Wallace the journalist was continuing to thrive. He was receiving lots of interesting assignments, not just from the *Daily Mail* but from other publications too.

In October 1905, he covered the funeral, in Westminster Abbey, of the great Victorian actor Sir Henry Irving and, in light of the widespread political and social unrest which had spread through Russia that year, he was asked by Alfred Harmsworth to do a series of articles on the bloodthirsty rule of the Tsars, entitled 'Red Pages from Czardom'.

The first, on Peter the Great, appeared on 21 November 1905. Wallace didn't mince his words:

> Peter the Great was a great butcher, an obscene, vicious neuromaniac, a lustful, bludgeoning, coarse brute of a man who got drunk on raw spirits, had respect neither for age, youth, sex, nor kindred. He flogged his wife, tortured with the most horrible torture his one legitimate son, and then burnt and knouted him to death ... The story of the Czars from Peter to Nicholas is the wonderful story in the world's history; you shall see how lunatics and wantons, imbeciles and horrible villains, governed Russia and hold the destinies of its millions in their soiled hands.

Wallace's articles on the excesses of Tsarist Russia perhaps explains why, when the communist revolution did come in 1917, he took a more nuanced view of the political changes than many other writers.

In early 1906 he was off on his travels again, firstly to Spain to report on the conference held at Algericas, to settle spheres of influence of the colonial powers in Morocco. The French were in opposition to the Germans and the Italian delegate Marquis Visconti-Venosta, acting under the instructions of the king of Italy, was attempting to bring the two sides together. Wallace was among the 'small army of correspondents' waiting near the telegraph office in Algericas for the results of the Italians' mediation efforts.

At eleven o'clock at night the Italians' secretary brought a huge wad of telegram forms into the office and gave them to the clerk. Without reading any of the cables, which in any case were in code, Wallace confidently wired off to the *Daily Mail* that the Italians' efforts had been a failure. How did he know? This time he didn't have 'inside' help, but merely deployed masterly logic. If Visconti-Venosta had succeeded, he surely would have sent just one short and triumphant cable to Italy. The fact that the message was so long showed that he had failed. 'The long message, I guessed, was an explanation – and one only explains failures,' Wallace later explained.

The conference dragged on, and in March, Wallace was sent to Lens in France to report on the French miners' strikes. There had been a terrible colliery disaster in Courrieres which had led to riots. The miners believed that engineers had shut down the mines while they were burning and had left their comrades – over 1,000 of them – to their deaths. Wallace was invited to go down one of the still-burning mines, but for once his courage deserted him and he declined. He noted that only one journalist did take up the offer, Albert de Courville, who later found fame as a film director and impresario. De Courville was described by Wallace as 'the most courageous kid I have ever known'. On hearing from his colleague, who saw dead men at the bottom of the shaft, Wallace concluded that the miners' anger was fully justified.

Wallace next headed to Madrid to cover the wedding of King Alfonso, which we have already described, and it was there that he received some very welcome news – a cable from Alfred Harmsworth (by now ennobled and going under the title of Lord Northcliffe) to say that he was prepared to advance him the sum of £1,000 (to be deducted in monthly instalments from Wallace's salary) in order for him to clear his *Four Just Men* debts. Northcliffe may have felt that the charges of 'fraud' levelled against one of his top correspondents were starting to damage his newspaper. Wallace doubted that it was his scooping of the bomb story which had influenced his employer, and put his generosity down to the fact that the owner of the *Daily Mail* liked him. Whatever the reason for Northcliffe's change of heart, Wallace now had the fear of bankruptcy removed from his mind and he could properly enjoy his foreign assignments again.

After Madrid, he received instructions to travel to Lisbon, with the information that a letter would be waiting for him there. When he reached the Portuguese capital, he was given a highly confidential document from the news editor containing unconfirmed information that an attempt was going to be made to assassinate King Carlos. Wallace, through the 'good offices' of a journalistic contact from his days in South Africa, arranged a meeting with the king. The king 'pooh-poohed' the idea that he was in immediate danger, but all the same Wallace decided to stay a week in Lisbon in case there was an attempt on the monarch's life.

After Portugal, it was off to Norway for the coronation of King Haakon on 22 June 1906. 'If it was too far south for the midnight sun, at least it was a land of midnight daylight,' he reflected. The British sent a cruiser to take part in the festivities and, clearly forgetting about Trondheim's northerly position, had organised a firework display as part of their evening programme. As Wallace noted, a firework display in blue, sunlit sky was not the most impressive sight.

Finally, after five months spent reporting from North Africa and Europe, it was time for Wallace to return to Britain. He looked forward to seeing Ivy and Bryan again, and to sorting out his financial affairs. Lord Northcliffe had saved Wallace from bankruptcy with his £1,000 loan, but the author of *The Four Just Men* continued to make decisions which would leave him out of pocket. In an act of great folly, he sold the entire rights of the book to the publisher George Newnes for just £75, instead of holding on to them himself. Perhaps it was because he was in desperate need of the money, but it was a terrible decision all the same.

The Four Just Men has proved to be one of his most enduring books, and has scarcely been out of print since it first appeared in 1905. No fewer than three film versions have been made, while in August 1906, a play of *The Four Just Men* opened at the Colchester Royal Theatre, starring H.A. Saintsbury, a leading actor famous for his portrayal of Sherlock Holmes, and for being the mentor of Charlie Chaplin. Yet Wallace had signed his rights away to the work for a relative pittance. This was no one-off mistake – he was to repeat it on further occasions later on.

For the moment, though, he was just relieved to still be in business. However, it wasn't long before he was in serious trouble again and it all came about over the price of a bar of soap.

In October 1906 Lord Northcliffe decided to launch a newspaper campaign against what he saw as the profiteering of 'the soap trust' – a few powerful companies, headed by Lever Brothers, who he believed were guilty of overcharging the public. The companies had agreed a hike in prices and, at the suggestion of Lever Bros, they were planning to amalgamate and thereby to eliminate the costs of competitive advertising. In the autumn of 1906 the soap companies were regarded as greedy profiteers and, in taking them on, Northcliffe clearly thought he was on to a winner.

The *Daily Mail* published a 'blacklist' of the firms that were planning to amalgamate. They put Edgar Wallace on to the case. He wrote an article entitled 'Cruel Blow to the Poor' highlighting the suffering caused to ordinary people by the soap trust's profiteering. He quoted an anonymous washerwoman, a widow who supported a large family of small children by taking in washing and who was now struggling to make ends meet. 'I stand at my washtub and very often well into the early hours of Sunday morning. To meet the competition of the laundries I have reduced my price to 9*d* a dozen – and at this price, the rise in the price of soap means all the difference between bread-and-butter for my children and dry bread.' As an alternative to a price rise, Lever Bros had decided to reduce the weight of a standard bar of soap by 1oz and was encouraging other manufacturers to do the same. Wallace claimed that such actions had cost the poor widow an extra 1*s* 6*d* a week.

The *Daily Mail* campaign was relentless, and caused Lever Bros great commercial harm. Sales fell, the company's share price slumped, and they were forced to drop their amalgamation scheme and restore their soap bars to their previous size. To counter the negative publicity, they launched a massive advertising campaign, but still the attacks from the *Mail* came. Lever Bros knew they had to stop the campaign and the company took legal advice from two of the greatest legal minds of the day, Sir Edward Carson and F.E. Smith. Counsel told them they had a strong case, and so they decided to sue the owner of the *Daily Mail* and the *Evening News* for libel.

Attention was drawn to the article entitled 'Cruel Blow to the Poor'. Sir Edward Carson, prosecuting, said that if it was true that the washerwoman had lost 1*s* 6*d* a week through the increase in the price of soap, she must have used ninety-six 3*d* tablets. There was laughter all around the court.

While his article was being ridiculed by Sir Edward Carson, Wallace was away reporting in Narbonne, in France, where a strike of wine-growers had developed into a riot. On his return to Britain, he found that he was in deep trouble with his employer. Lever Brothers had won their case, and were awarded £50,000 in damages and costs, the largest sum that had ever been awarded in a libel action in Britain at that time. Worse still for Lord Northcliffe, other soap companies, emboldened by Levers' success, came forward to bring lawsuits against his newspapers. The press magnate was liable for damages of around £250,000.

If that wasn't bad enough, he also had another potential libel case to deal with because of Wallace's failure to check his facts. There had been a minor naval mutiny at Portsmouth, and Wallace had travelled there to investigate. The officer involved was a man called Lieutenant Collard, who stood accused of having improperly given the order 'On the Knee' – i.e. requiring men to go down and kneel, and with having used bad language. Wallace heard from one of the seamen some information about the officer that he decided to include in his report. 'It is a significant fact,' he wrote, 'that four years ago Lieutenant Collard was involved in a similar case, which resulted in a court of enquiry, and Lieutenant Collard losing six months' seniority.'

The trouble was this 'significant fact' was not a fact at all. Wallace had allowed his sympathy with the men's cause to override his journalistic judgement. In his defence, he had sent a telegram to the news editor at the *Daily Mail* asking him to confirm the story about Collard, but alas, no checking was done. Collard's solicitors contacted the *Daily Mail*, who printed an apology. The officer, though, was still not satisfied and sued for libel. This time Northcliffe, no doubt scarred by his experiences with the soap companies, decided to settle out of court for £5,000. Edgar Wallace, for all his brilliance, his ingenuity and his enthusiasm, was proving to be a very expensive employee for the *Daily Mail*.

12

IN DEEPEST AFRICA

'I want to go to Africa,' said William James with the blue light of resolve in his nice blue eyes. 'Yes, sir?' said the agent, and waited. 'Africa,' repeated William, with an air of finality.

Edgar Wallace, 'The Linchela Rebellion', from the *Weekly Tale-Teller*, 1909

In late 1906, before he knew about Lieutenant Collard's libel claim, Edgar Wallace was heading back to Africa for the first time since 1903. This time, however, his destination was not South Africa, but the Congo. The brief he had from the *Daily Mail* was to try and find out if the terrible stories of atrocities carried out by the colonial administration there were true.

The country, then called the Congo Free State, constituted an area around five times the size of France, and had been acquired by King Leopold II of Belgium at the 1885 Conference of Berlin. The colony did not officially belong to Belgium, but was the king's private fiefdom. While all the imperial powers were, at one point or another, guilty of heinous crimes against the native population of the countries they colonised, word started to emerge that, even by the standards of European imperialism, King Leopold's rule in Congo was outrageously brutal. Missionaries told how the natives were treated as slaves, and murdered or mutilated by Leopold's enforcers, the Force Publique, if they did not do what their 'masters' demanded. All that the king cared about was getting as much rubber and ivory from the Congo as he could, regardless of how many people died in the process.

Two brave men did much to inform the world of the horrors that were taking place. In 1904, Roger Casement, the British consul in the capital, Boma, published a white paper in which he detailed the crimes committed against the Congo natives. In 1906, E.D. Morel, a campaigning journalist and member of the Congo Reform Association, published his book *Red Rubber*. Like Casement's report, Morel's book caused a sensation: 'Here is raid, massacre, mutilation, torture, incendiarism, and destruction visited upon a people, not in a state of war at all; but merely as incidental features in the raising of taxation! Since Pharaoh enslaved the Israelitish nation to minister to his ambitions, there has been no parallel to this!' he declared.

Britain's liberal press, led by the *Daily News* and the *Star*, enthusiastically supported the Congo Reform campaign. There were calls for an international conference to be held and for the Congo to be taken away from King Leopold. The public outcry over the Congo atrocities put Lord Northcliffe in a tricky position. It was the *Daily Mail*'s Liberal rivals who were making the running on this issue. The *Mail* obviously couldn't come out in support of Leopold, but there was a school of thought that held the stories were faked or deliberately exaggerated, and part of a cunning German plan to obtain the resource-rich Congo from King Leopold at an international conference. There was also scepticism expressed by some prominent members of the Roman Catholic Church, after Leopold had cunningly portrayed himself as a victimised Catholic, with mistruths being put about by Protestant missionaries.

So it was that the *Daily Mail* decided to send Edgar Wallace out to find out the truth – no doubt hoping that he would come back and report that the stories had indeed been fabricated. Wallace's journey to the heart of the Congo and 'atrocity country' was an arduous one. He travelled in a Belgian steamer from Antwerp to Lulanga. He then spent two days on a train to Leopoldville, the capital, before a ten-day journey on a slow-going river steamer to Lulanga. He still wasn't finished, as he needed to get to Bongandanga, the mission station where Roger Casement had written his report. With the Belgian officials unwilling to help him for obvious reasons, he was forced to rely on a mission steamer called *Livingstone*, with a 'throbbing donkey engine fed on wood chopped nightly by the natives' to get him to his final destination.

It was some experience, even for a man who, at 31, had already had experienced so much. The crew of the ship were cannibals. The landscape they passed was classic jungle, equatorial forest and swamp, with crocodiles in the water and wild beasts prowling at the edge of the river. The missionaries refused to accept any money for taking their extra passenger, but Wallace, in spite of their kindness, was wary of becoming too friendly with his hosts. He was concerned that they may be trying to influence his reporting. 'There was bad blood between the British missionaries and the Belgian officials, and we regarded the missionary angle with a little scepticism,' he later wrote. At first he refused to join in daily prayers, but relented after a missionary told him, 'Oh, don't feel uncomfortable Mr Wallace. You aren't the only heathen on this boat.'

Wallace had scarcely put his foot down in the Congo when he was bitten by a mosquito, 'I paid the penalty for my temerity in appearing at sundown without mosquito-boots' and, fourteen days after the bite, went down with Blackwater fever. As he sat convalescing on the boat, reading Charles Dickens' *Little Dorrit*, he heard a commotion. Forty-three natives, who had come out in an iron-barked canoe to board the vessel, had bumped into it and their canoe had capsized. 'I have the most vivid recollection of watching these drowning people, never dreaming that they could not swim, for the river folk are as much at home in the water as the indigenous crocodile,' Wallace wrote, 'In fact I was rather amused at their horrified faces, thinking that they were putting up a little stunt for my amusement, since the cannibal has a great sense of fun.' Wallace never did finish his reading of *Little Dorrit* and was put off the book for life.

There were shades of the classic film *The African Queen* in the way that the pipe-smoking, and not-very-religious man of the world, Wallace, gradually got to like and respect his more pious companions. 'I have nothing to say against missionaries,' he wrote, 'they treated me royally whilst I was their guest.' In a story he wrote six years later[1] he was even more effusive in his praise:

> You must understand that missionaries are very good people. Those igno-ramuses who sneer at them place themselves in the same absurd position as those who sneer at Nelson or speak slightingly of other heroes. Missionaries take terrible risks ... they cut themselves adrift from the material life which is worth the living ... they suffer from tempestuous illnesses which find them hale and hearty in the morning and leave their feeble bodies near death at sunset.

When he arrived at the missionary station he was given accommodation in the bungalow of the Reverend H.S. Gamman, who gave him his report detail-ing over 500 different cases of atrocities carried out by the Belgian officials against the natives. Wallace, though, was eager to find out for himself what had been going on, and with the aid of an interpreter, set out for tribal villages to gather first-hand testimony.

He had always had the natural curiosity which is essential for a good reporter, and he was genuinely fascinated by the people he was encountering. Other British journalists might have felt out of their element in the jungle in the middle of Africa, but for Wallace it was all tremendously fresh and excit-ing. He learnt about tribal culture – about witchdoctors and jujus, fetishes, sacrifices and palavers. He took a great interest in the Lomongo language, the tongue spoken by the Mongo and Ngombe tribes of that region, diligently studying the grammar compiled by the Reverend Gamman when he was back at the bungalow.

According to Gamman, Wallace was convinced that the atrocity stories were true. He not only believed the natives' accounts but he told the Reverend that he had seen evidence of atrocities with his own eyes.[2] Lane also cites an article of Wallace's published in February 1907 for the *Congo Balolo Mission Record*, in which he mentioned the 'oppression and neglect' of the natives, and of 'unimaginable cruelties'.[3] He wrote:

> Already the Congo is to me as a dreadful nightmare, a bad dream of death and suffering. Such a dream as one sees o' nights when nothing is right, when every law of man and nature is revolted, and the very laws of life are outraged … In another place, and in other columns than these, I shall take upon myself the journalist's privilege of prejudging posterity's verdict.

Yet Wallace's account of the Belgian atrocities did not appear in 'other columns'. When he returned to Britain, he was in for a real shock – Lord Northcliffe summoned him to his office and gave him the sack.

According to Margaret Lane, Wallace claimed, in a letter to Reverend Gamman's father, that Northcliffe had supressed his articles on the Congo and had fired him because he refused to change his line on the atrocities.[4] Yet in his autobiography, written nearly twenty years later, Wallace makes no mention of this and more or less confirms that he was dismissed because of the Lieutenant Collard libel case. 'I was entirely in the wrong. I had sent off an account from Portsmouth of a naval "mutiny" without being careful to verify the facts before I wrote the story,' he admitted. Wallace noted that he was the only man who had ever been fired by the *Daily Mail*.

He had been a favourite of Lord Northcliffe's and had provided the newspaper with some memorable scoops, and his reports had no doubt helped boost the newspaper's circulation, but his failure to check important facts carefully had made him a luxury the newspaper could no longer afford.

Before we describe how Wallace dealt with this huge blow to his pride – and to his bank balance – there's an interesting and intriguing postscript to the tale of his adventures in the Congo. Although he never had the opportunity to publish his reports in the *Daily Mail*, he did write about his time in the country in his autobiography. But there, he took a very different line to the one in the *Congo Balolo Mission Record*: 'I saw no evidence of atrocities that were not fourteen years old,' he declared.

Not only that, but he attacked the two men who did so much to expose the horrors to the world. 'Germany coveted the Congo, and I am perfectly satisfied in my mind that, in so far as Morel was concerned, he was a propagandist agent working on behalf of the German Foreign Office. With him was Sir Roger Casement, a man who in all sincerity hated England and the English, and was, moreover, a decadent of decadents.'

How can we explain the fact that Wallace regarded the Congo as a 'bad dream of death and suffering' in 1907, but dismisses the whole thing as a German propaganda campaign twenty years later? Well, of course the First

World War had occurred in the meantime, and it became easier to see events in the years which led up to that terrible conflict as part of a dastardly German plot. Moreover, Belgium, the villain of the piece in 1906 had become the 'plucky little Belgium' the victim of German aggression in 1914.

E.D. Morel and Roger Casement, who had been regarded as heroes, also fell foul of the British Establishment in the intervening years. Morel, a committed pacifist, opposed Britain's entry into the First World War, and was sentenced to six months' imprisonment for his anti-war agitations. Roger Casement fared even worse; he was found guilty of treason for his dealings with Germany before the 1916 Easter Rising in Ireland and duly executed. To blacken his name still further after his conviction, the authorities released what they claimed were Casement's diaries which detailed his homosexual affairs – hence the labelling of Casement as 'a decadent of decadents' by Edgar Wallace, who shared the predominant attitudes of the age towards homosexuality.

It is perhaps understandable that Wallace didn't feel like taking an anti-Belgian line in 1926, and why he felt ill-disposed towards Morel and Casement, but even so, it's disappointing that he decided to go with the times and the Establishment – and not with the truth. King Leopold's bloody rule of terror in the Congo cost the lives of around 10 million people. It was one of the greatest crimes in history – but it's one which tends to get overlooked in comparison with other horrendous crimes which followed in the twentieth century. Wallace was there, and saw with his own eyes what was going on, yet felt obliged to record a very different version twenty years later. It's interesting to reflect that, if he hadn't been fired by the *Mail* on his return and his original work had been published by the newspaper in 1907, he would have been able to successfully prejudge 'posterity's verdict' as he had earlier promised. Alas, it was not to be.

13

CAPTAIN TATHAM AND COMMISSIONER SANDERS

There are many things that happen in the very heart of Africa that no man can explain; that is why those who know Africa best hesitate to write stories about it. Because a story about Africa must be a mystery story, and your reader of fiction requires that his mystery shall be, in the end, X-rayed so that the bones are visible.

Edgar Wallace, *Sanders of the River*, 1911

Edgar Wallace was used to bouncing back after setbacks, but to be sacked by the *Daily Mail* was a hammer blow. He had acquired a reputation as a journalist who – for all his brilliance – was far too cavalier when it came to checking his facts, and for newspapers, fearful of being involved in expensive libel cases, he represented too big a risk.

If Wallace had managed to accumulate some savings during his time at the *Mail*, then things would not have been so bad, at least in the short term. But Wallace being Wallace, he still had debts to settle. Some of *The Four Just Men* debts were still outstanding, as was a milkman's bill for £70. He began to sell off his and Ivy's more valuable possessions in a desperate effort to keep the bailiffs away. It was hardly the best time for the couple's third child to be born, but in September 1907 Ivy gave birth to a baby girl, who was christened Patricia.

To escape his creditors, and to cut their living expenses, Wallace decided the family had to move again. So, in January 1908, they left Notting Hill Gate for Brockley, in the borough of Lewisham, in south London, not too far from where Wallace had grown up. Their new house was No. 6 Tresillian Gardens, where conveniently there was a back gate through which the master of the house could escape when the creditors came calling at the front. Once, though, a bailiff did get through but Wallace challenged him to a game of whist and won back all the money he owed during a marathon all-night session.

Not surprisingly, the straitened financial circumstances and Wallace's lack of a regular income put Ivy and Edgar's marriage under increased strain. 'The constant worry made Edgar gloomy and irritable, and Ivy, unable to summon an artificial gaiety, became silent and nervous, and at the first sign of a quarrel took refuge in tears,' says Margaret Lane.[1] It couldn't have been much fun for either of them, not knowing where the next pay cheque was coming from, and with a baby to look after, along with Bryan.

For Edgar these were depressing times, easily the worst period he had known in his adult life. Desperate to do anything to get his 'lucky run' going again, he became intensely superstitious. Lane records how he insisted on working by the light of an old orange lamp, just because a bazaar fortune teller had once told him that orange was a lucky colour. He gave Florence Thornton-Smith his tie to take to a palmist, but was disappointed when she told him that the clairvoyant had warned her never to trust its owner with money. He tried to 'turn a key' in the Bible.

But to his credit, Wallace never gave up. It was hard at first, but having no regular job to go to at least gave him more time to write. 'He worked, how he worked! He wrote anything, everything for anyone who'd pay – fiction, articles, serials, sport – anything. Edgar Wallace didn't have the divine inspiration – he didn't need it. He had relentless industry. He survived,' wrote James Cameron.

In addition to his articles and short stories, Wallace had two novels published in 1908. His reputation as a journalist may have been tarnished, but as a novelist the success and popularity of *The Four Just Men* had ensured that his stock was high. *The Council of Justice* was a sequel to *The Four Just Men*, but like many follow-ups, was not as good. Whereas *The Four Just Men* rattles along at a terrific pace, *The Council of Justice* tends to drag in places. While in the first book our heroes are doing their best to outwit the authorities, in the latter they are clearly on the side of the Establishment, in their battle against a group of revolutionary anarchists called the 'Red Hundred', led by the mysterious 'Woman of Grazt'. Our sympathies are unreservedly with the men in the first book, but in the sequel, there are times when we're left wondering if the enemy is really all that bad. The Four Just Men, or rather the Three Just Men as they now were, had become too conservative, too keen on the status quo – and the book suffers because of it.

The foreword is one of the most interesting parts of the book, as Wallace expounds on his support for vigilantism:

> Frankly I say of *The Council of Justice*, of the three men who killed Sir Philip Ramon, and who slew ruthlessly in the name of justice, that my sympathies are with them. Were I clever enough, or bold enough, or free from responsibilities; were I, in fact, any of the things that man never is, I should be proud and happy to make a fourth in this remorseless Council. ... There are crimes for which there is no adequate punishment, and offences that the

machinery of the written law cannot efface. Therein lies the justification for *The Council of Justice* – a council of great intellects, passionless.

The other book Wallace had published in 1908, in July, was *Angel Esquire*, which had first appeared in serial form that year for *Ideas* magazine. It told the story of the millionaire owner of a gambling establishment who, in his will, gets his possible legatees to compete against each other to solve an ingenious puzzle, with the winner receiving the prize fund. The battle is between Kathleen Kent, the heiress of one of the men old man Reale had duped, and the men who helped him do the fleecing. 'Angel Esquire' is the nickname of Mr Christopher Angel, the first of many gentlemen policemen from Scotland Yard who appear in Wallace's novels. Another regular fixture in Wallace's books – the crooked lawyer – also makes his debut in the shape of Mr William Spedding.

Wallace now had a new assistant to help him. Cassidy had been a friendly window cleaner who had come to clean the windows of the Wallace household. Ivy liked his demeanour and his appearance, and asked him if he would like to do odds jobs around the house for a few shillings. Cassidy proved to be a real godsend. He did everything in the Wallace house from brushing and pressing the master's clothes, administering first aid to the children when they fell, and giving the alert when creditors appeared at the front door. Away from the house, he would take Wallace's articles off to Fleet Street and bargain for cash payment for them, and also appear in the County Court in his master's stead to answer summonses. To Cassidy we must give a lot of the credit for Ivy and Edgar's surviving the two difficult years following the Edgar's dismissal from the *Daily Mail*. They would simply not have been able to cope on their own. Sometimes Wallace couldn't afford to pay him, but he always made it up in the end and Cassidy, to his credit, never made a fuss.

In the spring of 1909, Hulton published a collection of twenty-four 'Smithy' stories that had appeared in the magazine *Ideas*, until the title *Smithy Abroad* and two more books by Wallace appeared that year.

Captain Tatham of Tatham's Island, published in April by Gale & Polden, was 'a novel of romance and adventure', concerning a charismatic American, who sets out to form an independent state on a solitary uninhabited island in the middle of the Pacific, which he believes holds large reserves of gold. 'Who else but Edgar Wallace could have conjured up such a character as Captain Tatham?' the blurb on the back of a later reprint declared. 'One-time newsboy, soldier, pirate and a filibuster in the grandest manner!' The novel is unusual in that it is told not in straight narrative form, but by means of a series of individual statements made by parties to the story. It was Wallace's best book since *The Four Just Men*, perhaps partly because he put so much of himself and his own experiences into it.

Wallace made Edward G. Tatham a Virginian, but other than his American background, it's not hard to work out who he was modelled on. He was born on 1 April 1873, two years to the day before the author. His parents died when he was young, leaving him to be reared by a foster parent. At the age of 12 he crossed the Atlantic and was convicted and fined 2s 6d for selling newspapers in the street. He was charged with assaulting another young vendor. 'I have seen in a newspaper file of the period an account of the trouble which arose as a result of young Tatham's first interference with vested interests – for Patrick Moriarty claimed the monopoly of selling *Freeman's Journals* in that particular section and resented the appearance of a newcomer', a narrator tells us. Interference with vested interests? Wasn't that something Wallace had done with his articles against Lever Bros' Soap Trust?

The biography of Tatham continues along familiar lines:

Of his life in London as a boy little is known. He worked, that is certain. But he was never more than two or three months in any one job. I have traced him to printers, shoemakers, milk vendors. He seemed to be consumed with a spirit of restlessness which made the monotony of any form of employment maddening.

Tatham attends evening classes, and one of his history essays was printed in the council magazine. 'He was quick to learn, immensely alert, "and," said a master who remembered him, "gifted with an extraordinary imagination".'

There are biographical similarities too with other characters in the book. 'Second witness' Ernest Stuckey sailed to South Africa in 1899 to fight with the British Army. Like Wallace, he too was involved with Henniker's column and went to Wynberg hospital, where he met Tatham and clashed with De Wet.

'Fourth witness' Richard Callus is a 'journalist, traveller and novelist', a man – like Wallace – 'with a fine nose for a good story and the gift of telling one'. 'A journalist differs from all other writers in his overmastering passion for facts,' says Callus in his testimony – perhaps this is the author expressing his regret that he had not been more careful with his facts when working for the *Daily Mail*?

It's also interesting to read derogatory references to the Congo Free State in the book, which show that in 1909 Wallace was still holding to his original position on the atrocities of King Leopold's forces. Captain Tatham reveals that he has chosen to steal a steamer called the *Pealo* 'because it belongs to an unpopular government, in fact a government that isn't a government at all. No court of law with a sense of humour would pursue a charge of piracy brought by the Congo Free State – the very idea is so grotesquely comic that the case would laugh itself out of court.'

If we take Tatham's contempt for the Congo Free State as a sign that he's enlightened on the matters of race, then we're cruelly disappointed later on. In an altercation with a rival suitor and his father from Brazil he uses the 'n' word and contemptuously refers to the men being half-breeds. 'With Tatham a man was either black or white; he recognised no intermediary stage. Once let him depart from the pure white stock, and in Tatham's eyes he might as well be coal black. On this point he was a fanatic,' we are informed. Thankfully, Wallace makes it clear that he does not approve of his hero's blatant racism: 'Tatham in his insolence was the most offensive man I have ever met,' Richard Callus notes in his testimony, and he labels 'half-breed' as a 'horrid word'. Wallace may have included the scene – and others in which Tatham comes across as a rather overpowering bore – to prevent us from regarding him as a paragon, which it certainly does. It was one of the strengths of his writing that his heroes were rarely without flaws and his villains were seldom wholly evil.

Captain Tatham of Tatham's Island was written when Wallace was at a low ebb, but the plot of the book and his portrayal of Tatham reveals much about how Wallace hoped to overcome his own difficulties. Tatham is a dreamer, but he's also intensely practical. He is a man bursting with ideas. On one page alone he invents a new gas 'Tathogem' and announces a scheme for producing coal gas. Whatever the obstacles he encounters, he never allows himself to become despondent: 'Nothing seemed to depress Tatham however; he was as cheerful as cricket, so cheerful in fact that Callus set himself, out of sheer cussedness, to tone him down.'

Compare that with a description of Wallace penned by his daughter, Penelope, many years later: 'I think his most useful characteristic was his optimism. A play which failed? Something to be learned in future attempts. A bad day at the races? A frequent occurrence – a good day tomorrow. From every dismal valley, he could see the sunny uplands.'

Tatham finds a thoroughbred racehorse on his island and takes 'The Flying Scout' to England to race, where he lands some monumental gambles – winning the equivalent of over $50,000 on one race alone. How Wallace the compulsive, horserace-loving gambler would love to do that! Tatham possesses enormous nerve. Desperate to get back to London as soon as possible from Doncaster races, he cheekily boards an empty smoking carriage on the royal train. 'All you have to do,' he tells Callus, 'is to sit tight; meantime, busy yourself by putting your coat and hat upon the rack. So long as you are standing so that some enterprising detective cannot see your face you are all right.'

Wallace clearly believed that he could overcome his difficulties if, like Tatham, he carried on thinking big and coming up with new ideas – and provided he kept his nerve. The moment he stopped dreaming, he would fail. So long as he carried on 'attacking' life, be it in front of a typewriter or at the racetrack, he would be fine.

The Duke in the Suburbs, Wallace's next book, was a romance in which the Duke of Montvillier and his American buddy, Hank, move to Brockley and find themselves living next door to an impecunious mother and her daughter, Alicia Merrill. Alicia's father lost the family money speculating, but the kind-hearted duke sets out to help her.

Already in his first five novels Wallace had shown a remarkable range, but he didn't make as much money from the books as he should have, as he repeated the mistake he had made with *The Four Just Men,* and sold all his rights away. Lane says that he sold his rights for the first four books after *The Four Just Men* for sums between £70 and £80, although another source[2] says that Ward Lock purchased *The Council of Justice* on a 15 per cent royalty. It was the desperate need to raise money quickly to pay the bills that led Wallace to take the short-term view when it came to selling his work.

Wallace was out of favour on Fleet Street, but he hadn't given up hope of making contacts which could revive his journalistic career. He was a regular visitor to the Press Club, and it was there that he had an introduction to George Beech, the manager of Shurey's Publications. Beech commissioned a couple of horse racing articles from him, and then mentioned him to Shurey's fiction editor, Isabel Thorne, who edited two magazines, *Yes & No* and *The Weekly Tale-Teller,* which was launched in May 1909. Wallace sent Mrs Thorne two short stories and, on Beech's request, she agreed to meet him. It was a meeting which would have very happy consequences for Wallace and get him back on the road to success.

According to Wallace, Mrs Thorne told him that she would pay for one of his short stories, but the other wasn't good enough for publication. Wallace then asked her for some frank advice on how he could break into the short story market. He told her how he had written four novels in the past two years but hadn't made much money from them. What was the secret for making it big in the financially lucrative short story market? Lane records how Mrs Thorne gave Wallace an hour of her time, which included an 'explicit lecture' on what a short story for the *Weekly Tale-Teller* ought to be. Wallace left her office 'looking subdued and thoughtful'.

Who knows what might have happened had Mrs Thorne and Wallace not met again by chance a few evenings later? Wallace was sitting on the top deck of a bus bound for London Bridge Station, on his way to chair a meeting of the Congo Reform Association in the East End. Mrs Thorne boarded the bus, and the first vacant seat was next to Wallace. They got chatting and Wallace told Mrs Thorne where he was going, and of his adventures in Congo, and what he had heard about Sir Harry Johnston[3] and other commissioners in Africa on his journey there. 'But good heavens!' Declared Mrs Thorne, 'why are you worrying about good material for short stories? You've got everything there – colour, excitement, an exotic background and some wonderful characters! Why on earth don't you utilise your knowledge and write me some African stories for the *Weekly Tale-Teller?*'

Wallace was so excited by this suggestion that he forgot to change buses and journeyed with Mrs Thorne to London Bridge. 'There they walked up and down the platform, arguing, questioning and planning, and Mrs Thorne's train was allowed to go, and several of its successors, before they could relinquish the discussion of an idea which seemed to both of them little short of inspiration,' says Lane.[4]

Wallace couldn't wait to get home to start work on the outlines for the stories. In his enthusiasm he completely forgot that he was supposed to be chairing a meeting on the Congo. Typically, when an idea grabbed him, he worked at a feverish rate until the job was complete. Everything else was sacrificed. He went to see Mrs Thorne the next morning with the outlines for the stories. Lane informs that the 'first six or eight were each minutely discussed.' Wallace wasn't writing stories about Africa for the first time – it is likely that his story *The Forest of Happy Thoughts*, about a man who becomes a fugitive from justice in Africa, and which was turned into a play called *The Forest of Happy Dreams*, was written before he penned any Sanders tales. But now, with the district commissioner as his main character, he had the framework for a whole series of stories.

In 1909 the first of Wallace's Sanders stories appeared in the *Weekly Tale-Teller*. They became a huge success.

Wallace got his ideas from a number of sources. Firstly, there were the tales he had heard as a medical orderly in South Africa when he treated wounded soldiers returning from Admiral Rawson's Benin Expedition in 1897. Secondly, there were the stories he had heard about Sir Harry Johnston and other British commissioners while on his way to the Congo. Finally, there were his own experiences in the Congo. 'The material for the best of these stories came to me when I was a thousand miles upriver, suffering from Blackwater fever, for in that period I was brought face to face with the primitive in its most hideous and at the same time its most fascinating aspect,' he recalled in 1925.[5]

Wallace didn't set his African tales in the Congo, as it wasn't British territory and so decided to transport all that he had encountered in central Africa – the tribal languages, the tribes, the animals and even a gunboat called *Zaire* – to an unspecified part of west Africa, where he could have the British flag flying proudly.

Wallace's hero was Mr Commissioner Sanders – a no-nonsense, cigar-smoking colonial administrator who spoke the local tongue and who was loved and feared in equal measure by the ¼ million cannibals he ruled over. 'There is one type of man who can rule native provinces wisely, and that type is best represented by Sanders,' informs Wallace:

> You may say of Sanders that he was a statesman, which means that he had no exaggerated opinion of the value of individual human life [we are told at the beginning of the first story *The Education of the King*] When he saw a dead leaf on the plant of civilisation, he plucked it off, or a weed growing with his 'flowers' he pulled it up, not stopping to consider the weed's equal right to life. When a man, whether he was *capita* or slave, by his bad example endangered the peace of his country, Sanders fell upon him. In their unregenerate days, the Isisi called him 'Ogani Isisi', which means 'The Little Butcher Bird' and certainly in that time Sanders was prompt to hang.

In the third story, we are introduced to Bosambo, who becomes the native hero of the Sanders canon. Named after the Bosombo River in the Congo, Bosambo is an escaped prisoner from Monrovia in Liberia, who flees to 'Sanders country' and becomes chief of the Ochori. Sanders decides to pay a visit and Bosambo feigns illness. Sanders goes into his tent and touches the prostrate body, he feels 'a scar of singular regularity' and recognises it as the convict brand of the Monrovian government. He gives Bosambo a kick and tells him he has a mind to hang him, but he thinks better of it and asks if Bosambo can make men of the Ochori. The Monrovian says he can, and so Sanders allows him to remain as chieftain 'for I see you are a clever man!'. 'Master by the fat of my heart I will do as you wish,' replies Bosambo, 'for I have always desired to be a chief under the British.'

Bosambo is a bit of a rascal, but loveable and he loyally supports Sanders and the British Empire in his work. When the commissioner has gone, an awe-stricken councillor asks Bosambo, 'Did you know the great one?' 'I have cause to know him,' Bosambo replies, 'for I am his son.' 'Fortunately Sanders knew nothing of this interesting enclosure,' Wallace adds.

Later on, two more important characters are added – Lieutenant Hamilton, 'Captain of the Houssas' was Sanders' sidekick; like his master, a cool colonial type; the humorous element was provided by Lieutenant Tibbetts, nicknamed 'Bones', a pre-Bertie Wooster monocle-wearing 'silly arse'. 'I first met the real Bones on a German steamer, coming up from Mossamedes to take over his duties at one of the little stations which are to be found in such queer places on the coast. A lank, irresponsible youth, who had remained a child in mind, he told me stories of his Sanders that got me thinking,' Wallace later wrote.[6]

Bones may be a bit of an idiot but he knows no fear and often saves the day. In one later Sanders story, Bones' terrible bagpipe playing scares off a king and his spearmen who have prepared an ambush, but Bones being Bones is puzzled as to why the men had run away. Bones' popularity with readers soon began to surpass that of Mr Commissioner himself. In 1911, Wallace's first batch of Sanders stories was published in book form. It was dedicated to 'Isobel Thorne, who was largely responsible for bringing Sanders into being'.

While they were a big hit with readers when they first appeared, and indeed for many years afterwards, the Sanders stories are, out of all of Wallace's work, the most uncomfortable to read today. By the standards of 1911, Wallace's Africa tales are not particularly objectionable – in fact they would be regarded as at the 'progressive' end of the spectrum. Wallace believed in the right of the British to rule over Africans and other nationalities, but he did not believe that the imperialists should behave with wanton cruelty. The colonial rule should be firm but fair, unlike for example, the maladministration he had witnessed in the Congo Free State.

That said, for today's readers, the books are still marred by their patronising view of the 'natives' and the way that Sanders and the author treats them like children who need looking after. Here is an early passage from the first Sanders story:

> By Sanders' code you trusted all natives up to the same point, as you trust children, with a few notable exceptions. The Zulu were men, the Basuto were men, yet childlike in their grave faith. The black men who wore the fez were subtle, but trustworthy; but the browny men of the Gold Coast, who talked English, wore European clothing, and called one another 'Mr' were Sanders' pet abomination. Living so long with children of a larger growth, it follows that he absorbed many of their childlike qualities.

In similar vein, here's an extract from 'The Tamer of Beasts', a story from *The Keepers of the King's Peace*, published in 1917:

> Native folk at any rate, are but children of a larger growth. In the main, their delinquencies may be classified under the heading of 'naughtiness'.

Then there are the racist stereotypes, for example in the story where Bosambo is first introduced:

> With all due respect to the Republic of Liberia, I say that the Monrovians are naturally liars and thieves.

There is, though, a difference – albeit a subtle one – between the earlier Sanders stories and the later ones, which reflects the changing political climate. In 'The Magic of Fear', written in 1926, Wallace shows his contempt for a racist and arrogant British politician called Nickerson Haben who visits Africa in his capacity as under-secretary of foreign affairs. Haben sneers when Sanders introduces Agasaka, a native woman who, he says, has a 'peculiar brand of magic'. The politician accuses Sanders of absorbing native philosophies and superstitions, and uses the 'n' word. Sanders winces. '"N" is a word you do not use in Africa,' writes Wallace, who clearly disapproves. Agasaka, it is claimed, has the power to bring before the eyes of men and women that which they least desire to see. Haben reveals, under the influence of the native woman, that he has murdered his wife. 'Go to your room, sir,' says Sanders, and he spends 'the greater part of the night composing a letter to the Foreign Secretary.'

If we can imagine ourselves as British readers of the Sanders stories in 1911, and holding the 'mainstream' attitudes towards the British Empire of that era, then it's not hard to understand why the stories were so successful. They were well written, very entertaining, and had 'twist in the tail' endings. What comes over most of all in them, is Wallace's love of Africa – its customs, its superstitions, its colour, its magic and its mystery. It's easy to criticise the Sanders tales today, but they did enable millions of ordinary Britons, who would never have visited Africa, nor were ever likely to, to get a feel for what life was like in the 'Dark Continent'. Sanders' adventures broadened people's horizons, took them away from their daily worries and dull, parochial affairs, and transported them to an exotic land where anything could happen – and usually did. They learnt about palavers, juju, tribal customs and even a little bit about languages.

Wallace had good cause to love Africa. It is no exaggeration to say that the continent made him. We have seen how the young Dick Wallace who boarded the *Scot* in Southampton in 1896 bound for Cape Town returned from South Africa as a celebrated war correspondent. It was in South Africa that he met Kipling and began his writing career. Now the Sanders stories had given that career a timely boost, just when it had needed one. Between 1910 and 1926 Edgar Wallace was to write over 100 Sanders tales. If he had never written anything else it would still have been a great and lasting achievement, but there was so much more for readers to look forward to from a man whose sole mission was to keep them entertained.

14

BACK ON FLEET STREET

Fleet Street is a Mecca,
Fleet Street is a star,
Calling sage and magi
From the lands afar
Fleet Street is a tyrant
Fleet Street is a wife,
Once you're wed to Fleet Street
You are hers for life.

Edgar Wallace, 'Madame Fleet Street'

Wallace was on a roll. Not only did he have the *Weekly Tale-Teller* publishing his Sanders adventures, but his Smithy sketches were also appearing in a penny weekly called *Ideas*. *Ideas* was happy to receive as many Smithy sketches as their author could write, and Wallace was happy to oblige. Once, though, he forgot to file. Lane records how the panic-stricken editor rang him up asking where his copy was. 'It's on its way down,' Wallace replied, 'you'll have it within an hour.'[1] He then sat down to work at his usual breakneck pace and sent Cassidy to take the sketch by taxi to the *Ideas* office. The deadline was made.

Even more pleasingly, Wallace had also got an offer to return to Fleet Street as a reporter. The newspaper in question was the *Standard*, a London daily whose news editor was an old *Daily Mail* pal of Wallace's called Charles Watney. It was three years since Wallace had been unceremoniously sacked by Northcliffe. Now he was back where he felt he belonged, and where he loved to be. It was a sad occasion, but how proud he must have felt to be covering for his new employer the funeral of King Edward in May 1910. One month later, Wallace was at Royal Ascot to cover his favourite race meeting of the year, with a 'free ticket and a gold sovereign'.

His good run of luck continued when he landed substantial winnings of £1,000, not perhaps in the Captain Tatham league, but proof to him once again that fortune favours the brave. He was so elated by his success that he forgot about filing his report, and it wasn't until midnight when he was drinking champagne and stout with his friends at the Press Club that he was reminded that he had a column to write. Fortunately his pals helped him out. 'As we celebrated so we collaborated, and the story duly appeared,' remembered Fleet Street colleague, James Dunn.[2]

In the meantime, he was still working on short stories, serials and novels. In September 1910 *The Nine Bears,* Wallace's gripping tale about a group of crooked financiers out to make their fortune on the stock markets by 'anticipating' disasters which they themselves helped to bring about, was published by Ward Lock, with the story having earlier appeared in serial form. In chapter fifteen there is a wonderful description of life in a newspaper office in the early years of the twentieth century, showing Wallace's deep love for the craft of newspaper production:

> The door that opened into the tape-room was swinging constantly now, for it wanted twenty minutes to eleven. Five tickers chattered incessantly, and there was constant procession of agency boys and the telegraph messengers passing in and out of the vestibule of the silent building. And the pneumatic tubes that ran from the front hall to the subs' room hissed and exploded periodically, and little leathern carriers rattled into the wire basket at the chief sub's elbow.
>
> News! News! News! A timber fire at Rotherhithe; the sudden rise in Consols; the Sultan of Turkey grants an amnesty to political offenders; a man kills his wife at Wolverhampton; a woman cyclist run down by a motorcar; the Bishop of Elford denounces Nonconformists-News for tomorrow's breakfast table; intellectual stimulation for the weary people who are even now kicking off their shoes with a sleepy yawn and wondering whether there will be anything in the paper tomorrow.

1910 was also the year that Wallace took his first steps to break into the American market. He signed a contract with Dodd Mead, a New York–based publisher, for a story also entitled *The Nine Bears*, and gave them what was essentially a revised and longer version of the book published by Ward Lock, with the name of the principal villain changed from Silinski to Poltavo. The American novel appeared in March 1911 under the title *The Other Man*. 'Whether or not Ward Lock and Dodd Mead knew or became aware of each other's interest in a similar story is likely to remain a mystery,' commented Wallace expert John Hogan in 1977.[3]

Towards the end of the year there was more good news on the professional front. Two new publications were launched by Wallace's former *Daily Mail* colleagues – a new London evening newspaper called the *Evening Times* and a penny weekly called *Week-End*. Charles Watney, who had taken Wallace on at the *Standard*, was the man who had done most of the planning for the former title. John Cowley, the *Daily Mail*'s general manager, who had given Wallace his job as a reporter when he returned from South Africa in 1902, was the paper's general director. The *Evening Times* was financed by two Conservative MPs, Captain Morrison and Sir Samuel Scott, with the idea being to revive Toryism in the capital. Wallace, to his great delight, got jobs on both of the new publications. He was appointed *The Week-End*'s racing editor, and then soon afterwards he was appointed racing editor and special writer to the *Evening Times*. They were both dream jobs.

Horse racing was the sport in which everything that Wallace loved all came together. The 'mystery' element of trying to solve the puzzle of which horse would win; the sense of theatre at the racetrack; the excitement of the race itself; the colourful characters who frequented the racing world – the jockeys, the aristocratic owners, the bookies; the plots and schemes, the great gambles, lost and made, and the air of skulduggery. 'For Edgar Wallace the racecourse was much more than a pastime, much more than a habit. More even than an obsession, it was an addiction. He liked the feel of the place, he liked the sort of people who came here,' said James Cameron.

Wallace threw himself into his work with his usual vigour, diligently studying the form to improve his chance of picking winners. Soon, the *Week-End* became known for the quality of its tipping. 'Whenever he [Wallace] tipped a long-priced winner, up went the circulation, and to capitalise these successes we displayed, for the edification of small, gaping crowds round our windows, the identical tips cut from the paper,' recalled Wallace's colleague, Bernard Falk.[4] In fact, Wallace did so well at picking winners that, at his suggestion, the magazine abandoned its non-racing features and was relaunched as the *Week-End Racing Supplement*. At the *Evening Times*, Wallace employed various noms de plume to give readers the impression that there was a team of tipsters employed.

As 'Nick O'Lincoln'[5] he tried to tip sure-fire winners. As 'Clever Mike' he offered tips concealed in cartoons. As 'R.E. Walton' he promised to readers who sent him half a crown an envelope containing the name of a 2–1 winner. It didn't all go to plan. Nick O'Lincoln decided to give tips for the 1911 Cambridgeshire Handicap through an imaginary discussion between Sherlock Holmes and Dr Watson. The great detective, employing his famous logic, reduced the field to a shortlist of six, but the race was won easily by a complete outsider at odds of 33–1 called 'Long Set' who wasn't even mentioned in Holmes and Watson's discussions. There was nothing very elementary, Wallace found, about solving the puzzle of large-field flat race handicaps. Such failures, however, only made him all the more determined to get it right next time.

So bitten was he by the racing bug that Wallace at this time entertained serious thoughts of giving up his other writing and concentrating fully on racing journalism. In addition to his work as racing editor of two publications, he started two independent tipping sheets of his own, *Bibury's* and *R.E. Walton's Weekly*. The publications were staffed by himself, the indispensable Cassidy and an office boy, and the team operated from a room in Thavies Inn. It was all tremendous fun.

There seemed to be no limit to Wallace's industry. In 1910 he was married with two children, the racing editor of two publications, in charge of running two other tipping sheets, and let's not forget writing Sanders of the River stories for the *Weekly Tale-Teller* and Smithy sketches for *Ideas*, as well as numerous other short stories. As if that wasn't enough, he was also penning music hall sketches for the theatre. His collaborator was Albert de Courville, the brave young journalist who had earned Wallace's admiration by going down the burning mines at Corrieres in France. De Courville was now building a career in the theatre, and encouraged Wallace to write for the Hippodrome reviews with which he was involved.

Despite his heavy workload, Wallace still found time to make new acquaintances and to reconnect with his roots. He learnt that his late half-sister, Joey, who had died at the tragically early age of 25, had left a daughter called Grace Donovan, who lived with her widowed father in Cheshire. His niece was approaching her 21st birthday, and Wallace wrote to her and sent her a cheque to buy herself a birthday present.

It was no one-off event, as for the rest of his life Wallace proved to be the perfect uncle. He visited Grace in Cheshire, and then wrote to invite Grace to visit him and Ivy and their children for a week in the spring of 1911, and for another week in July. 'I will get you your railway tickets so you need not bother your head about that,' he told her.

Two weeks later he wrote again:

> I give you a great deal of thought my dear, and it is pleasant to know that I shall be much nearer to you again this week when I come up to Chester for the Stalybridge murder trial. I may come up and see you. PS If I do not write to you as quickly or as frequently as I want to it is because I am a hurrying, scurrying individual.

He signed his letters to Grace 'Your loving uncle'.

'I have often thought,' Grace wrote many years later, 'of the innate kindness of Edgar, as shown by the manner in which he would come to the station himself to meet me, and himself carry my suitcase. And even many years later when again I visited him – this time in Portland Place – when he was very rich and famous, how he arranged for me to see all the best shows, and was still the kind uncle.'

The kindness that Wallace showed towards his niece could be seen as evidence of how much he valued family, having been separated from his mother at such an early age, and having never known his father. But in truth, he behaved in the same warm-hearted and generous way to everyone he befriended, and even towards people he hardly knew.

15

THE CURIOUS CASE OF THE CONFESSION OF DR CRIPPEN

'Sensation,' said the foreman, waving deprecating hands, 'newspaper sensation.' Any lie to sell the newspapers – that's their motto.

Edgar Wallace, *The Nine Bears*, 1910

At the beginning of November 1910, Wallace could reflect on what had, up to then, been a wonderful year for him. He was the racing editor of two publications, he ran his own tipping sheets, he was writing for the stage, and regularly producing Sanders stories and Smithy sketches as well as other short stories. On 17 December, *PIP* (*The Penny Illustrated Paper*) published Wallace's 'The Murder at the Porthelm', billed as 'The Most Extraordinary Crime Story that has ever been Written'. It was a cracking tale and genuinely 'extraordinary' in that the obvious suspect was the murderer and the average policeman detected it, something which didn't happen too often, if at all, in detective fiction.

The *Evening Times* was going well, and gaining readers all the time, with its circulation up to 100,000. But 1910 was to have a nasty sting in its tail for both Wallace and the newspaper he worked for. The big crime sensation of that year was the arrest and subsequent trial of Dr Hawley Harvey Crippen. As I wrote in 2010[1] on the occasion of the trial's centenary:

> Crippen's was the first murder case to get global attention. The case contained all the elements of a classic Agatha Christie novel: an overpowering, promiscuous wife who had bullied and nagged her mild, self-effacing husband, apparently disappearing into thin air; the badly mutilated remains of a body found in the cellar; the flight of the wife's husband, with his mistress disguised as a boy, on a transatlantic liner; the fugitives' dramatic arrest in Canada.

Adding a further element of drama to the tale, Crippen was also the first criminal to be captured with the aid of wireless communication.

After a five-day trial at the Old Bailey in October, Crippen was found guilty of murdering his wife, Cora, and was sentenced to be hanged at Pentonville

Prison on 23 November. The question was – would there be a pre-execution confession? A few days before the doctor was due to be hanged, a man arrived at the *Evening Times* offices and asked to see the editor. He told the paper's news editor, Bernard Falk, that Crippen had made a confession to his solicitor, a Mr Arthur Newton, and that Newton was willing to sell the confession to the *Evening Times* for £1,000. There was much discussion at the paper as to what to do next. Was the confession genuine?

Newton explained that the 'confession' was not actually a written document signed by Crippen, but consisted of his own notes of verbal comments that he said his client had made. He told the *Evening Times'* representative, Arthur Findon, that for the sum of £500 he would dictate a full statement from the notes, which could be published on the day of the execution, providing the *Evening Times* with a brilliant scoop. Newton insisted that his name was kept out of the story. More negotiations followed, and the solicitor gave a promise that he would dictate the confession to the newspaper on 22 November. The *Evening Times* then 'went public' with its sensational news and put out posters across London announcing that the following day they would be publishing Crippen's confession. But then, Newton got cold feet. The newspaper had to threaten to publish the whole story of his offer, and the fact that they had already paid him £5,000 to get him to change his mind. Newton then promised to dictate the confession to a friend who would then deliver it to the flat of Arthur Findon. The friend did not give Findon the 'confession' but dictated it, and then insisted that it be burnt in front of him. As soon as the man went, the *Evening Times* team went to the fire to rescue the charred remains of the 'confession'.

Edgar Wallace now enters our story. He was there at the newspaper offices, eagerly awaiting the confession with the rest of his colleagues. Like almost everyone else in Britain, he had been fascinated by the Crippen case. The name of Dr Crippen had, in fact, come to his attention long before the doctor achieved notoriety. Once, when sitting with a number of other journalists in the governor's office at a prison, awaiting the hanging of a murderer, the discussion had got round to cures for earache. One of the reporters said that he had been treated by a 'little doctor' in north London, who had cured him without his experiencing the least pain. 'I remember the name,' Wallace later wrote, 'because in those days I used to be a writer of limericks, and I remember the first two lines, which began:

There was once a doctor named Crippen,
Who at plugging an ear was a pippin.

Then two years later, Crippen cropped up in Wallace's life again. He had been rehearsing a sketch for production at a music hall. One of the artistes told him that he had just missed a treat, a stage-struck woman had just been having an audition and she had been 'the worst ever'. The artiste pointed at the woman's 'poor blooming husband', who was 'talking, almost pleading' with the stage manager. It was Dr Crippen. 'Poor Crippen,' Wallace wrote, 'He spent left and right to satisfy his wife's overweening vanity; paid for expensive singing lessons, marvellous stage photographs showing her curtseying to applause that she never earned and wonderful stage dresses she never wore. But the only time she ever appeared in public she was jeered off stage.'[2]

While not doubting that he was guilty of the crime he was accused of, Wallace was nevertheless sympathetic to the mild-mannered Crippen. 'I have met very few people who knew him who did not like him,' he wrote, 'but, with the exception of one or two ladies who saw the best side of her, I never knew anybody who said very much in favour of Crippen's wife.'[3]

He must have been flattered too to learn, in the statement of Captain H.G. Kendall, that Crippen had been 'busy reading' *The Four Just Men* on his transatlantic journey on the SS *Montrose*, prior to his arrest. Over seventy-five years later, in March 1987, the actual copy of *The Four Just Men* that Crippen had been reading – a first edition – went up for sale at the Bloomsbury Book Auction in London, and was bought for £121 by Captain Kendall's grandson.

Wallace attended Crippen's trial, presided over by Lord Alverstone, the lord chief justice of England, calling it 'the most brilliantly conducted trial in the history of criminal jurisprudence'. When the transcript of the Crippen 'confession' finally arrived at the *Evening Times* offices, Wallace was instructed by the editor, Charles Watney, to give 'half a column of good intro' to it for the day's paper. It was the early hours of the morning on Wednesday 23 November 1910, and time was of the essence. 'This statement printed below is Crippen's own statement,' Wallace wrote on the front page, 'It bears in every line the stamp of authenticity. It is unnecessary to say that no journal – even the least responsible of journals – would print this confession of Crippen's without unimpeachable authority. That authority we possess.' That day, by one o'clock, the *Evening Times* sold 200,000 copies – more than double its daily circulation. Overall sales passed 1 million, but its rivals hit back. They contacted Pentonville Prison and Crippen's solicitor for confirmation of the 'confession'. When none was forthcoming, the *Evening News* and *Star* felt confident enough to print bills to be posted on London's streets proclaiming 'CRIPPEN: NO CONFESSION'. The *Evening Times* couldn't produce evidence to back up its claim, as all it had was some charred embers.

The next day, with its credibility torn to shreds, sales of the paper slumped to 60,000. By 26 November, circulation had fallen to 30,000. Once again,

Wallace's carelessness had caused a newspaper he was working for great trouble. In his introduction to the 'confession', he should not have claimed its 'unimpeachable authority', or ended with the line, 'That authority we possess.' Nevertheless, it would be unfair to blame him for the entire fiasco. He did, after all, have to write his introduction at a breakneck speed in order to make that day's edition and there was little time for reflection. The real problem had surely been the decision by the newspaper to deal with a man as slippery as Arthur Newton in the first place, and not cancelling its offer when it heard that he didn't have a document signed by Crippen himself. 'I can say nothing about the confession, but beyond this I cannot discuss the matter,' the duplicitous man said when challenged by Arthur Findon.

What the *Evening Times* should have done was to publish the whole story behind the 'confession' and, had they done so, it would have been Newton who would have been shown up and not them. But despite their solicitor advising this, Sir Samuel Scott, one of the MPs who financed the paper, decided against it, believing that the affair would eventually blow over. Alas, the circulation of the newspaper never did properly recover from the Crippen affair. 'For months we struggled on under the shadow of the discredit which came to us,' Wallace recalled.

Had the 'confession' been genuine? Wallace always maintained that it was, but the reality is that we have no way of knowing, and Arthur Newton's backtracking hardly inspires confidence. The question surely remains – why, if Crippen had wanted to confess, did he not make a signed statement?

As for Crippen himself, Wallace was characteristically charitable:

Except for this crime he was a lovable little chap, more the victim of his wife's overweening vanity than he was of any self-evolved passion; and despite the gruesomeness of his method of disposing of the murdered woman, I shall always regard him as the kindest and most moral murderer that has been hanged in the past fifty years.[4]

16

MORE BRIGHT IDEAS

'Jim,' she asked suddenly, if – if you are going to make your fortune … you will try something very rapid won't you?' … 'It will be something infernally rapid,' he said.

Edgar Wallace, *The Daughters of the Night*, 1925

The year 1911 began with another dramatic news event: the Sidney Street siege, where two or three Latvian anarchists/burglars, supposedly led by the mysterious 'Peter the Painter', were cornered by around 200 policemen – and later a detachment of Scots Guards – in London's East End. The gang had murdered three policemen and injured two others in an interrupted robbery of a jeweller's shop in Houndsditch in December.

'The Sidney Street siege gave us a lift,' Wallace noted, in relation to the *Evening Times*' circulation. He had come to work at 4.30 a.m. on 3 January 1911, and learnt from his colleagues about the events that were unfolding in Stepney. He rushed through his tipping work, 'in my agitation picking five winners out of the six races that were to be decided that day' before dashing off to Sidney Street.

It was the first 'battle' he had experienced since South Africa. 'It was rather like old times, though queerly unreal, listening to the klik-klok of rifles in that dingy thoroughfare,' he wrote. Wallace, like the good reporter he still was, tried to get as close to the action as he could. 'By good luck I got into a house almost opposite that where the murderers were at bay, and could, I think, have got one of them if I had a rifle, for he showed himself for a second at the window.'

Also at the siege was another veteran of the South African campaign, Winston Churchill, now Home Secretary. It was Churchill who called in the army, and who controversially refused to allow the fire brigade access to the building where the anarchists were when it caught fire. Churchill was also criticised for putting his own life at risk – it was claimed that a bullet fired by the anarchists went through his top hat. Wallace had to leave the siege to go to a race meeting, and when he returned that evening two burglars lay dead (three policemen and a firefighter also lost their lives) and the house where they had hidden was a smouldering ruin.

When sensational news stories were lacking, Wallace tried his best to return the *Evening Times* to the level of popularity it had enjoyed before the Crippen confession disaster. He devised a competition to try and boost sales, which involved readers cutting out a coupon from the newspaper to vote for their favourite pantomime principal boy of 1911. The prize for the winner was an enormous seven-tier 'panto-cake' which was exhibited in a shop window in the Strand. 'No matter how far down your nominee is on the list SHE CAN WIN IF YOU GET BUSY!' the *Evening Times* declared. Pantomimes were as popular in 1911 as the 'X-Factor' is over 100 years later, and pantomime principal boys enjoyed pop star status, as Wallace well knew.

The winner of the competition was Miss Ethel Hall, who played Robinson Crusoe at the Elephant and Castle, and who received 35,856 votes. Wallace presented her with her award – and an inscribed silver cake knife – on the stage at the theatre after the show. 'Edgar made a pleasant speech … and playfully invited her to put the cake in her pocket – a witticism which, in view of the scantiness of Robinson Crusoe's attire, was received as the very cream of daring irony, and brought the pleasing ceremony to an end with loud and prolonged cheers,' Margaret Lane records.[1]

The year 1912 did not start well for Wallace and his colleagues, when Captain J.A. Morrison, Conservative MP for East Nottingham and one of the backers of the *Evening Times*, decided to withdraw his support. Morrison's move pushed the newspaper into liquidation, but its devoted staff weren't giving up just yet. Salaries were cut – Wallace's was reduced to £3 a week – and the gallant John Cowley tried to keep the newspaper going with his own money until a wealthy backer could be found. The financier Alfred de Rothschild sent in a cheque for £1,000, urging the men to persevere with their efforts.

The newspaper was offered to the Conservative Party, to Sir Max Aitken (later Lord Beaverbrook), the Anglo-Canadian businessman, who later became the owner of the *Evening Standard* and *Daily Express*, and to Lord Northcliffe, but no one was interested.

On 25 April 1912, just two weeks after the sinking of the *Titanic*, the *Evening Times* hit the newsstands for the very last time. It was the end, not just of the *Evening Times*, but also of the *Week-End Supplement*. 'I do not know how much John Cowley lost,' Wallace wrote, 'but if ever I am asked to name the bravest deed I ever saw, I shall endeavour to describe Cowley with a cheque book and a fountain pen striving to hold the fort.' What made the demise of the paper so galling was that the *Evening Times* so nearly made it through.

'Only by the meagre sum of £152, no more than the price of a few columns of advertising space, did we fail to balance accounts in the last week of our existence. A guaranteed page advertisement a day would have saved us,' lamented Bernard Falk.[2]

Unsurprisingly, the closure of the two publications he had worked so hard for left Wallace, at least for a while, disillusioned with Fleet Street:

> Journalism is a rotten profession in many ways, it knows only one cry, and that cry 'Give'. You must give of your best on a Monday, slave, sweat, earn the mumbled thanks of a busy editor as you meet him in the passage (you on your way to hard labour, he en route for the Carlton) and strive – for what? For forgetfulness on Tuesday. Your *Magnum opus* – if you will pardon the expression – is waste-paper by Wednesday. Your achievement of Monday does not excuse your failure on Thursday. All you have done is forgotten, past, done with.[3]

Again, though, what looked like a major blow to Wallace's career actually helped him, as it enabled him to focus once again on his other work. In any case, he was never one to be despondent for too long. 'There are two deterrents to happiness,' he wrote in an article entitled 'How to be happy', 'One is ill-health in oneself – and even that is a handicap which can be overcome; the other is ill-health in those who are dearest to us. And when you dismiss those two factors, you have practically disposed of all the barriers and obstacles which stand between you and good cheer.'

In May 1912, a month after the *Evening Times* closure, The Four Just Men reappeared in a story called 'The Poisoners' in *The Novel Magazine*.[4] In the introduction, the vigilantes were hailed as 'probably the most remarkable figures that fiction has produced during the last decade'. Once again there were cash prizes for readers who could solve the mystery, but this time, the prizes were properly limited: £5 for the 'best and most concise solution, gathered from the clues'; £2 for the 'next best' and £1 each to the 'next best three solutions'. In August, the magazine proudly announced that the £5 prize had gone to a Miss E.W. Fyfe, No. 3 Blenkarne Road, Wandsworth Common, SW – but that instead of awarding a prize of £2 and three of £1, a further five readers had been awarded £1 because 'the next best answers' had been 'so equal'. 'The results were most pleasing,' noted the editor Robert Brennan, 'so great was the cleverness of my readers, many of whom would be serious rivals to Sherlock Holmes himself.' Wallace must have been delighted that this time the competition had gone well.

In 1912, Ward Lock published Wallace's *Private Selby*, one of several books and plays which appeared before 1914 featuring an imaginary German invasion of England or warning of one.[5] The character of Dick Selby had first

appeared in a serial in the *Sunday Journal* in March 1909, and was clearly modelled on the author and his early experiences. Wallace tells us:

> If reading this story, you happen upon improbable combinations of circum-
> stances, unlikely situations, events that stand on the outward rim of your
> belief, I would ask you to remember that Dick Selby had up to this time
> lived a most ordinary life … This story is not intended to go forth as one
> founded upon fact: more extraordinary things have happened and will
> happen than are chronicled here.

He was right, as his own extraordinary life had proved. Already in 1912
jokes were being made about Wallace's output. This item appeared in the
Press Club Bulletin of June 1912: 'During his wife's absence in Johannesburg,
Edgar Wallace is staying at the Hotel Grand Central. The manager is already
complaining that the hotel is practically monopolised by publishers who are
phoning for novels all day.'

Two more novels by Wallace appeared in 1913: *The Fourth Plague* and *Grey
Timothy*. The former was an exciting tale about the attempts to break up a
murderous Italian secret society called 'The Red Hand', which threaten to
inflict a deadly plague on Britain unless its demands are met. The latter was
a romantic adventure set in the world of horse racing, in which a cheerful,
optimist punter from Australia called Brian Pallard clashes with a corrupt and
arrogant English lord who is out to ruin him.

Wallace was also busy in 1913 writing the lyrics for a new Albert de
Courville musical, *Are You There?* which opened at the Prince of Wales
Theatre on 1 November. Described as 'one of the most ambitious musical
plays ever put on the London stage', the play received a big thumbs down
from audience and critics alike. '"Rotten!", "Get off", "Silly pantomime",
"Go away", "No speech." – these were only a few of the remarks used by the
gallery,' reported the *Daily Sketch*. De Courville was roundly booed when he
came on stage afterwards, and no doubt Wallace was pleased that he had only
contributed the lyrics.

With every minute of the day having to count, Wallace was now honing
the production system with which he was to become famous. Always an early
riser, he routinely worked at least a couple of hours before breakfast. He had
dispensed with having a secretary to dictate to, and used a Dictaphone instead.
The secretary would then transcribe from the machine.

Wallace had also changed his smoking habit in order to increase his writing efficiency. In South Africa he had been a regular pipe smoker, but pipe
smoke got in his eyes while he was working and, moreover, a pipe needed
regular work to refill and relight. So he swapped his pipe for cigarettes, and

started to smoke them using a cigarette holder – an accessory which was to become his trademark. There was undoubtedly an aspect of style and glamour about smoking with a long cigarette holder, and we have already noted how one sub-editor at the *Evening News* watched 'admiringly' as Wallace puffed out smoke from his 'inordinately long' mouthpiece, but Wallace's use of one was primarily practical. 'There was nothing of the pose in Edgar's predilection for those extraordinarily long holders,' his secretary (and later the second Mrs Edgar Wallace), Violet King, claimed, 'He used short ones when I first knew him. Over the years, little by little, they became longer and longer. His idea was to keep the smoke out of his eyes. That was the only reason for them. Eventually he used to buy them in lots of fifty. His valet laid them out in little batches, keeping them always clean.'

Robert Curtis, another secretary of Wallace's, also mentioned the efficacy of Wallace's famous 10in-long holders. 'The length is purely practical, for when Edgar Wallace worked at his desk, a glass 'wall' was round it to keep out the draughts which he disliked. In the glass was a small hole through which a cigarette in the holder projected and which kept some of the smoke outside.' The cigarette holder may have made good sense as an accessory for a chain smoker who spent long hours working at a desk, but it also helped establish Wallace's public persona. It undoubtedly helped him stand out from the crowd, and was fully in line with the flamboyant, larger-than-life image he was keen to cultivate.

Professionally, things were going very well, but Edgar's marriage was now floundering. The shyness and the homeliness which had first attracted Edgar to Ivy now appeared to him to be less attractive. His boisterous, optimistic personality required a livelier female companion. Ivy didn't smoke, and she didn't like horse racing, her husband's favourite pastime. She wasn't too fond of the theatre either. Yes, she had borne him two lovely children, but Wallace wanted something more. He always enjoyed flirting innocently with the opposite sex and as we have seen was a man of enormous charm; but, according to Margaret Lane, it wasn't until 1910 that he fell in love with another woman. Lane called the lady in question 'Daisy' though hints that it wasn't her real name – probably in 1938, when her biography was published, Wallace's lady friend was still alive and Lane had no wish to embarrass her in a more circumspect age.

Lane describes 'Daisy' as 'an attractive woman in her early thirties' who was a few years younger than Edgar, and that Wallace found in her 'all the easy sociability and liveliness of spirit which charmed him in women'.[6] While Ivy preferred to stay at home, Daisy loved the theatre. She also enjoyed horse racing. Wallace introduced Daisy to Ivy, as he did all his lady friends, but Lane notes that Ivy received her rival 'sadly', as if she realised this was no short flirtation by her husband. Daisy became a regular visitor at Tresillian Crescent, and began to take over the role that Ivy had been used to playing. Despite the changed situation, relations between Edgar and Ivy continued on an amicable basis, though we can only imagine as to how hurt Ivy must have felt at being supplanted in her husband's affections.

Wallace was someone not known for his insensitivity to the feelings of others – far from it – he was noted for his considerate nature. So, why then could he not put himself in Ivy's shoes and realise how she felt? Lane believes that he deliberately ignored Ivy's unspoken jealousy. 'He had an extraordinary capacity for shutting the eyes of his mind to what he did not choose to see, and he certainly had no desire to see Ivy suffer.'[7] Perhaps, having been separated from his biological mother at any early age, brought up by a foster mother and also looked after by her daughter, he loved having two women around him. Wallace had absolutely no intention of divorcing his wife – or moving away from her to live with Daisy – he just thought, rather naively, that the three could all get on well together.

Ivy, meanwhile, looked forward to the times when she and Edgar could be alone together without Daisy, or just with their children. One such occasion was in the summer of 1913, when the Wallaces went on holiday to the seaside resort of Westende in Belgium. They took rooms in a quiet hotel, and while Edgar worked on his latest novel, Ivy looked after Bryan and Pat. 'The holiday at Westende had been a period of glorious freedom for the children, and a great success,' recorded Margaret Lane, 'Ivy had regained a little of her lost serenity, and had begun to hope that if only she and Edgar could be alone once more, a little less divided by his work and by more dangerous distractions, all might yet be well.'[8] Alas, for Ivy, there was to be no turning back of the clock. Her husband's workload would only increase and, as for 'dangerous distractions', there would be more – and none more so than the 18-year-old typist with dark hair and freckles from Clark's Secretarial College who turned up, wearing a hat with a veil, at Wallace's flat one night in 1915, in pursuit of a job.

Back though, to 1913, and in March of that year Wallace was back again in the editor's chair – this time as editor-in-chief of the Edward Hulton-owned publications *Ideas*, and *The Story Journal*. Hulton's publishing empire, with its headquarters in Manchester, was probably second only to Lord Northcliffe's at the time[9] and was to grow even larger in the years to come.

Hulton had decided to move the editorial office of *Ideas* and the *Story Journal* away from Manchester, to a basement office in Temple Chambers, London, and Wallace, who had been a regular contributor to *Ideas*, and had editorial experience, was an obvious choice for the newly-created position. He threw himself into his new job with typical enthusiasm. A. E. Wilson, the editor of *Ideas* at the time, remembered Wallace's extraordinary creativity: 'At ten in the morning Edgar would sail in rather resplendently, and there would ensue an erratic sort of conference at which he would smoke strange blends of cigarettes, drink innumerable cups of tea, and pour out amazing quantities of ideas for the paper. Some of them were wonderful, some of them hopelessly impracticable.'[10]

It wasn't Wallace's only project at the time. Although he never employed a ghostwriter himself, he did, at least once, work as a ghostwriter for others. Evelyn Nesbitt was an American chorus girl who had got embroiled in a famous murder case in New York. She had married Harry K. Thaw, a millionaire playboy. Before many witnesses, Thaw shot dead a certain Stanford White, owner of the Madison Square Gardens complex. It was alleged that Evelyn Thaw, as she now was, had been having an affair with White and that her husband had killed him out of jealousy. Somehow, Thaw escaped the electric chair (no doubt being able to pay for the best lawyers helped) and in 1913 his wife came to Britain to star in an Albert de Courville revue. She met Edgar, who agreed to ghostwrite her autobiography.[11]

No doubt working on the book proved a welcome diversion for Wallace from having to deal with Edward Hulton. While his magazines were light-hearted, Hulton himself was rather a dour man not renowned for his sense of humour. He liked to put those who came to him with ambitious schemes, which they felt sure would succeed, firmly in their place. 'You must think I'm a damned fool,' he would snap.[12]

It's not surprising that the hypercritical Hulton and the easy-going Wallace did not get along. The break with Hulton at some point was inevitable, and it came in late 1913. Wallace was writing a serialised life story of Evelyn Thaw for Hulton's *Daily Sketch*, no doubt trying to maximise his income from the biography project. He was one day short of an instalment and didn't have time to approach Thaw for more copy, so he decided, very foolishly, to lift, almost word for word, a previous interview he had done for *Ideas* with an artist, in which the latter expounded on his philosophy of life and views on modern art. One eagle-eyed reader – perhaps an enemy of Wallace's? – spotted what the author had done, and sent the two articles in to Hulton. The newspaper proprietor decided to enquire closer into the *Ideas* editor-in-chief's activities and was furious to discover that the typist whom Wallace employed on the company's payroll was busy working, not for Hulton publications, but in typing up Wallace's own outside work.

In Wallace's defence, Hulton wasn't paying him enough for him to be expected to devote all his time to his company, and he simply had to take on outside work. Moreover, it was the amount of work that Wallace was taking on that made him so careless and led to him 'borrowing' his work from other publications. Hulton, though, wasn't interested in excuses and Wallace was summarily sacked. He could now say – if he had wished to boast – that he had been shown the door by Britain's two biggest media barons. But of course, being Edgar Wallace, the blow wouldn't keep him down for too long.

17

FOR KING AND COUNTRY

'I must confess,' said the Director of Counter Intelligence, 'that Haynes gets me rattled.' His chief of staff sniffed. 'For God's sake don't sniff,' said General Marriness irritably, 'you don't like Haynes, Colonel. His methods aren't the methods we're used to – but we're fighting a new kind of war and dealing with a new kind of enemy.'

Edgar Wallace, *The Adventures of Major Haynes*
(of the Counter-Espionage Bureau), 1918

In the New Year 1914, no one mentioned war. 'The war danger had become too much a commonplace to be taken in earnest,' wrote historian Donald Read. 'During the first half of 1914 in particular, neither the British public nor the British government were expecting war.'[1]

At the start of the year Wallace was without a regular income, but in the spring his luck changed again when Kennedy Jones, another of his old chums from the *Daily Mail*, gave him the assistant editorship of the weekly magazine *Town Topics*, which he financed. Wallace stayed on the editorial team for five years, and it proved to be one of his most enjoyable working experiences. *Town Topics* has been described as 'a raffish, waggishly facetious weekly for the man about town who was, in the cant of the time, "a bit of a goer"'.[2] The founder and editor was Arthur Binstead, aka 'Pitcher' – a journalist of the 'old school', described by Wallace as a 'splendid wit and a man of great geniality'. Clubbable, and a man for whom 'the world's centre' was Romano's Restaurant on the Strand, he was certainly a very different character from the dour Edward Hulton. Wallace recalled one humorous incident with his boss thus:

One day Binstead was going down the stairs of the *Town Topics* and saw the office boy coming up, bearing on a plate a glass of milk and a few biscuits. 'Pitcher' stared at the sight. 'Where is that going?' he asked. 'It's for Mr Wallace,' said the boy. 'Pitcher' gasped. 'Isn't he WEANED?' he demanded.

Alas, 'Pitcher' died in 1914, and Wallace found himself promoted to managing editor.

The *Town Topics* team was a happy crew; battle-hardened Fleet Street veterans doing a job they all loved. Wallace tried to find as many jobs for his old friends as he could. The indispensable Cassidy was installed as a sub-editor, while Cora Lawrence, a former colleague from the *Evening Times*, was put in charge of the theatre section. Wallace even found a position for Cora's son, Vincent, as a gossip columnist. Advertising itself as 'the man's paper', *Town Topics* didn't just cover sport but carried jokes, restaurant reviews, short stories, articles and poems – and lots of gossip. It was just one of a rich array of weekly magazines and journals of the time, and undoubtedly one of the most entertaining.

One of Wallace's columns was entitled 'Adventures in Strange Places'. One week he wrote about a trip to Ayr in Scotland:[3]

> I have a tender feeling for Ayr … You can find quite a few statues to Wallace in Ayr. If you go round by Wallace's the draper's and stand over by Wallace's the saddler's, you can, by craning your neck, see a statue of Wallace above the Town Hall. (The Town Hall is between Wallace's the florist's and Wallace's the baker's). In Ayr, if you are arrested and desire to avoid disgrace, you give a false name and call yourself Wallace.

Wallace wrote for *Town Topics* not only in his own name, but also under the pseudonym 'X' and his childhood name 'Richard Freeman'. His short stories showed him to be a master of the craft.

'Evelyn: The Story of an Embarrassment' is a case in point. It starts with a woman telling her lover, Jack Terence, to climb out via the fire escape as she can hear her husband coming up the stairs. To delay her husband, she decides to play-act, and accuses him of coming from a rendezvous with an imaginary 'Evelyn' – the first name she thought of. She says she found a letter from 'Evelyn' addressed to her husband. To her great horror, her husband confesses to having an affair with 'Evelyn' – who actually exists. He was planning to meet his lover at his home, as he thought his wife would be away – and he has told her to wait at the fire escape. 'Tell me something – does she know Jack Terence?' She waited, holding her breath. 'She's – she's his wife,' he mumbled miserably, 'You've never met her – neglected and all that sort of thing. Oh, hell, I've made a mess of it!'. His wife draws a deep breath. 'Don't say "I" – say "we", Larry,' she said softly, 'husband and wife should bear one another's burdens.' The whole story is told in less than 800 words.

In the first half of 1914 there were plenty of interesting events for Wallace's magazine to cover. Charlie Chaplin made his film debut in the silent comedy

Making a Living. In April, George Bernard Shaw's *Pygmalion* opened in the West End. In the world of horse racing there was the sensational scratching, due to injury, of the wonder horse 'The Tetrarch' for the Epsom Derby in June. As a 2-year-old in 1913 'The Tetrarch' had won all seven of his races but, alas, race goers were sadly never to see him in action again. Wallace, as disappointed as any other racing fan, penned a poem for *Town Topics* under the title of 'The Grey Who Did Not Run'.

On Derby Day itself, Wallace took the train from London to Epsom Downs along with his journalist pals J.B. Booth and Horace Lennard. There was an old man in their compartment who told them how he had seen 'Thormanby' win the Derby in 1860. 'Man alive! How old are you?' asked an astonished Wallace. 'Eighty next October,' the man replied, 'and I can go back before "Thormanby". There aren't many Derbys I've missed since. This will be my fifty-second.'[4]

At the end of the month in which 'Durbar II' won the Derby, came the event which was to radically change the course of world history – the assassination, in Sarajevo, of Archduke Franz Ferdinand, heir to the throne of Austria-Hungary, and his wife Sophie, by a Bosnian Serb called Gavrilo Princip. 'There seems to be no reason why we should be anything more than spectators,' said Prime Minister Herbert Asquith about the British position in the light of a European war, but the German violation of Belgian sovereignty on 4 August changed all that.

Wallace was not surprised by developments, 'I say that war "broke" but to me there was ample warning,' he wrote, 'that fateful Sunday night when I read in the late edition of the *News of the World* the story of Sarajevo and the assassination of the heir-apparent to the Austro-Hungarian throne, it was as clear as daylight that war was inevitable.'

The outbreak of war meant he had to miss a much-deserved holiday in Chamonix in Switzerland. 'I am wondering whether I shall get a holiday next year. I owe the war this, that it robbed me of the nearest approach to a rest cure I have ever had,' he complained in an article entitled 'Francis Joseph and a Missed Holiday'.

Wallace had no doubts whatsoever that British involvement in the war was justified, and as a fierce patriot he rallied to the cause. 'Whatever this war costs us will be worthwhile if as a result we see a sane democracy overthrowing its masters – material, spiritual, and human,' he opined. He regretted the fact that at 39 he was too old for active service, and also that Kitchener's prohibition of him as a war reporter was still in force, meaning that he could not write from the front line, which he would have loved to have done.

J.B. Booth, a regular contributor to *Town Topics*, remembered a meeting with Wallace at this time:

For a time we talked of war, and then he began to speak of his old regiment. As he spoke he drew a sheet of paper towards him and began to scribble in pencil. For a few moments he was silent, and then he tossed the draft to me. I have them before me, those pencilled verses, breathing the old pride in the old regiment.[5]

Although Wallace could not fight, nor work as a war reporter, he would still do his bit for Britain as best he could. Sometimes that meant peddling official propaganda. The old adage that the first casualty of war is the truth was again displayed in the first weeks of the hostilities, as lurid stories of German atrocities towards Belgians appeared in newspapers and magazines to help boost the recruitment drive. Wallace joined in with the demonisation of the enemy, with *Town Topics* being transformed into a jingoistic, 'Hun-bashing' paper 'bristling with sentimental patriotism and snorting verses.'[6]

An example of a 'snorting verse' was a piece by Wallace entitled 'Ballad of Hate to Wilhelm II', which was published in *Town Topics* on 7 November 1914:

What of that tortured and mangled Louvain,
The work of a decadent ape?
What of the beasts without bowels or brain
That you loosed to their orgy of rape?
Hate us – we like it; from Things in your shape

'You are not far wrong if you regard the German as the scourge of God – you will be within the limits of safe prediction if you prophesy the ravelling of that scourge into the finest and most harmless oakum,' Wallace declared.

Wallace also did his bit to denigrate 'conchies' – the 'conscientious objectors' who refused to fight for king and country. For *Town Topics*, he created the character of Private Clarence Nancy, who is allocated to the Non-Competents Corps, having refused to even paint a red cross on an ambulance wagon. The effeminate Nancy travels to the camp with his pet cat, Tibby, and a caged canary. 'When I arrived at Bugville Station there was nobody to meet,' he bemoans in a letter to his 'Dear Papa and Mama,' 'I nearly *cried* with vexation. It was so horribly thoughtless remembering the enormous size of the Army that they couldn't spare a colonel or a sergeant to show me the way. And it was quite *dark* and you know how lonely the country roads are.' When Nancy arrives at the camp he meets a 'dear boy' named Hilary Fitzsimmons, 'who absolutely fell in love with Tibby,' and who kisses the cat so much that Nancy becomes jealous. At the camp he meets other 'conchies', all of whom are figures of fun for Wallace. His failure to understand the very principled objections that many people had to fighting in the war – and his portrayal of 'conchies' as camp, embroidery-loving, scent-wearing cowards – does him no credit at all.

Less objectionable – at least to the eye of the reader today – was his humorous piece 'Bye-Laws for Zeppelins', written in response to the criticism the government was receiving in dealing with the menace from the German airships. Among the bye-laws Wallace created were:

1 Licences. No Zeppelin captain will be recognised unless he takes out a licence to drive over England.

4 Rules of the Road. Zeppelins will keep to the left on entering the London areas.

8 Rules for bombers. For the convenience of commanders, certain London housetops will be illuminated to facilitate bomb dropping. The houses will be chosen by a committee consisting of Lord Northcliffe, Sir John Simon, Lord Fisher, and the Editor of the Morning Post.

Wallace's salary had been £10 a week in August 1914, but Kennedy Jones, mindful of the effect the war would have on the sporting and theatrical interests which supported the paper, cut his salary and that of other staff members in half. Moreover, other newspapers to which Wallace regularly contributed either closed down or reduced the size of their editions.

Help was at hand, however, in the shape of Charles Hyde, the owner of the *Birmingham Daily Post*, who appointed Wallace the newspaper's military correspondent. Although he couldn't report from the frontline, he could produce a daily column summarising the war news and giving readers his own particular take on developments. The only caveat was that the column must pass the military censor.

Wallace's first article appeared on the second day of the war, and over the next four years and three months he was to pen, by his own estimate, 1½ million words for Hyde's newspaper on the Great War. He wrote the column six days a week, usually late at night when his *Town Topics* work was finished, and when one considers the other work he was doing at the time – in addition to his editorial responsibilities he was also writing short stories, serials, novels and other books – the unbroken sequence must rank as one of his greatest achievements. He was paid two guineas for each column, working out to twelve guineas a week, which although it was quite a modest sum in 1914, still represented a regular income for which he was grateful.

Wallace, who could never refuse anyone in need, decided to do his bit to help the Belgian refugees who had fled the German invaders and escaped to Britain. With characteristic generosity he leased a house in Brockley and offered it to the manager of the Westende Hotel, where he and his family had enjoyed such a happy holiday the year before, as a place where the Belgian and his family could stay in peace and security. Refugees from the manager's family were also made welcome at the bungalow Wallace rented in the summer at Alfriston, and where Ivy along with the children spent long holidays. Wallace's idea of 'family' was an extended one, and included friends and their children too. Later on we shall see that he even invited the milkman and his bookmaker to go on holiday with him.

His *Birmingham Daily Post* column kept him busy six nights a week, but it was just one outlet for his war writing. In 1914–1915 he wrote no fewer than six paperback books on the war and leading military figures for the publishing firm Newnes.

That old reliable 'Smithy' was returned to action, 'Smithy's Friend Nobby' was serialised by *Town Topics* in 1914, and brought out in book form by Newnes as *Nobby*, two years later. 'Everyone with a sense of humour should read these very amusing, and true-to-life stories of the Army. They cause one perpetual laugh,' the blurb declared. In 1915, Pearson published *Smithy and the Hun*, a collection of twenty-one short stories.

Spy stories became all the rage during the First World War in a climate of media-induced paranoia about enemy agents, and Wallace showed that he could excel in this genre too. 'Code No. 2' first appeared in the *Strand Magazine* in April 1916, and tells the story of a Swiss clerk called Schiller who works for the 'Intelligence Department' in London and who mysteriously disappears on the eve of the war. Schiller is a spy who had hit upon an ingenious way of obtaining information from the safe of the Chief of Intelligence. 'What is most remarkable about this story is that it, in essence, it anticipated the technological developments of a quarter of a century later – the computer-controlled hidden camera and infra-red photography,' noted Donald McCormick.[7]

Wallace's main outlet for his tales of espionage was *Thomson's Weekly News*,[8] a publication which is still going strong today. He wrote a series featuring the redoubtable spy catcher Major Hiram Haynes of the Secret Service. A 'born gunman', Haynes 'spoke seven modern languages and read two dead ones, could and did quote Browning with remarkable fidelity' and like his creator, smoked cigarettes through a long amber holder. 'There were people who liked Major Haynes; there were others who disliked him intensely. No small proportion of the latter lie in a certain little burying ground not many miles from the Tower moat,' readers were informed.[9] Another series told of the escapades of a German agent – Hermann Gallwitz – under the title 'My Adventures as a German Spy'.

A third Wallace spy series for the same publication was 'The Secret Service Submarine' which told of the exploits of John Dudley Frazer in submarine

Z1. 'It is necessary for obvious reasons to present the story of Mr John Dudley Frazer in the form of fiction. Someday it may be possible to describe in a more official manner the activities of the boat I call *Z1*,' Wallace explains in the preamble. Frazer foils a German naval invasion, saves a female British spy from execution by impersonating a German officer, and even has the chutzpah to make one of his escapes on the Kaiser's very own train. It was all terribly thrilling and the readership lapped the stories up.

Wallace also took the war to the American market. The US was neutral until 1917, and Wallace was keen that readers stateside should get the British perspective. 'My idea was to convey to America a picture of English soldiers and English effort which would create an atmosphere of sympathy, if not for our cause, for the men who were fighting our battles. I have never worked so hard in all my life to bring the stories to perfection.' The result of Wallace's efforts was a series called 'Tam O' The Scouts' which featured a hugely likeable Scottish mechanic who rose to be an officer in the Royal Flying Corps. Tam proved a great success across the Atlantic, giving Wallace enormous satisfaction. 'The story of his exploits ran without interruption for two years in *Everybody's Magazine*,' he proudly recalled many years later. 'Tam Clubs were formed in many of the big cities, and I believed he even enjoyed the distinction of having a horse named after him!' After the war, he was flattered to be told by an American editor that Tam had been the inspirer of the American Flying Corps spirit.

In addition to Tam, he also revised and added to his Major Haynes spy stories for the US market, which appeared as a series entitled 'The Adventures of Major Haynes (of the Counter-Espionage Bureau)'.

Today, we can look back at Wallace's writings on the First World War with mixed feelings. Overall, around 16 million people worldwide were killed in the conflict and there were over 21 million casualties. Far from being 'the war to end all wars', the 'Great War' was followed by another bloody global conflict just over twenty years later which could be seen as a continuation – after a twenty-one year armistice – of the first.

Wallace was one of the writers who helped 'sell' the war against Germany and its allies as a noble, just cause. Was he right to do so? Probably the most objectionable of Wallace's war books, from a modern perspective, was the novel *1925: The Story of a Fatal Peace*, published in November 1915. It depicted what, for Wallace, was the nightmare scenario of coming to terms with Germany. 'My object ... is to bring home to readers the inevitable consequence of ending the present war in any other way than by the complete subjugation of Germany,' he explained in the introduction. But if Britain had reached a peace deal with Germany in 1915, as Wallace feared, there would have been no bloodbath at the Somme – where there were 60,000 British casualties on the first day alone, and over 1 million casualties overall – or at Passchendaele, where there were an estimated 610,000 casualties.

Given his fierce patriotism[10] and strongly pro-empire views it was no surprise that Wallace took such a jingoistic line. In his defence, he would have had no idea that the war would last so long – or that so many people would eventually be killed. 'I doubt very much that Wallace, or anyone else for that matter (except perhaps Horatio Bottomley), would have written such a book as *1925*, in 1917 or 1918 when there was genuine weariness of and revulsion for the war at every level of society,' argued Christopher Lowder, writing in 1978.[11]

Was British involvement in the First World War necessary? Would it have been better if Britain had stayed neutral in 1914 or, failing that, come to terms with Germany in 1915? Today, many would answer 'No' and 'Yes' to those questions, but it is perhaps hard to blame those caught up in the patriotic fervour of the time for taking a different line.

18

JIM

He was wonderfully alive, communicating to her a sense of immense completeness and above all a transcendent individuality. She was eager, impatient to know all about him, his beginnings, his life, his strange career.

Edgar Wallace, *The Terrible People*, 1926

During the first year of the war, there were changes in Wallace's living arrangements. Ivy and the children, along with their governess and a servant, moved to Clarence Gate Gardens, which had been Wallace's bolthole, while Wallace himself rented a service flat in Yeoman House, Haymarket. This all cost money as, of course, did renting the house at Brockley for his Belgian friends and the bungalow at Alfriston, and his extra outgoings meant that Wallace had to undertake more work. In addition to his columns, books, short stories and serials on the First World War, he also worked on his non-war based novels. In the period 1914–1918, no fewer than eleven such books were published.

His increased workload meant he was in urgent need of greater secretarial assistance. Robert Curtis had first met Wallace in 1913 when he was working for the Dictaphone Company. His job was to transcribe on to typewriter the matter dictated onto cylinders. 'From time to time there were delivered to me large batches of cylinders containing literary and journalistic matter from someone who, for some reason or other, never divulged his name,' he later recalled.[1] 'All I knew of the mysterious author was that his voice had a curiously husky quality, that his mispronunciation of various words made me shudder, and that he was always in a desperate hurry for the transcript.' Curtis was curious about who the 'mysterious author' was and made enquiries. He found out that the customer had an address in Haymarket. His manager, who was just as keen as Curtis was to find out who their client was, suggested that the typist went to Haymarket to personally deliver the next batch of manuscripts. Curtis arrived at Wallace's flat and was received by 'a short, slim, decidedly good-looking man, with a rather pallid face and a neat upturned moustache'.

Curtis introduced himself, but Wallace did not reciprocate. Playing the detective, Curtis's eyes wandered around the flat to look for clues. He saw 'a preponderance of novels by Edgar Wallace' on the bookshelves, and others lying about the room. He still wasn't sure though, and only by checking Wallace's writing on several letters which had already been sent to the company, with the handwriting on a manuscript sent in by an anonymous client a few days later, did he achieve confirmation.

Later, he discovered why Wallace had been at pains to hide his identity. The author had acquired his Dictaphone on hire-purchase, and his instalment payments were in arrears. If he revealed his identity he feared that he would receive a peremptory invitation to pay up, or be forced to return the Dictaphone. As he was hard-up and in the middle of some important work, either option would spell disaster – hence his desire to remain 'anonymous'. The next time Curtis met the Dictaphone Company's mysterious client, he addressed him as 'Mr Wallace'. Wallace smiled back. A few days later, Curtis was in for a pleasant surprise when Wallace suggested that he leave the Dictaphone Company and set up on his own. He guaranteed Curtis £1 a week more than he was getting at present, and that he would give him all his typing work to do.

Curtis decided to take the plunge, 'With my dilapidated typewriter and my debilitated Dictaphone I transcribed hundreds of thousands of words for Wallace.' The two men found they had much in common – not least a love of horse racing. Wallace's first words to Curtis when he turned up in the morning to collect the latest cylinders for typing were invariably, 'Hullo, Bob. Do you know anything?' Later on, the men discovered that Curtis had been born in a house adjacent to where Wallace had once lived in Greenwich. Curtis – who became the champion typist of England and Europe – was to be a huge help to Wallace as he sought to increase his output still further.[2]

One Friday morning, early in their association, Curtis called at Wallace's flat. Wallace greeted him, as usual, by asking what he fancied for that day's racing. The two men sat discussing the form, when Wallace suddenly broke off, 'By the way, I've got a serial to do. 75,000 words – and I'm going to turn it in by Monday morning. I'm broke and must have the money.' It was already midday on Friday, and Curtis thought Wallace was joking – he wasn't. 'I'll start dictating right away,' Wallace announced, 'We'll get a corps of district messengers to carry the cylinders to you at Hammersmith as fast as I can dictate them, and we'll work all day and night. You're on a pony.'

'The only impression of those seventy-two hours that remains with me is of a dilapidated typewriter ceaselessly clattering and of wrists and arms aching abominably,' Curtis wrote, 'but the story was finished according to plan, and by midday on Monday the manuscript was in the publisher's hands, the payment for it in Wallace's and my "pony" in mine. We had both earned it.' Curtis soon got to know the symptoms of 'an impeding spasm of high-speed work'. It was when his employer uttered the words, 'Bob, I'm broke!' 'While Wallace had money, he could rarely bring himself to settle down to writing, and at the first signs of financial tightness I came to realise that it would not be long before I heard the inevitable "Bob, I'm broke", and we should be plunging again into a whirl of furious activity.'

When Curtis told Wallace that he was joining up to fight in the war in April 1915, Wallace was furious. 'He took the view that I should have consulted him before enlisting, that I had shown an utter lack of consideration for him, and that I would make a rotten soldier anyway.' But, as always, Wallace's anger didn't last very long and when Curtis went to see him again it was a very different story. 'He was all anxiety to do everything possible to enable me to go with an easy mind. My whole family, he assured me, would be under his wing until I returned, and I was to worry over nothing.'

With Curtis gone, Wallace urgently needed a replacement. He placed an advertisement in the newspaper, and so it was, that at 8.30 one night in the spring of 1915, a Miss Violet Ethel King turned up at his flat at Yeoman House. She produced her credentials from Clark's Secretarial College, which she had just left. She assured Wallace of her proficiency as a typist – before admitting that she had never heard of him. 'He made me see plainly that he was hurt. He took it for granted – even then – that his name was a household word,' King later recalled. It was an inauspicious start, but the two stayed talking for a full three hours. At the end of the interview, without discussing wages or hours, Wallace told King she had the job and that she was to start work at 9 a.m. the following day. 'A new and vital relationship – perhaps the most important that Edgar had ever had with any woman – friendly, passionate, jealous and business-like in turn, had unobtrusively begun,' says Margaret Lane.[3] King later wrote:

> I haven't any idea why Edgar chose me out of the number of young women that applied for the post of secretary to him. He tells me it was because I could do arithmetic. Most of the other young women wanted to become his secretary because they knew he was the coming journalist and writer. They had literary ambitions of their own – and I suppose secretly hoped they would be able to advise or inspire him … I had no such romantic ideas, I knew I could no more write a story than ride a kangaroo and I told him so.[4]

Violet was only 18, yet tried to make herself look much older than she was. She was slim and pretty with dark, bobbed hair and, looking at photographs of her, it is not hard to see why Wallace would have found her attractive. For her part too, the author she had never heard of made a good first impression, 'In the one glimpse I had of him I liked his looks,' she later wrote; 'he was of medium height and a moustache stamped him as being no sheepish follower of the cult of the moment. There was an insolent uplift of his eyebrows that appealed to me. I liked the square cut of his jaw.'[5]

In 1915, Wallace was far from the portly figure he was to become, and puffing away on his elegant cigarette holder ('not the exaggeratedly long one of his later years, a little one' as Violet recalled), and immaculately attired as always, he would have seemed quite a dashing figure.

Years later, Wallace penned a little verse about his first meeting with Violet and how he came to engage her:

> It's very necessary,
> I should have a secretary
> And one night there came to me
> This same girl who seemed to be
> Very competent and handy
> (She was also slightly bandy)
> She wore ear-rings and a veil
> And was thinner than a rail
> Well, to cut the story short
> As she seemed a jolly sort
> I engaged her on the spot
> Soon on friendly terms we got.

It didn't take Violet long to realise that she was working for someone very special. She soon became in awe of her employer and his remarkable industry. 'My first week's work was a revelation to me. I realised that I was secretary to no ordinary journalist. I had worked for journalists before, but this man beat all records in the rate at which he turned out brilliant and finished articles and stories.' Her first-hand account of Wallace's writing routines gives us a valuable insight into how he was able to produce so much. Dictation was a key element:

> He would begin early in the morning – 8.30 usually – and then till lunch-time there was a steady stream of dictation. He used to pace the room like a hungry tiger, dictating his articles, his stories, his plot to me. I used to take them straight down to my typewriter because he had not the patience to let me transcribe from shorthand. After a short break for lunch on we used to go on again, Edgar – or Mr Wallace as he was then – dictating hour after

hour with scarcely a break, till late into the night. We used to go on until he had finished – it was often one or two in the morning before I closed my desk.

King's work was exhausting, but she loved her new job, 'I enjoyed working for Edgar Wallace more than I enjoyed working before. It was an education for me to see his masterly handling of things.' Wallace's use of dictation didn't just mean that he could produce far more than if he had typed up, or written his work himself in longhand, it also helped to give his work a much stronger narrative flow, as the critic and academic Wheeler Winston Dixon explained in *The Transparency of Spectacle*:[6]

> These dictated texts have an intensity of address and a spontaneity of construction mirroring the gift of a superb storyteller at work; it can be argued that when one reads Wallace's finest texts, the page upon which words are printed becomes an opaque or transparent medium designed solely as a matrix to convey the author's *voice* to the reader. The listener/reader is thus transported into Wallace's world directly through the speech of its author, and the actual text evaporates as the novel sweeps forward in an inexorable wave, enfolding both the characters within the text and the author of the tale being told.

As a technical explanation for why Wallace's best novels are so hard for the reader to put down, Dixon's analysis is hard to beat.

There was certainly plenty of work to keep Edgar and his new secretary busy. In addition to his daily columns for the *Birmingham Post*, there were serials for the magazine *Answers*, run by his Scottish friend Willie Blackwood, innumerable articles for D.C. Thomson Publications, and contributions to Albert de Courville's theatrical revues.

That was more than enough to keep one writer fully occupied, but one must also add in the war books, and the other novels which he continued to churn out. Some of his work had admittedly already appeared in serial form before the war. For instance, *The Admirable Carfew*, a light-hearted story about a young and adventurous man who tries his hand at several things – including being a newspaper reporter – was published in September 1914, having first appeared as a serial in the *Windsor* magazine from 1911 to 1914.

The Man Who Bought London, published by Ward Lock in December 1915, and first serialised in *Yes or No* from 1912–1914, tells the story of an idealistic American, King Kerry, who heads a syndicate of millionaires set on buying up large parts of London for the betterment of the general public. His plan involves the replacement of slums with 'co-operative flats', in which there would be baths, gymnasia, playgrounds, a hospital, a crèche and a free library. 'Each building,' King Kerry explains, 'will be self-governed, will contain its doctor, its dentist, and its trained nurses, all of whom will be at the disposal of the citizens of this little community free of charge.' It's not all plain sailing for Kerry, however, and he is up against Hermann Zeberlieff, a former business partner, who is out to thwart his plans. The romantic interest is provided by Elsie Marion, a former shop assistant whom Kerry appoints to be his agent, and who proves to be more than up to the job. Without giving too much of the plot away – and the truly sensational surprise ending – the book provides evidence of Wallace's sympathy with the feminine cause as well as his support for action to improve the lives of London's poor. It's evidence – and there is plenty more besides – to counter the claims made by some of his critics that he had no interest in social justice.

The novels from Wallace that appeared in the war years were once again a testament not just to his industry, but to his versatility. In May 1915, Arrowsmith brought out *The Melody of Death*, a story about a newly married man who, believing he is dying from cancer, takes to crime to make sure his wife is provided for. *The Tomb of Ts'in*, published by Ward Lock in 1916, involves an Indiana Jones-style search for hidden treasure in China, in which Captain Tatham, an earlier hero, reappears as 'Captain Talham'. It was based on the true historical record of the First Emperor of Qin, who unified China in 221BC, formed the Great Wall and also built an enormous imperial residence incorporating a burial chamber. In Wallace's book, the emperor's tomb is discovered, anticipating an event that didn't happen in real life until 1974.[7]

The Tomb of Ts'in contains sections which, apart from the different names of the characters, also appear word-for-word in *Captain Tatham of Tatham's Island*. The book is one of the rarest Wallace first editions, and there has been speculation that its rarity was due to the fact Wallace had bought up copies himself, as he was embarrassed by his self-plagiarism. However, in 1977, Wallace's bibliographer, W.O.G. Lofts, came up with a more credible theory: 'Probably the likeliest explanation of the scarcity of *The Tomb* is that with the acute paper shortage during the First World War, Ward Lock possibly only printed a fraction of their normal run.'[8]

A Debt Discharged, published by Ward Lock in February 1916, involves a clever gang of forgers and the hold they have over the heroine's uncle. In *The Clue of the Twisted Candle*, detective writer John Lexman becomes involved in a plot more fantastic than anything he had so far devised. He is tricked into murder by someone he believes is his friend, but who wants him out of the way so he can marry his beautiful wife. Unusually, some of the action in the book takes place in Albania, a country not often used as a location by British crime novelists.

'If, in the literary world, he was regarded by superior persons as a writer of "shockers", he had a large and increasing public who were fascinated by the wholesome and thrilling stories he wrote, and who held on breathlessly to the skein of mystery until they came to the denouement he had planned.' This was Wallace talking about Lexman, but seeing how popular his stories were becoming, it could just as easily have been the writer talking about himself.

Wallace was too old to serve in the army and was barred, thanks to Lord Kitchener, from reporting from the front line. But that didn't stop him penning a generous tribute to Kitchener when his old adversary was killed by a German mine while sailing to Russia in June 1916:

> That he frightened men, I know. I have seen a brigadier waiting an interview and fingering the brim of his cap with the nervousness of a delinquent school-boy. I have seen colonels of infantry shake at his summons, and supply officers prostrate after one of his unheralded inspections. Yet he was a man of curious tenderness. To say he was without sentiment is not true.

The First World War also saw Wallace's first venture into the exciting new world of moving pictures. In 1915 he was asked to write the scenario for the film *Nurse and Martyr*, about the nurse Edith Cavell who had been shot by a German firing squad for sheltering British soldiers. The film, released in November 1915, was not a great success, but it whetted Wallace's appetite for the movies and so, with typical enthusiasm, he decided to make films of his own. He set about transforming his Alfriston bungalow into a studio. He ordered a large motion-picture camera and a truckload of canvas scenery. Wallace's plan was simple – he would write his own scenario and his family and theatrical friends would act in the film. 'When this epic film was finished, he would make a second – a graphic representation of the Battle of Jutland – and both films would be sold to the distributors at a spanking profit,' records Margaret Lane.

Alas, it didn't go to plan. For the first film, his theatrical friends did not turn up. And it was while he was trying to recreate the Battle of Jutland that Wallace realised that film making was not as easy as he thought. He had bought more than 100 water-line models of battleships, with the plan being that they would be arranged on a canvas sea and filmed from above using the stop motion technique used in cartoons. But the problem was that a seaplane also needed to be filmed, and Wallace couldn't see how it could be done with his camera occupying the whole roof of the frame. 'He puzzled over it for some days, and then impatiently washed his hands of the whole matter. The scenery was dismantled in disgust, the camera sent back to London, and the water-line models of the battleships given to the children,' says Lane.[9] It was a setback to Wallace's ambitious plans to become a film director, but not the end of it, as we shall see later.

Despite Wallace's enormous workload, he was still keen to undertake civilian war duties. Through a barrister friend he was admitted to the Lincoln's Inn branch of the Special Constabulary. Among the duties of Section 9 was a very important one – to protect the person of King George V by making nightly parades in the grounds of Buckingham Palace. Wallace never did enjoy physical exertion – he believed that energy expended physically reduced the amount available for mental use – but he looked forward to the patrols. It wasn't just the feeling of belonging he gained from being a member of a unit and wearing a uniform again: for the first time since his discharge from the army, there was the company too. Wallace's career as a writer was a solitary one, and so this most sociable of men relished activities where he could mingle and chat freely with others. Wallace's friend J.B. Booth once asked him what he would do if there was an air raid while he was on duty. 'Turn out the guard and find a real policeman,' was Wallace's prompt answer.

It seems that Wallace's work did, though, gain the royal seal of approval. Early one morning, King George V was walking through the gardens and stopped before Special Constable Wallace. 'Good morning,' the king said with a smile, 'I see I'm well looked after in the night – judging from the number of cigarette ends I find about.'[10]

His job as a Special Constable was not the only official war work Wallace undertook. He also took on a confidential assignment from the War Office. From April 1917 onwards he interrogated returning British prisoners of war, with the aim being to take statements from them regarding their treatment in enemy hands. It wasn't an easy job, as many of the men were suffering from shell-shock and nervous disorders. However, Wallace was the right man for the task. 'He had the gift of inspiring confidence, and his calm personality and sympathetic approach made tolerable for many of these shattered men an experience which, less skilfully conducted, might well have been a painful ordeal,' was Margaret Lane's verdict.[11]

The men were interviewed at Clarence Gate Gardens, usually in the evenings, and Violet typed up their statements before carrying them down to the War Office.

As the war dragged on, Wallace kept hard at work on his novels and serials and 1917 saw three new crime novels published. *The Just Men of Cordova* was the latest in his Four Just Men series; *Kate Plus Ten* tells the story of a female head of a gang of thieves who falls for a man from Scotland Yard; while in *The Secret House*, Wallace brought back characters who first appeared in *The Nine Bears*.

Nigel Morland – whose mother had been befriended by Wallace, and who was employed by him as a 'presiding Mother-Friend-Counsellor-Manager-

PRO or what have you' – was a regular visitor to Clarence Gate Gardens in the latter years of the First World War, receiving lessons in the art of crime writing. His recollections[12] give us an insight into Wallace's working environment at this time, as well as providing us with further evidence of the author's extraordinary kindness:

> It was exactly like stepping into something noisily alive when I opened the front door with my key. A telephone was usually starting to ring; the air was usually warm, smelling of cooking and cigarette smoke … People were moving about; voices could be heard and there was an almost visible air of excitement as if a machine was moving into gear – but EW had probably been at work since dawn, unless he'd not been to bed at all.

On arrival, Morland always headed straight to Wallace's study:

> There he was behind his desk, beaming away with the long cigarette holder in his mouth. He always greeted me with his booming 'Niggie, come and listen to this' and with an air of breathless excitement would reel off word perfect and from memory something he had dictated in the past 12 hours, and nobody laughed louder than he at the funny bits.

Morland and his mother were treated as if they were members of the family, eating lunch with the Wallaces:

> Lunch often dragged on – EW usually had too much work on hand and should never have come to lunch at all, but to him every human being was far more important than deadlines; he found people, known or unknown quite irresistible and he had to talk to them all.

Every day at five o'clock, Nigel and his mother went home, but no matter how busy he was Wallace came to the door to see them off:

> If there was an air raid on or threatened he always personally found us a taxi, told the man where to go and even the route! The taxi was discreetly paid for our long journey and ordered to bring us back if the raid became rough – more than once this happened and somehow we found beds in that crowded flat.

Wallace made a huge impression on the young wannabe crime writer: 'Quite apart from the fact that he was the kindest man in the world to anyone who needed help, he was like a human dynamo to be with – you just could not get enough of his company. He was really larger than life size and more fun than any other person I have ever known.' Once, Nigel was in convalescence after an illness and Wallace heard that he wanted a scooter. Despite being in financial difficulties at the time, he went straight off to Harrods and bought an expensive scooter for his young friend.

In 1917 there was also a welcome visit to Wallace from an old friend. Robert Curtis had been invalided home in 1916 and, after his discharge from hospital, became confidential clerk to Sir John French, the man Wallace had met in South Africa, and who was now commander-in-chief of the Home Forces. Curtis remembers:

> As soon as I was discharged from hospital I called on Wallace and found him sitting at his desk, with his usual smile, and his Dictaphone mouthpiece in his hand. He might have been sitting like that ever since I had left him. 'Hullo, Bob,' was his greeting, 'Know anything?'
>
> 'All I know', I answered, surveying him critically, 'is that while I have been away you've added several inches to your waist measurement.'

Wallace told him that since he had been away, he'd had nine different typists – only one who could spell (presumably Violet King), or understood the uses of a comma – and that he had just started a new serial that he wanted Bob to write. He would, though, have to wait until 1919, when Curtis was officially demobbed, for the men's partnership to continue.

From 1915 until the end of the war, there were three women in Edgar's life: there was his wife Ivy who, in September 1916, had given birth to a second son, Michael; there was Daisy, his companion; and then there was Violet King. Ivy may have hoped that the birth of another child would have brought her and her husband closer together, but there was to be no turning back of the clock. She could see quite clearly that her main rival was now no longer Daisy, but her husband's pretty young secretary. 'There was no love lost between Ivy and Violet King, though they erected a façade of charming consideration and friendliness, and conducted their stealthy instinctive hostilities behind it,' records Margaret Lane.[13]

Violet attracted a series of dashing young officers who would call on Clarence Gate Gardens to take her out. Dressed up to the nines 'wearing a velvet opera cloak, a bandeau of artificial leaves, and high-heeled tango shoes tied with criss-crossed satin ribbons high up the ankle'[14] she cut a glamorous figure, and the knowledge that she was being pursued by other men only made her more attractive to her employer.

Lane tells us that the strongest antagonism between the three women in Wallace's life was between Violet and Daisy. The former could not understand what Edgar saw in Daisy, and Daisy no doubt realised that the secretary was now her greatest rival and not Edgar's wife.

Most of this friction passed over Edgar's head. He was too busy with his work and, moreover, was no doubt happy with the status quo. He had a wife whom he was fond of and who was still bearing him children; he had a delightful female companion with whom he could enjoy his racing and theatre; and he had a young and pretty secretary and general assistant with whom he worked for most of the day, and whose company he also greatly enjoyed.

If it had been left to Edgar it's likely that he would still have been sharing his life with Ivy, Daisy and Violet for many years to come. He certainly had no wish to divorce his wife. However, in 1917, things changed again. We have mentioned earlier how Edgar, with his usual generosity, had offered hospitality to Belgian refugees who had fled their country in 1914. One of them, a man called Leon, became a close friend of the family and began to spend more time together with Ivy. He seemed to be a kind and intelligent man and he was popular with the children too. Ivy fell in love with Leon, and confessed as much to Edgar. She told him she wanted a divorce and that once she had got her freedom she would marry again and go abroad to build a new life with her second husband.

Wallace quizzed his wife on the strength of her affections for the Belgian, and also on whether her new love was genuinely committed to her. When he was convinced of the answers, he agreed to a divorce. It was a sad end to the romance which had begun in South Africa twenty years earlier, but at least there seemed to be the promise of future happiness for Ivy. The divorce petition was presented in the summer of 1918 and the decree absolute was granted on 2 June 1919, with Ivy's adultery cited as the reason.

Ivy took Michael with her to live in her new home in Bournemouth, Bryan was sent away to prep school, while Pat stayed at Clarence Gate Gardens. Ivy thought she had a second marriage to look forward to, but the Belgian, who had gone back home at the end of the war, suddenly cooled on her. 'His letters dwindled, became conversational and cool, and at last ceased,' records Lane.[15] Ivy learned that the man she had pinned all her hopes on was already married. It was a bitter blow. She went to see her father, who was now living in Bournemouth, but that most unchristian of men closed his door on her. Then she learned that her mother had suddenly died in South Africa.

Ivy probably thought that anything would be better than being just one of the three women in Edgar Wallace's life. But, as her ex-husband's career went from strength to strength in the 1920s, and he became established as the most widely read author in the world and an international celebrity, the life of the woman who had shared so much with him, and who had born him four children, was to go rapidly downhill.

Sadly, 1918 was, in many ways, the toughest of the war years, certainly in regard to food shortages. On 22 January, the Ministry of Food announced drastic restrictions limiting the consumption of basic foodstuffs. Queues were reported at butchers for horsemeat. 'The dinner party today is about as gloomy as entertainment as can be imagined. I have just heard of one to which each guest was asked to bring something as a contribution to the feast! And another, given by a well-known bishop, at which there were twenty guests who dined off soup, potatoes, and tapioca pudding without the milk,' reported the *Daily Express* on 12 March.

Meanwhile, Edgar Wallace simply kept his head down and carried on working. Thankfully for him, tea and cigarettes – the two things he most needed – were not on ration.

In June, *Those Folk of Bulboro* was published by Ward Lock. This was unusual in that it was not a mystery, adventure story or thriller, but simply a 'novel' and noted as such on the title page. Wallace expert John Hogan believed the book was written pre-1914 – most probably in the fallow period 1908–1909 – and that Wallace dug out the manuscript to fulfil his contract with the publisher. The book concerns religious intolerance in a northern town and features, as the main character, Dr Anthony Manton, who returns from the Congo to take up his uncle's medical practice.

The Man Who Knew, published in the US in 1918, and in Britain by George Newnes a year later, was a story of intrigue and death with the mystery having its roots in South Africa. The ending is truly sensational, even by Wallace's standards. 'Those practised readers who begin this narrative with the weary conviction that they are merely to see the workings out of a conventional record of crime, of love and mystery, may be urged to pursue their investigations to the end,' Wallace warns the reader at the start of chapter three. 'There is a strangeness in the story of *The Man Who Knew* which brings it into the category of veracious history.'

In 1919, Wallace was helped by the return from military service of his trusty typist, Robert Curtis. Curtis tried to re-establish his typewriting business, but found new clients hard to come by. He told Wallace his predicament. Wallace asked him to join him full-time as his secretary. 'I've got no money but I'll guarantee you four pounds a week.' It was an offer Curtis could hardly refuse. 'Wallace told me later that he had always wanted me in his permanent, whole-time employment, but had never till then dared to commit himself to paying even a small regular salary,' Curtis wrote.

In August 1919, Edgar Wallace finally decided to take a break from work. The war was over, Ivy had gone, and it was now Violet who was supervising the household. Wallace told her to prepare for a family holiday to Switzerland. Typically, no expense would be spared. Violet, Edgar, Pat and Bryan would stay in the very best hotels, travel first class on the trains and have a whale of a time. Violet made all the arrangements. 'It was the first time she had ever been out of England, and Edgar was delighted with her naïve excitement,' Margaret Lane writes.[16]

We have come to regard Edgar as something of a workaholic, but he was a man who was always able to switch off and relax. His Dictaphone was left at home, and he forgot about books and articles for the duration of the break. 'He worked harder than any man I have ever known. But it was only because he loved his work,'Violet later wrote, 'had his passion for work given place to, say, an equally overpowering love of idleness, he would undoubtedly have been a magnificent idler.'

When Wallace wasn't working, he certainly knew how to enjoy himself. We know he loved nothing more than a day at the races, but he also loved playing cards – in particular piquet – 'the happiest days of his life were spent in the card-room of his beloved Press Club,' wrote Violet, and he loved seeing new places. He had shaved off his moustache before the holiday, believing it made him look too old in comparison with his youthful female companion. 'He certainly looked younger without it, and more attractive – the clean, powerful lines of his face were more clearly striking than before, and emphasised his air of calm self-confidence,' noted Margaret Lane.

They were good friends beforehand, but the holiday in Switzerland brought Edgar and Violet much closer together. 'It was an enchanting holiday in which the worries and disappointments of the last few years seemed to have dropped behind, and even Daisy was forgotten,' records Lane; 'Miss King – alert, intelligent, agreeable, admiring – was better company, he found, than any of them.'[17]

The woman who, four years earlier, had come into his life looking for a job, was making him feel young again. He bought Violet a gold and steel paperknife, engraved with the inscription 'To V.K. from E.W.' in Interlaken, and while in Lucerne he bought her (and Pat too) a shady hat. Their new intimacy meant a change in how they addressed each other. Violet preferred to be known as 'Vivette', but one of Edgar's idiosyncrasies was giving people his own pet names. He first called Violet 'Annie', then 'Sunny Jim' and then simply 'Jim'. Edgar, for his part, had always been called 'Dick' by those closest to him – with Edgar being only his 'professional' name.

'My name is Edgar – it's a rotten name, it's a ladylike name, it's a Nancy-like name,' he had written in a humorous piece for *Ideas* in August 1913, 'People who come to see me for the first time expect to find a willowy lad sitting by the side of canary embroidering pink roses on a table centre. When they find me eating raw red beef at Simpson's and discussing the Cambridgeshire weights they are disappointed.'Violet expressed her preference for 'Richard', the name he had been christened with. So, henceforward, they would address each other as 'Jim' and 'Richard'.

The journey home to England from Switzerland was broken with a stop in Paris, to celebrate Pat's 12th birthday, on 1 September. Once again, no expense was spared to make sure everyone had a jolly good time. 'An open taxi was hired for the day, and there was an orgy of present buying, followed by a drive in the Bois and the ceremonial consumption of cakes and ice-cream at the Café de la Cascade,' writes Lane.[18]

After Paris, Edgar took his children to Ostende, the main coastal resort in Belgium, where their mother was spending the summer with Michael, who was now 3. Wallace handled his separation with Ivy in such a way as to minimise any distress to his children. They would no doubt have been reassured to have seen their parents remain on friendly terms, and Wallace stressed to Pat and Bryan that they could see their mother whenever they wished.

The European holiday had been enjoyed by all, with no thought given to its cost. With his batteries fully recharged and his spirits high, it was time for Edgar to return home and get back to work.

19

THE FICTION FACTORY

Mr Gilbert Orsan was an industrious writer: he might not perhaps rival that inventer of tales who, if rumour does not lie, produces a novel a week and a play a fortnight.

Edgar Wallace, *Again the Ringer*, 1929

In the autumn of 1919 Wallace threw himself into a new project: co-writing a major West End theatrical revue for his friend Albert de Courville who, by now, had become a famous producer, notwithstanding the panning that *Are You There?* had received. De Courville asked Edgar to collaborate with Wal Pink and himself in creating a new show called *The Whirligig*.

Although he had written sketches and verses for the stage in the intervening period, including a sketch for de Courville's wartime operetta *Soldier Boy*, which the producer praised as one of the funniest in the show, this was Wallace's first major theatre work since the disastrous *An African Millionaire*, and he was determined to make a success out of it. Nothing was left to chance. 'He haunted rehearsals at the Palace Theatre, counting the number of laughs, and making optimistic calculations of the number which might be expected on the opening night,' says Margaret Lane.[1] Wallace even went to the lengths of employing a mechanical counter during actual performances to record the number of laughs.

The Whirligig premiered on 23 December 1919 and proved hugely popular with audiences, running for 441 performances. The sketch said to have produced the most laughs was one that Edgar wrote for the star of the show, Maisie Gray, as the comical cockney charwoman 'Mrs 'Arris'. 'Her blowsy respectability, her husky voice and beady eye, the predatory way in which her hand strayed as if unconsciously to her employer's cupboard, delighted 1920 audiences to the point of hysteria,' writes Lane.[2]

Wallace was overjoyed to be back in the world of theatre again. He loved mixing with theatre folk and became friends with almost all the cast. He generously invited the leading players to come round to Clarence House Gardens for dinner every Wednesday, between the matinee and evening performances, while on Saturdays, he and Jim hosted all sixteen of the Tiller Girls from the chorus, treating them to roast lamb, ice cream and champagne.

In 1919, in addition to his work on *The Whirligig*, Wallace was kept busy with his other writing. *The Green Rust*, published by Ward Lock, had as its villain a German scientist who sets out to poison the wheat harvest as revenge on the Allied powers for winning the Great War.

As the year – and the decade – came to an end Wallace could look back at ten years of solid achievements. He was established as one of the country's most popular writers, and if he was not yet a household name, he was at least on the way to becoming one. His output had been prodigious – in the period 1910–1919 he had produced over twenty novels and countless short stories, serials and newspaper and magazine articles. He had now written a popular West End revue too. He had arrived there by sheer hard work, but remarkably in the decade to come he would increase his production still further. The 1920s would be *his* decade – the decade in which the illegitimate board school boy from south-east London would become the most widely read author in the world, and a very rich man indeed.

Up to now his life story had been remarkable enough, but just like in one of his gripping, fast-paced serials, the tale was to get even more incredible as it progressed. Wallace was literally working round the clock, but was not yet receiving the income his incredible creativity and industry deserved. Jim later revealed that, despite his huge output of work, Edgar's income during the first five years she was with him (i.e. from 1915–1919) was 'considerably less' than £50 a week. *Answers* paid him 50s per 1,000 words for serials. He was paid 12 guineas for his weekly column on the war for the *Birmingham Daily Post*. He got around 20 guineas a week from elsewhere.

As to the financial situation in and around 1920, Robert Curtis tells us that when Wallace wrote a serial story he was 'perhaps' receiving between £200 or £300 for the serial rights, and £100 for the book rights, plus a little bit more for the American rights. He adds that: '£500 or £600 was not much return for the labour involved in writing 80,000 words of more or less good English with a thrill or a chill in each instalment.' Wallace was doing well, but he was far from being a rich man. With money going out faster than it was coming in (both Pat and Bryan were at private schools) he knew he had to increase his income.

The American market was one area where his work could do with a boost and where there were potentially very rich pickings to be had on the back of his 'Tam' stories. He decided to go out to New York himself to see an American agent, and meet up with publishers and magazine editors. Jim arranged for his steamship ticket and, while he was away, he left everything in her capable hands – including his daily betting. Wallace was only away for a fortnight, but it was a successful trip. He tied up a contract with a literary agent and made several useful contacts.

It wasn't all work, however; he came back with a diamond ring for Jim. 'Absence makes the heart grow fonder' as the old saying goes, and it seems that while he was away in New York, Wallace decided that he wanted to marry the woman who had come into his life in 1915 professing that she had never heard of him.

His proposal, appropriately enough, came in the middle of dictation. Jim recalled:

> He was dictating 'The Three Oaks Mystery'. He stopped in the middle of a sentence and looked down into my eyes. In his own was a suspicion of a twinkle. 'What about knocking off for a bit?' He began. I thought he meant a nap. 'Don't you think we've waited long enough?' He went on. I let him know I did think just that. 'Right,' he said. 'What about popping round to the Registry Office and finding out what is it we have to do?'

The wedding took place without a great fanfare. Wallace was reluctant to break the news to Daisy before the marriage, and preferred to present her with a fait accompli. 'He had a horror of emotional scenes not of his own making and believed that a penn'orth of decisive action was worth a pound of discussion,' says Lane.[3] The only witnesses were Wallace's cook and his chauffeur.

A news agency reporter did, however, recognise Wallace's name on the register, and a small item about the marriage did appear in an evening paper. Lane tells us that the agitated bridegroom took a taxi to Fleet Street and by 'personal appeals' persuaded the principal newspapers not to report the story.

Newly married, Edgar and Jim went back to what they had been doing when Edgar had proposed – namely finishing off 'The Three Oaks Mystery' serial they were working on for the *Daily Express*. That story, which told of robbery and murder and how two brothers set out to solve the crime, would eventually be published by Ward Lock in 1924, but in the first two years of the 1920s a further four Wallace titles appeared.

The Daffodil Mystery was an gripping tale in which the heroes are a Detective Jack Tarling and his Chinese assistant, Ling Chu. The villain, Thornton Lyne, who is found murdered, dressed up in woman's clothes with a bunch of daffodils laid on his breast, is one of the most repulsive characters to have yet appeared in a Wallace story. 'Poet and poseur, he was, the strangest combination ever seen in man,' we are told in chapter three. Lyne is a millionaire heir of a department store, but is imbued with characteristics we often see in Wallace villains – he is pretentious, pompous, vicious, snobbish and extremely creepy. In other words, he embodied all the things that Wallace most despised.

No one buys Lyne's book of 'poetry' but that makes sure that he becomes 'the idol of men and women who also wrote that which nobody read'. It's hard not to regard this as Wallace getting his own back at the rather superior, waspish critics who sneered at writers of 'penny dreadfuls' such as himself, and who felt that the work had to be of little artistic worth because it sold so well.

Jack O'Judgment, the book which followed, was another top-notch effort. Who is the mysterious vigilante, dressed in a black silk cloak, felt hat and mask, who threatens members of a gang of blackmailers, and whose calling card is the Jack of Clubs? The identity of Jack kept readers guessing right until the final chapter.

The Book of All Power, published by Ward Lock in June 1921, is one of Wallace's strangest and most interesting works. It's an adventure story set in Russia, both before and after the Bolshevik revolution of 1917. An old Jew, Israel Kensky, is the owner of a much-coveted book that contains 'the magic of power and the words and symbols which unlock the sealed hearts of men and turn their proud wills to water'. The secret of the book is not revealed until the very last page. Although it's true that the 'Red' characters in the book were largely portrayed as swinish brutes – the stereotype in most popular fiction of the time – Wallace at least showed an understanding of why the revolution had occurred. 'Wallace's attitude to the revolution is quite sympathetic and could be unique among popular novelists, and may be due to his knowledge of Russian life and customs,' noted Peter Coussee in 1994.[4] It could have been that he remembered the articles on the crimes of the Tsars that he had written for the *Daily Mail*.

Although his novel writing was going from strength to strength, Wallace was keen to return to the theatre. With the run of *The Whirligig* finished, he decided to write his own play. 'There's big money in the theatre,' he told Curtis, 'I'll write a play today. Why haven't I thought of this before?' Wallace's writing system for plays differed from his writing of books and serials in that he did not dictate, but wrote out everything by hand. He still worked at a breakneck speed, though, completing his new play in just fourteen hours.

The plot of *M'Lady* involves the wife of a convict, Mrs Carraway, who decides to bring up her little child, Marie, to believe that she is the orphan daughter of a foreign countess and that her mother is merely a nurse. Wallace was confident – as he was before every major venture – that it would be a success, but *M'Lady* was to be one of his most embarrassing failures.

It opened at the Playhouse Theatre in the middle of a heatwave in July 1921, hardly the best start. The proud playwright and his wife, wearing her first expensive evening dress, attended on the first night, and Edgar made a speech after the final curtain. It didn't prevent the play receiving a thumbs down from critics. 'Mr Wallace is evidently dramatically inclined, and should try his hand at another play' advised the *Daily Mail* – and that was one of the kinder reviews. 'I do not remember such unanimity as was displayed the next morning in the Press notices of the play; they were the worst I have read concerning any play,' noted Robert Curtis.

Audiences slumped and *M'Lady* was taken off after a fortnight. It was a bitter reverse, coming after the success of *The Whirligig*, but typically Wallace didn't allow the despondency to linger more than a few hours. In fact, the failure of *M'Lady* proved, like so many previous setbacks, to be a blessing in disguise. He had made significant financial losses on the play since he had formed a syndicate to finance it and had leased the theatre, and the creditors needed to be paid. That only meant one thing – shutting himself away with his Dictaphones and cranking up his production system of books, short stories and serials still further. Edgar Wallace, out of financial necessity, became a fiction factory.

It was one thing to produce a flood of books, short stories and serials; it was another thing to maximise the income that the author could obtain from them. We've seen how Wallace, needing the money there and then to pay his creditors, would sell all his rights to a title, and then watch as the book continued to sell, and not receive a penny. All his books up to now had been sold outright for under £100. It was true that some – indeed, many – of these started out as serials for which he had also been paid, and that he had been proficient in recycling work for different markets, but even so, he was missing out on an awful lot of royalties.

It was Jim who encouraged him to take a more businesslike approach to his work. What Edgar needed most of all was an agent. Jim arranged for him to see the agent, A.S. Watt. Watt was shocked when he heard of the cavalier way Wallace had sold the rights to his work. He also knew of a publisher who had been monitoring Wallace and who believed he could be a major money-spinner for his company. This publisher saw in Wallace huge commercial possibilities – he knew British readers had an insatiable appetite for well-written, fast-paced thrillers and mystery novels, and Wallace, with his prodigious work rate and incredible imagination, would be the man to keep them happy.

The publisher was Sir Ernest Hodder-Williams, head of Hodder & Stoughton. Very quickly a deal was struck. Wallace would receive £250 in advance royalties on delivery of each manuscript, with a rising scale of payment according to the sales of the book. For the first time in his career, Wallace could look forward to an income stream from his books after they had been published. 'This would have been a satisfactory arrangement with any sound publisher, but Sir Ernest was more than that; he had, where Edgar Wallace was concerned, a prophetic intuition which told him that this none too successful man, already nearing his fifties, had the makings of one of the greatest popular entertainers of all time,' says Margaret Lane.[5] It's harsh, and inaccurate, of her to say that in 1921 Wallace was 'none too successful', as he had already behind him a vast amount of published work, but there's no doubting how important the deal struck with Sir Ernest Hodder-Williams was.

The original contract was for six books. 'It is wonderful to have royalties at all, and royalties that come after the bankruptcy proceedings of Christmas that leave a man with only his furniture to eat – and that properly seasoned – are most wonderful of all,' Wallace enthused in a letter to Sir Ernest. In January 1924 Hodder-Williams, fully convinced that Wallace could produce the goods, told him that he was prepared to publish his books as quickly as he could write them. 'As regards a new contract, I shall be delighted to sign one,' Wallace wrote, 'I can only assure you that never again will I stray from the path of virtue and sell my books to the longs and the shorts of the publishing business. Until I came to you I had never seen a royalty cheque, and had come to regard my book rights as a kind of bonus for my serials.'

Wallace's reference to the 'longs and the shorts of the publishing business' was an allusion to the publisher John Long, who had published two of his books in 1923, but despite his promise he continued to write for them and other publishers too.

Some have argued that the deal with Hodder & Stoughton locked Wallace into a system of mass production, and forced him to put quantity before quality. His friend Willie Blackwood, the editor of *Answers*, implored him to cut his output and spend time on improving his style, but he and others who gave similar advice were missing the point. Wallace had learnt to write quickly and without revision during his time as a reporter and journalist. He did not waste time agonising over the *mot juste*; neither did he see writing as a chance to show off his superior vocabulary to the reading public. His aim was to tell the story as quickly and as entertainingly as he could.

The critic Wheeler Winston Dixon has paid tribute to the 'sheer force of Wallace's fictive voice'[6] and how it made his books so hard to put down. Wallace proves the truth of the old adage that simplicity is genius. 'Simplicity, he held, was the first requisite of greatness in writing,' Jim later revealed: '"Every time I read the Bible," he would say, "I am more and more impressed by its simplicity. It is its simplicity that makes it the most beautiful piece of literature in the world".'

If Hodder & Stoughton had contracted Wallace to produce one novel a year, it is likely that he would have delivered a ponderous book, nowhere near as good as the work he did produce. Sir Ernest, shrewd man that he was, knew that the faster Wallace worked the better he worked. The books that Wallace wrote for him, and others at this time, testify to this.

The first of Wallace's novels for Hodder & Stoughton was *The Law of the Four Just Men*, published in October 1921:

> There will always be a public for a writer like Mr Wallace who carries us along with a heartening swing from incident to incident until we reach the climax – with never an anti-climax. His style, with its crisp, straightforward sentences void of all irrelevance of thought or suggestion, is admirably adapted to the work in hand.
>
> Review in The Bookman

It was followed in May 1922 by *The Angel of Terror*, a chilling tale which has as its villain the murderous Jane Briggerland, who targets a young heiress Lydia Meredith, with the action moving from London to Monte Carlo and finally to Tangiers.

The Crimson Circle ran as a series in the *Daily Express* in 1921/22, and was published by Hodder & Stoughton as a novel in September 1922. It was the author's own favourite, and not hard to see why – as thrillers go, it's a book that has everything. Right from the very first sentence, the pace is unrelenting and the reader is in Wallace's grip until the final denouement. I have lent copies of *The Crimson Circle* to people of ages ranging from 13 to 82, and all found it impossible to put the book down once they had started it. This is how Wallace begins his story:

> It is a ponderable fact that had not the 29th of a certain September been the anniversary of Monsieur Victor Pallion's birth, there would have been no Crimson Circle mystery; a dozen men, now dead, would in all probability be alive, and Thalia Drummond would certainly never have been described by a dispassionate inspector of police as 'a thief and the associate of thieves' …

After reading that, how could you possibly not want to know more?

The prologue describes how an English malefactor named Lightman escapes the guillotine in France due a nail being put in the wrong place by an executioner who had had a bit too much to drink. 'Eleven years later that nail killed many people,' Wallace tells us. Lightman, under a new identity which is not revealed until the penultimate chapter, comes to Britain and heads a sinister gang of blackmailers and extortionists, who send their threats on letter cards stamped with a large crimson circle. A private detective called Derrick Yale, with strange psychometrical powers, assists Scotland Yard in their investigations, but it is the 'stolid, stupid-looking' Inspector Parr who finally solves the baffling case and unmasks Lightman.

The Crimson Circle proved to be a huge commercial success, and by 1938 had sold over half a million copies in Britain alone. A crimson circle, with his underlined signature written over it, became Wallace's logo, printed on the front of his later Hodder & Stoughton books, while many years later, the name was used for the monthly magazine of the Edgar Wallace Society. In 1970, in a poll of Edgar Wallace Society members, the book was a favourite with most correspondents.

In 1922, Lloyd George resigned as prime minister, the BBC began its radio service and Howard Carter found the tomb of Tutankhamen. It was proving to be a real *annus mirabilis* for Wallace. In July, Hutchinson published his racing story, *The Flying Fifty-Five*, which also appeared as a serial in the popular Sunday newspaper the *News of the World*. Wallace 'affectionately dedicated' it to his 'colleagues and friends of the Sporting Press'. Like *Grey Timothy*, it was another very entertaining novel about his favourite pastime. Wallace sets the scene brilliantly for the book's climax with his description of the Epsom Downs on Derby Day:

> The hill was covered with humanity, the rails lined from starting gate to winning post on both sides of the course. Colour there was in plenty. The scarlet, blue and green banners of the outside bookmakers, the variegated colours of the women's dresses. All these, against the emerald green of the Downs, made a picture which she would never forget.

Wallace followed *The Flying Fifty-Five* with an altogether more macabre book, *Mr Justice Maxell*. Not for the first time, Wallace sets some of the action in Morocco, a country he knew well from his earlier days as a correspondent. The book is particularly interesting for the moral ambiguity of its main characters: it's a thriller without a clear villain or hero. Wallace loved to point out how 'such great events hang upon slight issues' – in *The Crimson Circle* a dozen lives are lost due to a nail not being knocked in properly on a guillotine, while in *Mr Justice Maxell*, the decision of Cartwright, one of the main characters, to take his *petit dejeuner* sitting outside a café in Paris and not inside, has disastrous consequences.

Three further titles appeared in 1922. *Captains of Souls*[7] was a strange semi-science fiction tale involving the transmigration of human souls from one person to another. The subject matter showed that Wallace was never afraid of experimenting. *The Valley of Ghosts*, Wallace's first book for Odhams Press, was a more traditional thriller involving blackmail and the exposure of an evil moneylender. There was also another book from the River collection – *Sandi the Kingmaker*, the eighth in the series, was published in May by Ward Lock.[8]

In May, Wallace, clearly pleased at how he was finally gaining a proper reward for his talents, wrote a letter of thanks to A. S. Watt, his agent: 'My Dear Watt, May I express my deep appreciation of all you have done for me, especially in regard to the sale of film rights? You have secured better prices for my work than I could have procured, and you have splendidly protected me against my own amiability.'

On 5 May, he also wrote an effusive letter expressing his gratitude to his old employer, Lord Northcliffe, who was suffering from ill health:

> I don't know whether you realise that when you gave me my chance I was semi-illiterate – a man entirely without education or any of the advantages which men had, even if they had only graduated in Fleet Street ... I shall be a spendthrift all my days, But I will pay you, in my heart, and by my spoken and written word the homage and love I feel for you.

Three months later Northcliffe, the man who had given Wallace his first big break in British journalism, was dead, at the age of 57.

Away from his novel writing, Wallace maintained his interest in real-life crime. In April 1922, he had a nine-day working holiday in Hereford, where he attended the murder trial of the 'Hay poisoner' Herbert Armstrong, a *cause célèbre* of the early 1920s.

A Hay-on-Wye solicitor and clerk to the local magistrates, Armstrong was accused of murdering his wife by giving her arsenic. He had been arrested in December 1921 for the attempted poisoning of a professional rival. He was found guilty, though Wallace had his doubts. Armstrong was hanged at Gloucester Prison in May 1922, and two years later Wallace's account of the case was published in a Newnes collection, entitled *Great Stories of Real Life*. To this day, Armstrong remains the only solicitor in Britain to be hanged for murder.

Wallace's semi-regular column in the *Sunday Post*, the D. C. Thomson-owned newspaper, gave him the opportunity to spout forth on a wide variety of topics, including issues of law and order. 'Are we drifting back to slavery?' he asked on 12 June 1921. In other weeks he discussed Parliament, the judiciary and whether Britain needed a 'national organiser'. Wallace's versatility was extraordinary, as was the way he could work on two or three projects at the same time. 'He could switch from an article on "Should Women wear high heels?" to "What's going to win the Manchester November Handicap?" – like that. His mind would switch over instantly,' said Pat Wallace. She also revealed how her father got ready to start work, and how he stopped:

He'd work very concentrated, as if a current built up in him and he used to sit and think before he started. He would put his hands together as if the current passed through them and after that he never hesitated. If he was working very long hours without a break, he had his own way of knowing when it was wise to switch off. He'd put his hand on his head very tenderly – he had a place on the top of his head which used to get very hot – and if it did he'd stop.[9]

20

THRILLING A NATION

It was typical in this period of excitement, when the name of the Crimson
Circle was on every tongue, that sensation should follow sensation.

Edgar Wallace, *The Crimson Circle*, 1922

With cheques from publishers, newspapers and magazines coming in all the
time, Wallace's income was rising fast and by 1923 he was earning around
£150 a week. Even so, the money was pouring out even faster. As far as
Wallace was concerned money only had one use – it had to be spent. Not for
him studying the share prices of the financial press and making careful invest-
ments. In any case, he had speculated on the South African stock exchange
and it had been a disaster.

We have seen how the urgent need for money to pay off creditors had been
a major factor spurring him to activity. When he had money, and thought his
creditors were at bay, he would put down his Dictaphone and head to the
racecourse, but as soon as the next bill arrived he would be back at his desk
again. Of course, there were always plenty of bills.

Robert Curtis recalled how in the years following the Great War, Wallace
would eschew travelling by bus, Tube or even taxi, and instead hire expensive
limousines to take him from Clarence Gates Gardens to wherever it was he
needed to go: 'His bills from the hire company were appalling.' In addition to
his children's expensive private school fees – Pat was at Cheltenham Ladies'
College and Bryan at Oundle – from 1923 he also had racehorse training fees
to pay.

His first horse, bought that year, and registered to run in Jim's name, was
appropriately named 'Sanders'. If the horses he bought had been good ones
he would at least have got back some of the expense, but invariably they
were moderate. In the words of James Cameron: 'He would buy them for a
thousand and sell them for a hundred.' Not that Wallace minded too much.
By becoming a racehorse owner he had achieved one of his most cherished
ambitions. It enabled him to become even more closely involved with his

favourite sport than he had been when a tipster or racing columnist. Now he was on the 'inside' of the racing world, regularly mixing with trainers, other owners and jockeys, and standing proudly in the parade ring as his horse prepared to race.

Wallace spent a lot of money on his own pleasures, but a fortune on other people. 'He was incurably generous,' wrote Curtis, 'It was one of the most loveable traits in the character of the most loveable man I have ever known. He scattered his benevolence with as lavish a hand as he scattered money on any other object.' Curtis recalled how an old friend called on Wallace one day with a familiar request: 'Can you lend me a tenner?' Curtis knew that money was tight at that particular time and was curious how Wallace, who never turned anyone in need down, would respond. 'A tenner, I really don't know old man,' Wallace replied, 'Wait a minute and I'll see how the Pals' Account stands.' The Pals' Account was a special fund to help his friends which Wallace paid into whenever he could. The friend who had asked for a tenner, left with a cheque for £15. Many a time Curtis warned his boss that the person he had lent money to would never repay him. Wallace's reply, 'Being let down doesn't matter.'

Perhaps it was good karma for all his kindness, but 1923 turned out to be one of the happiest years of Wallace's life. Becoming a racehorse owner fulfilled one ambition, being elected chairman of the Press Club in March another. Back in 1905 he had written to Ivy: 'I do not care for the Press Club, such a rotten class of people go there,' but he changed his mind in the fallow days which followed his sacking from the *Daily Mail*. Then the club had been a welcome bolthole, a place where he could make new contacts and where he could sit and smoke and play poker with old colleagues. Now, fourteen years after he had first stood for chairman, he had been elected. He was determined to make an impact during his year in office. Wallace came up with a capital idea which linked two of his greatest loves: journalism and the turf. The Press Club would hold a special Derby lunch, on the Monday before the big race, to which all the leading owners, trainers and jockeys would be invited, with the 17th Earl of Derby, a man who Wallace greatly admired, the host.

Wallace planned everything for the inaugural lunch, even down to the flowers, which he had arranged in the racing colours of the different owners. Eminent guests included the Aga Khan, the newspaper owner Lord Rothermere, Captain Boyd-Rochfort who later became the trainer to the Royal Family and the leading jockey Steve Donoghue, who was asked to stand on a chair so that he might be seen.

Taking the chair, Wallace made a pleasing speech, mixing humour with sentiment, and got everyone in the right mood for the occasion. 'He could set an atmosphere as well as any master actor in a theatre,' recalled Horace Sanders, a former Press Club chairman, 'One was always sorry when Edgar sat down, but he always sat down at the right time.' The Derby luncheon was a great success and became established as an annual event. Wallace always regarded it as his proudest achievement.

In late May there was another cause for celebration, as Jim gave birth to the couple's first child. Margaret Penelope June Wallace was born on 30 May 1923. Of all Wallace's children, Penny, as she was to be known, was the one who would most take after her father – she became a crime writer, had the same engaging, optimistic personality and even shared Edgar's penchant for smoking with a cigarette holder.[1] 'Penny had the Wallace chin, the Wallace nose and the Wallace unstopability,' it was later said of her.[2] She was to become her father's favourite, but her birth, coming just two weeks before Royal Ascot, did pose him an immediate problem. Jim was not only his wife, but his enthusiastic racing companion and she had never before been to the world-famous race meeting. Edgar, with typical extravagance, decided to buy a private box for Jim at Ascot, intending to keep it as a surprise.

He couldn't wait for his favourite event of the year to come. 'Ascot was a sort of dream place, it was society, celebrity and horses all at once. What more could Edgar Wallace ask for?' said James Cameron. The trouble was, Royal Ascot 1923 was fast approaching and Jim was still in a nursing home recovering from giving birth. Two weeks after Penelope had been born, Edgar arrived to visit Jim and told her about the box. Jim's doctor had forbidden her to leave the nursing home for another two weeks, but Edgar was having none of it. He came to see his wife again on the morning of the first day of Royal Ascot and was followed in by his chauffeur who was carrying several boxes. He had bought new outfits for Jim to wear on each day of the four-day meeting. Edgar had thought of everything and to get medical approval, he even invited Jim's doctor to come along too to join in the fun and keep a watchful eye on his patient. The party set off to enjoy the festival.

Wallace, as always, was an incredibly generous host. He not only plied his guests with as much food as they could eat and as much champagne as they could drink, but put bets on for them with his own money. He made sure that his guests always won. Carol Reed recalled:

> I remember once going to Ascot with a party that he gave there, about fifteen of us and he had a box there with a dining room at the back – all very grand – and I remember him saying 'everyone in the room is on for a tenner for the winner in the last race.' 'So,' we said 'what's that – what's the horse's name?' He said 'I can't tell you.' I knew he hadn't done anything at all. So the race comes on after lunch and up comes this horse who was an outsider – and it came in at 15–1! Everyone looked at Wallace and asked

'Was that the horse?' And he said, 'Yes, that was the horse, you've all won. And he paid out. 15–1! He loved to do generous things without anyone knowing about them.[3]

Putting bets on for friends on unnamed horses and telling them after the race that their horse had won was a favourite trick of Wallace's. How much it must have cost him we can only guess, but the main thing was that he was making people happy – and whether it was by writing hugely entertaining thrillers, or providing them with winners at the race track, making others happy is what he most loved doing.

After years of struggle, 1923 was the year that Edgar Wallace had finally arrived. He was chairman of the Press Club, a box holder at Royal Ascot and now also a patron of a good cause. At the end of October, 'Fleet Street Week' for St Bartholomew's Hospital was held – a series of charity events to raise money for the great teaching hospital in London's East End. Wallace was deputy chairman of the joint executive committee (in his Press Club capacity) and edited the illustrated souvenir programme. He also penned an introduction:

Fleet Street has precious little sentiment. It lives too near to the cause of things, has too clear a view of the machines that work and the strings that are pulled, to harbour many illusions. But Fleet Street whole-heartedly advances the cause of Bart's, and holds out a confident and receptive hand for your bounty.

Wallace, along with all his good works, public and private, continued to delight his ever-growing readership with more imaginative tales. *Chick*, a light-hearted story which first appeared as a series for *Windsor* magazine in 1921–22, was published in book form by Ward Lock in February 1923. In it, Charles 'Chick' Beane, a humble insurance clerk, unexpectedly inherits the title of Marquis of Pelborough and has to learn how to act and behave like an aristocrat. His work colleagues also have to decide how to address him. Bennett, the head clerk, is a communist, but still thinks Beane should be called 'My Lord'. 'I regard titles as a ridiculous survival of class privilege,' he says, 'But Chick Beane has always been respectful to me and I regard him as a comrade and an ornament to the proletariat.'

In July, Wallace's third book for Hodder & Stoughton, *The Clue of the New Pin*, an ingenious 'locked room' mystery with a Chinese businessman called Liang as the main character, was published. There's a line in the novel in which Wallace is perhaps expressing regret that he has had to work so hard and is aware of the costs to his health. 'Mr Wellington Brown was a born loafer; it is a knack which would prolong many lives in this strenuous age, if it could be acquired.'

The Green Archer, which had first appeared as a serial in the *Chicago Daily News* in 1922, was published by Hodder & Stoughton in November. A tale of a seemingly haunted castle, owned by an American millionaire ex-gangster called Abe Bellamy, it was billed by the publishers as 'the most exciting novel Edgar Wallace has written' and proved to be a huge hit with the reading public.[4] Reviewers were impressed too: 'It is impossible not to be thrilled, impossible too not to exert all one's ingenuity in attempting to solve the enigma of the identity of the archer in the green. The whole story goes with a swing from beginning to end, and is excellent entertainment,' enthused the *Sunday Times*.

In *The Missing Million*, bridegroom Rex Walton seems to vanish into thin air on the morning of his wedding, having withdrawn £1 million out of his bank account in the week before the wedding. Wallace himself was not yet a millionaire, but his stories were now bringing him the sort of income he could only have dreamt about in his days as a humble foot soldier in Aldershot.

The years 1924–1926 were when Edgar Wallace became established, not just as a best-selling author, but as a household name. It was in 1924, the year that Britain saw its first Labour government and Lenin, the leader of the Russian Revolution, died in Moscow, that Hodder & Stoughton first used the phrase 'It is impossible not to be thrilled by Edgar Wallace.' Thought to have been lifted from the first line of the *Sunday Times* review of *The Green Archer*, to promote their author's work, it was no idle boast, but one that millions of Britons would have agreed with.

How can we explain the national addiction to the works of Edgar Wallace which was developing? Wallace's strong fictive voice, highlighted by Wheeler Winston Dixon, undoubtedly made his books hard for readers to put down. His matter-of-fact style, honed after years as a reporter, also helped to make even the most fantastic happenings seem believable. Wallace's novels provided the 1920s reading public in Britain with the excitement and thrills which they craved.

They had endured the Great War, and the harsh, grey years following the Armistice. They had had rationing, unemployment, government-imposed austerity and political unrest. Now they wanted some enjoyment. Wallace's thrilling tales took readers out of their monochrome lives into a Technicolor world where everything was possible. The secretary on the 5.20 from Charing Cross could imagine that she was like Thalia Drummond in *The Crimson Circle*, pitched head-first into an amazing adventure and breathtaking romance; the lowly journalist on a suburban newspaper could fantasise about being involved, like Peter Dewin, in a mystery like that of *The Feathered Serpent*.

Wallace himself had no grand literary pretentions, and set out only to entertain his readers. 'If a man puts down a book of mine and says he enjoyed it, I don't ask for more,' he once told Nigel Morland. As the crime writer

Julian Symons stated, 'before Wallace, English crime writers were middle-class people writing for a largely middle-class readership. Edgar Wallace changed all that. For the first time we had a crime writer who came from the working-class. Wallace's portrayal of working-class characters and policemen rang true because he knew what he was writing about. His time spent as a crime reporter also gave him the edge over his rivals.'

Wallace's books appealed not only to the working class. He had fans in high places too. King George V and Prince Albert, later George VI, were both devotees. It was said that during the king's illness, Queen Mary bought the four latest Wallace titles to read to him.[5] 'During a recess Prime Ministers do not as of old hie themselves to the classics and thank their God for Virgil. They batten instead on the works of Edgar Wallace,' observed H. Douglas Thompson.[6]

Stanley Baldwin, Conservative prime minister from 1924–1929, was one of Edgar Wallace's fans in the Palace of Westminster. As was Arthur Balfour, who had served as prime minister from 1902–1905. A rather aloof and detached upper-class intellectual, who wrote a book on philosophy in his early thirties, Balfour, like so many, was bitten by the Wallace bug. 'I remembered Lord Balfour talking with the greatest gusto about a novel of Edgar Wallace's he had just read … (*The Hand of Power*). He was fascinated by the machinery of the plot. He wanted to know all the details of Edgar Wallace's life and was disappointed that the outline I was able to give him was so sketchy,' noted a journalist on the occasion of Wallace's death.

Leading Tory politician Lord Birkenhead, formerly F.E. Smith, was another who was hooked. 'He was amazed at the man's [Wallace's] industry and ingenuity. He admitted that he had never read an Edgar Wallace story which did not excite him.' Birkenhead invited Wallace to lunch, and the author explained his method:

> He said he allowed an idea to occur to him and then wrought out of that single notion a web of plot and contrivance. Giving 'F.E', an instance, he explained that he once saw a piece of candle lying on the floor which had been a full three inches long, but had become contracted and bent under heat and was shorter than its full three inches, by, let us say, an eighth of an inch. He conceived the notion that this candle might help him with a plot. Could he not have a man murdered in a room and allow the murderer to escape by leaving the latch propped up from the inside with this candle … Out of this germ of a notion Edgar Wallace built a good story, *The Clue of the Twisted Candle*.[7]

It wasn't just Wallace's plots that fascinated readers, it was the author himself. 'In the twenties, Wallace provided what the war-strained British needed:

something exotic, something to do with the new word glamour. Edgar Wallace with his long cigarette holder, gangster hat and ever-ready cheque-book, was a shadowy giant with whom the ordinary reader could identify,' noted Tom Pocock.[8]

Up to now we have tried to give short synopses of Wallace's books, but because of the number of titles which appeared from the mid-1920s onwards, it is impossible in a book of this size to include descriptions of everything he wrote. While he still penned the odd non-thriller (for example the historical series for children *The Black Avons*), since his tie-up with Hodder & Stoughton Wallace increasingly concentrated on writing thrillers. Although they were all different, given the sheer number of books he produced, there were inevitably some similar plot lines.

In a number of his thrillers there was a mysterious criminal organisation – usually a gang of murderers, blackmailers and extortionists, whose leader is often the very last person you'd expect and whose identity is usually kept under wraps until the final denouement. *The Crimson Circle*, *The Fellowship of the Frog* – which Wallace believed was his best crime story – *The Hand of Power*, and *The Terrible People* all fit into this category. Forgery is also a common theme and features not only in the 1927 novel *The Forger*, but other books such as *Penelope of the Polyantha*, *Private Selby* and *The River of Stars*, as well as numerous short stories. And of course, there are lots and lots of murders.

Jockey Jack Leach recalled going up to visit Wallace once evening at his Portland Place flat. The great author was there:

> … Striding up and down the room, chain-smoking through that famous long black holder, writing four books at once plus a racing article. [Wallace it seemed, was getting muddled up.] Suddenly he turned to me and said: 'There are too many characters in one of these books; I must try and get rid of some of them, they worry me.' He then murdered four of them in one chapter. It was fantastic to listen to.[9]

Unlike other writers of 'The Golden Age' of crime fiction, Wallace usually employed a different detective or sleuth in each book. Among those who did appear more than once were the gloomy Elk, who features in *The Fellowship of the Frog*, *The Twister*, *The India Rubber Men* and *White Face*, and whose police rank changes from book to book; T.B. Smith (*The Secret House*, *The Nine Bears*); and the philosophical 'Sooper' – aka Superintendent Minter (*Big Foot*, *Lone House Mystery*). There was also a very popular series of short stories with the fastidious, umbrella-carrying Mr J.G. Reeder from the Public Prosecutor's Office.

The job of smashing the criminal gang is often left to a regular police inspector, in association with a gentleman detective – who invariably falls for the beautiful female lead. The heroine is usually a shop assistant, secretary or actress, struggling to make ends meet, yet on more than one occasion she turns out to be an heiress to a large fortune and/or the daughter of another character in the book. As to the baddies, they come in all shapes and sizes and are often disguised as the most innocuous character in the novel.

When trying to solve a Wallace mystery, it's wise to suspect everyone, save the romantic leads. 'No one save the detective hero and the pretty heroine is what they seem,' observed crime writer H.R.F. Keating. The female lead is invariably kidnapped by the criminal mastermind – still wearing a mask – towards the end of the book, prompting a frantic night-time car chase through the Home Counties to rescue her from the disused factory, farmhouse or cellar where she is being held captive.

Wallace's books are always fast-moving, and new technology helps speed things up. Cars and telephones, the wireless, ingenious listening devices and electric gadgetry all feature prominently, while aeroplanes also make regular appearances. Some of Wallace's work may appear dated today, but to the reader in the 1920s they must have seemed strikingly modern.

The journalist James Dunn once asked Wallace where he got his ideas from. 'There are plots everywhere,' Wallace replied. The two men were walking in the old Alsatia area of London at the time:

> Pointing to a tiny window covered by a shabby curtain he [Wallace] said: 'Here's a plot! There's a murderer behind that curtain. He's hiding there just like the old cut-throats did. Here he is in the heart of Fleet Street where everybody is looking for him and no one knows where he is. The Flying Squad is out. The Police Gazette has got his picture. Every station in the country is warned: but there he is, quite safe, and he will come down and have a steak in that little restaurant over there with a cop walking past the door. Damn it – I'll write it!'[10]

Most of Wallace's thrillers are set, at least partly, in London, with villains having their headquarters in Deptford or Limehouse, and the River Thames features in many of them. Although action does occasionally move outside of the metropolis too, with the Marlow area of the Thames Valley being a popular setting for some of the action after Wallace moved there in the late 1920s. Seemingly haunted houses and mysterious mansions with secret passages and sealed-off rooms, known only to the villain, also regularly appear. Wallace was a big fan of 'the locked room' mystery, and several of his books include 'impossible' crimes: murders of people in rooms where there is no obvious answer as to how the malefactor could have got in and out.

Margaret Lane was of the view that Wallace's 'heroes are all heroic, his hero-ines all pure and his villains unequivocally villainous'[11] but that's not strictly true. Even the blackest Wallace baddie usually has some redeeming feature – for instance Abe Bellamy in *The Green Archer* and Colonel Dan Boundary in *Jack O'Judgment* possess great courage which the reader can't help but admire. 'I often think that where the writers of fiction stories and plays make such a mistake is in their delineations of villains,' Wallace had written in his 1926 work, *The Gaol Breaker*, 'It is my experience that there are no villains who are villainous in all things, but that their evil acts are born of circumstances and of their own selfish plans and enterprises.'

Wallace's characters are rarely cardboard cut-outs and more morally ambiguous than he is given credit for. In many a criminal gang there is at least one member who tries to go straight, and sometimes those on the side of the law – such as the pompous judge Sir Ralph in *The Fourth Plague* – are made very hard to like. Then there's the fact that many of Wallace's heroes are, technically speaking, criminals themselves – vigilantes, or moral avengers acting outside of the law. Wallace began this theme with *The Four Just Men* and continued it with characters such as *The Brigand* – aka Anthony Newton, a Robin Hood of the 1920s, who sees it as his job to fleece the undeserving rich – and his female counterpart, *Four Square Jane*.

While there's murders a plenty, car chases, abductions and lots of secret passages, one thing you don't get in Wallace's books is sex. At the most, the heroine and the male romantic lead share a kiss and hold hands at the end, but that's about as far as it goes. 'I try to write clean adventure stories, entirely free from sex interest, because I hold pretty definite views on sex stories,' Wallace explained in an article for *The Bookman* in January 1930. Robert Curtis recalled:

> He hated the sex novel, which he used to say was the easiest thing to write provided one's mind was dirty enough. Once when he was in Paris en route from Switzerland to London, he bought a copy of D.H. Lawrence's *Lady Chatterley's Lover*. When I met him the next day: 'Bob,' he said, handing me the volume, 'I nearly chucked this into the Channel; it's the most obscene thing I've ever read. But you're a bit of a highbrow – have a go at it and learn the meaning of nausea.' – I did.

Despite his disdain for sex scenes in books, Wallace had too good a sense of humour to be too po-faced about the subject. Once, when asked by an interviewer what useful purpose he thought he served in life, he replied with a grin, 'I've kept more women awake at night than any other living man.' It was probably true, given the popularity of his books.

With his work going so well, Wallace felt justified in splashing out even more on his greatest passion, horse racing. In 1924, he bought a second race-horse, who he called 'Bosambo'. 'What this animal cost him from start to finish I do not care to think,' wrote Robert Curtis; 'Edgar, I imagine would have found it less expensive to run a steam yacht.' Wallace, ever the great optimist, brushed off poor performances and continued to back heavily on his horses, always believing that in the next race they'd show their true form. 'He would never accept the explanation that they were second-rate horses for which he had paid too much money. Next time, he was certain, one of his string would win – eventually become a Classic horse, and win the Derby,' said Margaret Lane.[12]

On one occasion, Wallace was so confident that Bosambo would win at Warwick that he promised Jim he would take her on her first visit to America with the money he was going to win from his bets on the race. He was so sure of victory that he wrote the telegram booking their passages during their journey to the racecourse in a hired Daimler limousine. The result – Bosambo came last, and the trip to America was cancelled. Wallace, according to Curtis, backed Bosambo every time he ran, except the one occasion when he should have. 'That day at Nottingham, when neither Wallace nor I had backed him, he won his one and only race, and his starting price was 10–1,' Curtis lamented.

Whenever Wallace received a large sum of money he tried to increase it by gambling: 'Let's play up the luck' was one of his favourite sayings. According to Jim, the first 'big' money he ever received was a cheque for £1,000 from America in advance of royalties. Most people would simply have banked the money and had a celebratory glass of champagne. Not Edgar Wallace, he had to 'play up the luck'. The cheque arrived on a day when there happened to be a race meeting at Newmarket. Wallace hired a chauffeur-driven car to take him and Jim to the races. 'I know a good thing in the first,' he told his wife on the journey. Jim was delighted to see that the horse which Edgar had mentioned in the car had won the first race. But alas, Edgar had changed his mind and backed three other horses, having listened to advice from other people when he arrived at the track. More bad bets followed, as Wallace tried to get back the £300 he had lost on the first, and by the end of the day's racing there wasn't enough money from the £1,000 to pay for the hire of the car. Wallace had blown his American royalties on one afternoon at the races.

In his book *Sods I Have Cut on the Turf*, the jockey Jack Leach[13] mocked Wallace's approach to gambling. 'In many ways he was a strong personality, but there was one very weak link in his make-up – he thought he knew everything about racing. I never met a man who knew less.' When it came to his own horses, Wallace refused to listen to honest assessment of their abilities.

'The trouble is that he was in love with his horses, and wouldn't hear a word against them. If his trainer, or any of the crack jockeys who rode for him from time to time, told him the horses were no good, they immediately got the sack.' But, as Leach conceded, everyone liked Edgar, and even the trainers and jockeys he dismissed remained good friends with him.

Again, Wallace's gambling and the way he refused to be downcast by heavy losses highlighted his extraordinary optimism. 'Edgar never lost confidence; he always thought the next one was a certainty.' And even if it wasn't, he knew that all he needed to do to get back the money he had lost was to pick up the Dictaphone and start working again. As to why Wallace gambled, Robert Curtis recalled a conversation he once heard between his employer and an eminent psychologist. Wallace had had a disastrous week at Ascot, where he had lost in the region of £20,000. The psychologist explained to him that 'the Englishman's passion for betting was in reality the outcropping of his innate spirit of adventure, to which modern life denied expression in its more romantic forms'. That might be a generalisation, but Curtis thought it was certainly true of Wallace, 'He had no use for a life without a tang in it. He hungered for thrills, and he found them in plenty on the racecourse.'

While Wallace lost a fortune on the horses, we must not forget that the sport did also provide him with plenty of material for his work. One of his most memorable creations was the little cockney tipster, 'Educated Evans', who first appeared in book form in May 1924, and who was based on real life tipster, Pat 'Ringer' Barrie[14] whose memoirs Wallace had ghosted for *John Bull* magazine.

The buzz that Wallace got from gambling was being experienced by millions of Britons through his books. In the years 1924 and 1925, no fewer than eighteen Wallace novels appeared, many of which had already been published as serials. Among the most popular was *The Fellowship of the Frog*, published by Ward Lock in January 1925[15] which, along with *The Crimson Circle*, has strong claims to being the best thriller Wallace had written. Again, the plot concerns a secret criminal organisation, headed by the mysterious 'Frog' whose identity is carefully concealed until the forty-first of the book's forty-two chapters.

A King by Night, which Wallace dedicated 'To my Friend, P.G. Wodehouse', was another top notch effort, involving the hunt for a mysterious prowler. 'The characters march with a lively gait and the narrative from first to last is handled with the consummate touch of a master,' the blurb on a later edition declared. A prowler features again in the *Blue Hand*, while in *The Strange Countess*, an orphan finds she is the daughter of a convicted murderess and sets out to clear her mother's name. Wallace dedicated the book to the publisher D.C. Thomson, 'with the author's happiest memories of a long business association'.

There were hints of what was to come a few years later with *King Kong*, in *The Hairy Arm*. It features an orang-utan which climbs buildings and chases swooning lady film stars. First published in America in 1925, it appeared a year later under the title *The Avenger* in Britain. In 1925, Wallace's work appeared in a new medium – radio, or the wireless as it was then popularly called. He wrote a twenty-five minute radio play called *The Little Quaker*, which was set off the Cornish coast on the bridge of an Atlantic liner, and which was broadcast on the '2LO' station on 22 June.

'Make this an Edgar Wallace year,' declared Hodder & Stoughton in early 1926, and millions of Britons did just that. Eighteen Wallace novels had appeared in the years 1924 and 1925: eighteen now appeared in 1926 alone. In the second half of 1926, Hodder & Stoughton sold 488,612 of his books, and his other publishers sold 300,000. In other words, Wallace chalked up sales of over ¾ million in just six months. Among the new titles were *The Black Abbot*, about a sinister, ghostly figure and a hunt for buried treasure, which was said to have been Hollywood star Clark Gable's favourite book, and *The Terrible People*, a brilliantly plotted thriller about a gang of criminals who seek revenge for the hanging of their ring-leader. In *The Day of Uniting*, Wallace tried his hand at science fiction and the result was impressive – an exciting tale in which the Earth is threatened by a giant asteroid.

It was in 1926 that Wallace began to make big money very quickly. It wasn't just on account of his novels, which were now being printed and sold in larger numbers than ever before, but a highly successful return to the London stage.

21

ENTER THE RINGER!

Who had not heard of the Ringer? His exploits had terrified London. He had killed ruthlessly, purposelessly, if his motive were one of personal vengeance.

Edgar Wallace, *The Ringer*, 1926

On 1 May 1926 Britain was hit by a coal strike which, two days later, would lead to the country's first General Strike. It was probably not the best time to have a new play opening in London's West End, and no doubt Edgar Wallace went to the first night of *The Ringer* at The Wyndham's Theatre full of apprehension. His last theatrical effort, *M'Lady*, had been taken off after a fortnight. Would his new play be any different?

To his great relief, *The Ringer* was a resounding hit with both audience and critics. 'The play was a tremendous success,' he enthused in a letter to Sir Ernest Hodder-Williams, 'Coal strike or no coal strike this "drammer" looks like lasting out the crisis.' After the curtain went down on the first night Wallace, the cast, and friends headed to the Carlton for a fabulous party attended by over 100 people. There was much to celebrate. Wallace had finally made it at the West End at the age of 51. *The Ringer* not only established him as a popular dramatist, it also led to many more successful plays which netted him around £100,000 in profits over the next six years.

For the genesis of the play we have to go back to 1924. Wallace had been commissioned to write a serial for the American magazine *Short Stories*. He gave them *The Three Just Men*, and at the end of the story the heroes follow a man to London where they see a real murder done in front of them at a theatre, while a 'stage' murder is occurring at the same time, in a play called 'The Ringer'.

Wallace then wrote a serial called 'The Ringer' for the *American Detective Story* magazine, which was subsequently published as the novel *The Gaunt Stranger* by Hodder & Stoughton in July 1925. Ever since the disaster of *M'Lady*, Wallace had been looking for the right vehicle with which to return to the London stage. He believed *The Gaunt Stranger* had all the right ingredients for a thrilling play. What Wallace had lacked in the past was someone with the theatrical experience to help him dramatise his work. Sir Gerald du Maurier was to be the 'missing link' – the man whose expertise helped turn Edgar Wallace, the successful novelist, into Edgar Wallace, the successful playwright.

Du Maurier was a famous actor-manager who co-managed the Wyndham's Theatre from 1910–1925. According to Margaret Lane, Wallace had submitted a draft of a dramatised version of *The Gaunt Stranger* to du Maurier in the winter of 1925/26. The two men met for lunch, and by the end of the meal the actor-manager had agreed to cooperate with Wallace on his new play. He thought that the draft had plenty of theatrical potential but advised a change of title. *The Gaunt Stranger* became *The Ringer* and the two men began work. However, according to Nigel Morland,[1] Wallace had not yet written a dramatised version of *The Gaunt Stranger* by the time he first met du Maurier. It was only when Sir Gerald mentioned that he had an empty theatre on his hands, that Wallace 'caught fire' and talked about *The Gaunt Stranger* as a play which already existed.

Wallace made up scenes over the coffee as he went along. When du Maurier expressed his interest, Wallace told him that the play would have to be 'typed from its Dictaphone form' and then went home to write it out in just over forty-eight hours. There was radical revision of the play which Wallace had written so quickly. 'Du Maurier doctored the play into shape – virtually rewrote it in fact,' noted James Cameron. It was a thrilling plot: *The Ringer* – aka Henry Arthur Milton – is a master of disguise and ruthless destroyer of his enemies. He has sworn revenge on the crooked lawyer Maurice Meister, whom he blames (correctly) for the death of his sister. Meister seeks police protection, but will it be enough to save him?

The Ringer went into rehearsal at Wyndham's with an all-star cast. Leslie Banks, who played 'Bliss', a rather enigmatic detective, was one of the top stage actors of the day, and was later to appear as Sanders in Alexander Korda's 1935 film *Sanders of the River*. Nigel Bruce, who will forever be remembered for his portrayal of a rather bumbling Dr Watson alongside Basil Rathbone's Sherlock Holmes in the Hollywood series of films in the 1940s, played Inspector Wembury. Gordon Harker, another renowned character actor whose career lasted until the 1960s, played the cockney burglar and ex-convict Sam Hackitt. Leslie Faber, another star of the era, played Dr Lomond, the genial Scottish medic who assists Scotland Yard. The role of Cora-Ann Milton, the wife of the Ringer, was played by Dorothy Dickson, an American-born actress and singer who had appeared with the Ziegfeld Follies. The question was – would the audience be able to spot which of the play's characters was Henry Arthur Milton in disguise?

Gerald du Maurier's nephew, Nico Davies, was the ward of J.M. Barrie, the author of *Peter Pan*. The actor-manager suggested that Barrie come along to rehearsal to see what he thought of it. Barrie told du Maurier and Wallace that he had enjoyed it enormously and thought they had a winner on their hands, but he also added that he thought that it was ingenious of them to take the audience into their confidence so that they all knew from the start who the criminal was. Du Maurier and Wallace were shocked, but fortunately audiences did not find it as easy as Barrie to spot Milton, and the twist ending worked well.

'*The Ringer* was a smash hit – there was never an empty seat in the house,' Dorothy Dickson later recalled:[2]

> What really gave him [Wallace] the big kick was this success in the theatre which he hadn't had before. He would come down about three times a week just in time to watch the end of the first act which was really very effective and got a pin drop silence from the audience and he'd come walking back in the dressing rooms with his wonderful smile and say 'Well, it worked again, didn't it.' And I said, 'yes, it always works.'

Cora Milton made a big impression on one young member of the audience:

> A friend of the family took me to see *The Ringer* at a theatre in London and I was thrilled. Although I could not have been much more than thirteen, certainly under fifteen, I lost my heart to Cora Ann and hoped to marry her one day after the Ringer was finally caught and executed. Unfortunately he was never caught and executed so I decided to emigrate and spent about thirty-five years in Jamaica.
>
>   L.L. White, in a letter to the Edgar Wallace Society in April 1970.

Wallace received around £7,000 in royalties for *The Ringer*, half of which he insisted on giving to du Maurier. His generosity towards his collaborator was to have lasting consequences. With the money he received from Wallace, Sir Gerald bought a cottage at Bodinnick in Cornwall where his family could spend their holidays. His daughter Daphne, who became a celebrated novelist, was inspired by the beautiful landscapes and set her most famous works, such as *Rebecca*, *Frenchman's Creek* and *Jamaica Inn*, in the county. As her mother reminded her, the family's cottage in Cornwall only became possible because of the kindness of Edgar Wallace. Angela du Maurier, Daphne's sister, remembered Wallace in her 1961 autobiography *It's Only the Sister*:

> To as, us a family, he [Wallace] was amazingly kind. I can see, the cynics murmuring, 'And why not? Didn't Gerald du Maurier make him as far

as the stage was concerned?' That is not the point. My father helped a very large number of people, but even if they 'won through' they sometimes preferred to forget; Edgar was generous to us because he liked us, and I should think for no other reason. And because he was a generous man when he had the world's goods ... People who have been poor either become miserly if they one day achieve riches or they chuck their money about right and left. Edgar was a chucker, and there must be many people alive at this moment who look back on his memory with affection and gratitude.

Understandably keen to fully exploit his latest success, Wallace also wrote up *The Ringer* in story form and it appeared as a serial in *Answers* between October 1926 and January 1927. It was then published as a novel by Hodder & Stoughton one month later. Wallace dedicated the book to du Maurier. *The Ringer* was undoubtedly a milestone in Wallace's career, as it turned him into the hottest property in town.

'Whereas in previous years he had been content to dispose of the book rights of a story for £100 or even less, he now signed contracts under which he received £1,000 in advance of royalties, and within a year or two his book royalties from one publisher alone were in the region of £25,000 a year,' wrote Robert Curtis. The success of *The Ringer* also led Wallace to take a very bold, or some would say, reckless, step. The £7,000 he had made in royalties was a sizeable sum, but he noted that Frank Curzon, the producer had made £30,000. Wallace decided that from then on, he would not only write plays, but produce them too.

Wallace's triumph had, as ever, to be celebrated by some lavish spending. The Wallaces upgraded their living arrangements, moving from Clarence Gate Gardens to a new £1,600-a-year flat, No. 31 Portland Place, in Marylebone – their grandest abode yet in one of the most expensive parts of London.[3] There, Wallace employed a large staff of servants and had a special lift built in from the ground floor to the first floor to enable him to get to his desk more quickly. He also had a furnished flat in Haymarket, which was used as an office for Robert Curtis, and a suite of rooms at the Carlton Hotel (with a private telephone line through to Haymarket).

The man who used to hire a limousine to drive him round London also splashed out on his very own yellow Rolls-Royce. Robert Curtis remembers its arrival:

There glided up to our doorstep ... a luxurious limousine of the most expensive type available – to be superseded a year or so later by another, still more luxurious and expensive, which, as it stood shining and glistening by the kerb, made even Portland Place look poverty-stricken and in need of a fresh coat of paint.

The years of the mid-1920s were undoubtedly the happiest in Wallace's life. He had achieved the recognition he had deserved, now not just as a novelist, but a playwright too, and was at last earning some very serious money. Family life was also satisfying. His son, Bryan, had left Oundle and was studying engineering at Cambridge University. Pat had finished Cheltenham and was bound for finishing school in Paris. Meanwhile, Wallace had baby Penny to cherish – he loved to hold her in his arms and often did that while dictating the latest lines of a book or article.

Wallace was a kind and attentive father. His major fault as a parent was that he was over-protective towards his children. So worried was he that Bryan would be injured, he threatened to bar his son from his house forever if he took part in the bob-sleigh world championship in 1928. Bryan did compete, but his father, having sent his son's personal belongings to a room in the Park Lane Hotel, welcomed him back into the fold after just one week.

Wallace had a tendency to spoil his offspring, something Jim always fought against. On one occasion he 'kidnapped' Pat to take her away from her boarding school when she told him that she had been on a school picnic and was still hungry. 'He drove away from that school at seventy miles an hour, as though he were afraid that we should be pursued and I would be taken away from him by force,' Pat recalled. The whole of that term Wallace kept his daughter at home. 'Edgar arranged a thousand treats for me to make up for the fact that I hadn't happened upon a school where I received just the treatment that he thought I should.'[4]

While Jim called him 'Richard', to his children Wallace was known as 'Krazy Kat', after a popular cartoon character. 'My father was very fond of children,' Penny remembered, 'I was never forbidden the study when he was working. He would stop in mid-sentence as I asked questions or requested a drawing or a verse and, as I closed the door, he would take up his dictation where he had left off.'[5]

Pat, sixteen years older than her sister, was already attracting male admirers by the mid-1920s. Wallace, who hardly ever drank himself, was concerned when, one evening, Pat came in home late from a party. The next morning he presented her with a cigarette case, engraved with a picture of Krazy Kat smoking a cigarette and the words 'It is better to smoke'. Wallace couldn't bear the thought of his children drinking, but positively encouraged them to share his love of smoking. 'Edgar brought me up in a fairly Bohemian fashion. I was not sent to bed early, like most children, and I was always allowed to meet people he thought interesting and join in the conversation,' Pat revealed in a 1929 magazine interview.[6]

There were usually two Wallace family holidays a year – a trip to Babbacombe in south Devon in the spring, and then the annual Christmas vacation to Switzerland. Before departure Wallace would work even harder than usual to finish outstanding novels and stories so he could get the money for them to pay for the trip.

Wallace, his family and guests were booked each year into the luxurious Caux Palace Hotel, near Montreux, on the banks of Lake Geneva. The circle of friends invited by Wallace to Switzerland got wider with every year that passed. The extended family included friends, friends of his children, friends of the friends of his children, and later on, even the milkman and Wallace's bookie. Wallace picked up the tab for everyone and everything.

Daphne du Maurier and her friend Angela were invitees in 1926:

> We enjoyed every moment of it. Edgar was a wonderful host, and Jim, his attractive second wife, considerably younger than himself, was an equally superb hostess, joining in all the fun and teasing her stepchildren, ourselves and the rest of the party unmercifully, while positively encouraging us to tease her back.[7]

Unbeknown to her, Edgar and her father had got together in the autumn, and decided that a trip to Caux and mixing with other young people would do Daphne, considered to be something of a loner, the world of good. Daphne, who was 19 going on 20, enjoyed the fun and games – the skating, luging and skiing and staying up late in the bar drinking brandy and soda – but most of all loved talking to Edgar and his wife. 'They never talked down to me and although Edgar was a strict enough father to his own children, the absence of the parental tie between us made the talking much easier.'[8]

Wallace was no skier, but there was still plenty in Switzerland to keep him occupied. He enjoyed a gentle mountain stroll, with the emphasis firmly on 'gentle', and trying out the local cuisine. Although staying in a luxury hotel, he always preferred to eat his first course of soup at the nearby station restaurant, where he said it tasted much better, before going back up to the hotel for the other courses.

That Christmas, Wallace combined business with pleasure. He met with theatrical manager Bertie Meyer and at the latter's suggestion wrote, in just five days, a new play called *The Terror*. It was to be financed by Wallace, Meyer and the actor Dennis Neilson-Terry. *The Terror*, which debuted at the Lyceum Theatre in London in May 1927, proved to be another great success. *Theatre World* enthused:

> This new Edgar Wallace play is great fun. Everyone knows that as a purveyor of thrills – to name only one of Mr Wallace's innumerable literary

activities – this remarkably prolific writer is unequalled. He is in excellent form in this melodrama and skilfully manipulated thrills.

The review noted that Wallace had left nothing out that could keep the audiences on the edge of their seats:

> There are murders (two), arch villains, a not too arch heroine, detectives, mysterious music, ghosts, screams, darkness, innocent suspects, a seemingly inane youth who is 'really' somebody quite different, terrified women, blackmail, and stolen gold. Mixed by Edgar Walllace, whose wit enables him to make his audiences roar with laughter after they have nearly screamed with fright, they make an excellent mystery play.

The Terror had cost £1,000 to produce, but brought in £35,000 in profits.

Another successful West End production meant another no-expense-spared first night party. Carol Reed, Wallace's stage manager, recalled:

> He [Wallace] adored the first night. He used to come down – with a white tie, tails, sit in the box – bow to the audience – no nerves at all and he'd laugh louder than anybody at his own jokes but absolutely genuinely. There were enormous parties afterwards – presents for everybody.

It could never be said of Edgar Wallace that he didn't know how to celebrate his success, and in the mid-1920s, it seemed that everything he touched turned to gold.

22

PEOPLE

Ray Bennett had reached the stage of sane understanding where he did not
even regret.

Edgar Wallace, *The Fellowship of the Frog*, 1925

In 1926, amid all his other activity, Wallace still found time to write his autobiography – albeit a relatively short one, at around 40,000 words. The suggestion
had come to him from Lord Riddell, proprietor of the *Strand Magazine* and
the *News of the World*. Riddell had originally wanted it for the former publication, but when he saw the outline he asked for a longer version for his
Sunday newspaper – which had around 12 million readers. In April 1926, the
first instalment of 'The Life Story of Edgar Wallace: A Human Document of
Surpassing Interest – From Poverty to Success' appeared.

Later that year, Wallace's life story was published in book form under the
title *People, A Short Autobiography*, by Hodder & Stoughton, with the by-now-
familiar signature of the author written across a red circle displayed on the
front cover.[1] The book was very well received and saw Wallace being compared to Charles Dickens. 'Mr Edgar Wallace is above all a writer of fiction,'
wrote Brodie Fraser in *The Bookman*:[2]

> His books are classed among the best sellers. They are deservedly so classed.
> I cannot keep pace with them, but I have read as many as a busy life will
> allow. But he has never written anything so gripping, so entertaining, or
> even so exciting as *People*. The figure he has outlined in this book has all the
> illusive fascination of a David Copperfield … Mr Wallace's wanderings have
> been Homeric and they are told with Homeric simplicity and charm.

Wallace dedicated his autobiography to the Earl of Derby, whom he lauded as
'a friend of the people'. In his introduction he philosophised:

> I have sought nothing so illusory as 'success' – rather have I found new foot-
> holds from which to gain a wider view, new capacities for gratitude towards

my fellow-man, and a new and heartfelt sense of humility as, from my little point of vantage, on the ever-upward path, I watch the wondrous patience and courage of those who are struggling up behind me.

He also expressed hope that his rags-to-riches story would prove inspirational to others: 'If it encourages one ambitious child to strive to eminence, if it helps make lighter the lot of one man or woman and gives hope where there is no hope, it will not have been written in vain.'

There surely would have been many who read Wallace's extraordinary tale and thought: if an illegitimate son of a poor travelling actress could make such a success of his life, why can't I? Wallace had shown that anything was possible in life if hard work was combined with intelligence, a pleasant personality, a strong character and enormous self-confidence. But how many people could realistically replicate the achievements of Edgar Wallace? Wallace said that his autobiography was 'a tribute to the system under which we live', but such social mobility was rare (and arguably even rarer today), and by praising society rather than himself he was guilty of downplaying the extraordinary personal qualities which had propelled him to fame and fortune.

Wallace's fame as a crime writer meant that he was also enlisted by the press to help solve real-life mysteries. One such case was the strange disappearance of fellow crime writer Agatha Christie, an event which gripped the nation in December 1926. 'The disappearance seems to be a typical case of "mental reprisal" on somebody who has hurt her,' Wallace theorised. He suggested that Christie – whose car had been found by a lake in Surrey, had 'deliberately created an atmosphere of suicide.' 'If Agatha Christie is not dead of shock and exposure within a limited radius of the place her car was found, she must be alive and in full possession of her faculties, probably in London.'[3] Ten days after she had vanished Christie was found at a hotel in Harrogate, Yorkshire, where she had registered under the name of 'Mrs Teresa Neele' from Cape Town. Christie never explained her disappearance, but according to the 1998 book *Agatha Christie and the Eleven Missing Days*, by Jared Cade, she planned the event to get back at her husband, Archie, who had asked her for a divorce and who had told her he was in love with another woman, called Nancy Neele. Wallace may have been wrong about Christie being in London, but he does seem to have been right about Christie's motives.

In all, 1926 had been a remarkable year for Edgar Wallace, but there was one sad piece of news which took some of the shine off his success – the death of his first wife Ivy. Having been discarded by her un-Christian missionary father for disobeying him over her marriage, she went to live in Tunbridge Wells. Life without Edgar was lonely and boring, and she greatly looked forward to the school holidays when Michael and Bryan would stay with her.

Once a year, just before Christmas, she travelled with Michael by train to Switzerland, where she would hand her son over to the rest of the Wallace family and, after exchanging pleasantries and festive greetings, make her own way back home.

In December 1925 she was not well – she had been suffering from a pain in her breast for some time, but still made the journey to Switzerland. She handed Michael over to Edgar, Jim, Bryan and Pat as usual, but with the pain in her breast getting worse, consulted a doctor in France on her way home. He told her that she had cancer and that she needed an immediate operation. Ivy wrote to Edgar as soon as he arrived back home, informing him that she needed an operation, but not telling him that it was cancer. With typical generosity, he sent a sizeable cheque to pay for her treatment. The first operation looked to have been a success, but Ivy's symptoms returned and she was told more surgery was necessary. Edgar once again sent money, and started writing to Ivy on a daily basis. Later, Bryan broke the news to him that Ivy was terminally ill. Edgar was shocked, but didn't go to see his dying ex-wife.

It was a black mark against him, but it was not a sign of a lack of concern. Edgar still cared deeply for Ivy, but he was a man who liked to avoid distressing scenes as much as he could. Ivy died in early 1926. 'The death shattered Edgar as no other grief had done,' recorded Margaret Lane.[4] He was determined that his wife be properly commemorated so he composed an inscription for a memorial to be put up in the Rosebank Methodist Chapel where he and Ivy had been married. But Ivy's sister, no doubt fearing her family's reaction, advised Wallace to wait a year or two with his tribute. Alas, the inscription never went up.

It was ironic that Ivy died at the start of a year in which her husband enjoyed his greatest success. It had been she who had helped and encouraged him in his early years, she who had shared his early triumphs and crashing disappointment, and now she had died – just when millions of Britons were toasting her husband's name.

Wallace no doubt went through much soul searching when Ivy died. He invited two of her sisters with their families to England, paid for their travel and put them up in a flat he had rented for them in London. He even invited them to a winter sports holiday. Perhaps he was feeling guilty, but it must be remembered that when he agreed to a divorce, he did so in the belief that his wife would remarry and be able to live a full and happy with her new Belgian partner. He can be blamed for the way he and Ivy drifted apart, but he can't really be held responsible for Ivy's sad demise.

Success hardens many people, but not Edgar Wallace. He had always kept up with his old family and friends, regularly visiting Clara Freeman and inviting Grace, his niece, to London. Things didn't change now that he was rich and famous. Aaron Campbell, the umbrella-maker, recalled how Wallace would leave some money with him and then wire whenever he got a tip for the horses: 'He wired me all right and I put the money on, but I will admit that the horses didn't always win!'[5] When he was living at Tresillian Crescent in Brockley, Wallace used to drive up in his brougham to Campbell's shop and say 'Aaron, pick out the best umbrellas and send them up home.'

In 1927 Campbell wrote to Wallace asking if he would be able to come and present the prizes at the Clyde Rowing Club races:

> In reply I had a letter to this effect; 'My dear Aaron, I shall be only too pleased to come and do as you ask, and what is more I will present to the Clyde Rowing Club a silver cup to the value of 21 guineas'. He came down like a gentleman. He brought his wife and daughter too. When the carriage drew up at the door he jumped out and said 'Aaron old boy. I'm glad to see you.' He acted as starter and umpire for the races and at the end presented the prizes.

During the event, Campbell chatted to the now very famous writer whom he had known when he was a young lad cleaning out milk churns:

> I said, 'Dick, I'm very proud of you'. He said 'Why Aaron?'. I said: 'On the grounds Dick that you've risen to terrible heights and you haven't had a kick'. Meaning that he had never had anyone to push him on 'without influence', I told him. 'You've got right to the top and I thank God. We're proud of you, Dick.' 'Yes, Aaron,' he said, 'and I'm proud of it too.'

Those who met Wallace testified to his lack of pomposity. Cockney diarist and second-hand bookseller Fred Bason approached Wallace after the first night of one of his plays at the Apollo. He told him that he thought it was a very poor play and bet him 2*s* 6*d* against a signed book of his that it wouldn't run a week. 'Fifteen days later, when I saw him at another first night, he came over to me and asked me to go to his car with him. I did so, and he got out a signed copy of his latest book. It said "You win!" on the title page. Amidst all his work, all his trouble and worries, he remembered a bet made with a galleryite nobody.'[6]

The writer Robert Hichens remembered chatting to Wallace for about two hours in a railway compartment in the sleeping car from Montreux, when Wallace and his family were travelling back from their annual Christmas holiday. 'He was entirely unpretentious, and told me of his very humble beginnings, and of his varied life as a soldier abroad, and struggling journalist and author before he obtained his amazing financial success. "I'm entirely what's called a self-made man," he said, "I'm not a highbrow. I write to please the big public, and to make as much money as possibly without doing harm to anyone".[7]

Graham Greene was another younger writer on whom Wallace made a positive impression. 'I only saw Edgar Wallace once, but the moment has stayed in my memory like a "conservation piece",' he wrote in 1964. It was 1930, and Greene was 25 and had just published his first novel. He had been invited, as a junior guest, to a very grand publisher's do at the Savoy, to which famous writers of the day had been invited. He witnessed Arnold Bennett sternly rebuking a waiter for serving him the wrong drink with the words: 'A serious writer does not drink liqueurs.' He then saw Edgar Wallace talking with Hugh Walpole – a writer who did have a reputation for pomposity:

> I remember Walpole's patronising gaze, his bald head inclined under the chandeliers like that of a bishop speaking to with kindness to an unimportant member of his diocese. And the unimportant member? – he was so oblivious of the bishop's patronage that the other shrank into insignificance before the heavy confident body, the long, challenging cigarette holder, the sense that this man cared not so much as a fly button for the other's world. They had nothing in common, not even an ambition. Even in those days I found myself on the side of Wallace.[8]

Wallace had been kind to people when he was on the way up, and now he was rich he felt he could be even kinder. Every Christmas he would send a cheque for £50 to needy friends, and insist that they spent the money on themselves. Children of those who worked for Wallace were always in for treats. 'What I do remember was the joy I had on the occasional days when EW used to send his green liveried chauffeur with a white (or cream) Rolls-Royce car to our little house and lend us his slipper-stern boat for the day!' remembered the Reverend Michael Boultbee, whose father Frederick was Wallace's accountant. 'This was my only childhood link with boats – which led to me joining the wartime Navy and my continuing love of boats now,' he wrote in 1975.

It was not only his friends who benefited from his generosity, but total strangers too. Francis D. Grierson, writing in *The Bookman* in 1932, revealed how Wallace had helped a special writer on a London newspaper who had fallen ill:

> It was found that his finances were lower than had been suspected. He was unknown to Wallace. A friend of mine got up a subscription to help the sick man. My friend did not know Wallace, but he wrote and told him the

circumstances, and asked for half a guinea to swell the fund. I saw Wallace's letter in reply, from which it is enough to quote this passage; 'I am very glad you have given me a chance to help … I enclose a cheque, and if you want more please do let me know …' The cheque was for ten guineas!

Wallace loved to use his money to relieve suffering and unhappiness, as this story, told by Margaret Lane,[9] shows:

One night – and this was many years before he became really rich – he noticed that a girl in the box office of a theatre was silently crying. He stopped to ask her what was the matter, and, since she seemed incapable of telling him, gave her his address and told her to come to his flat the following morning. She came, and told him that her young child was ailing, and that the doctor had diagnosed tuberculosis. She had no money to pay for a cure, and had only her job at the theatre to support her. Edgar's response to her story was to wave the magic wand of immediate generosity, and with far more thoughtfulness and delicacy than would have been implied by the mere reaching for his cheque-book. The girl was offered a nominal job as his secretary, so that she could leave the theatre, the boy was sent immediately to a sanitorium, and when the time came for the annual visit to Caux both he and his mother were taken for a holiday in Switzerland.

Romantic novelist Berta Ruck also experienced Wallace's kind-heartedness at first hand. She sent him some newspaper correspondence in which she had put the case for 'despised-because-popular writers'. 'He answered delightfully in his own hand; further he enclosed two autographed photographs of himself in winter sports-kit, adding in a postscript: "You might like to pass these on to your boys. Boys seem to care for these things". And he signed himself. "Yours fraternally, EDGAR WALLACE."

A few years later, Ruck wrote a novel entitled *To-day's Daughter*. The main character was given a 'book-father' called Twyford Elliott, a dressing gown-wearing author of thrilling detective stories, who was clearly modelled on Wallace. Her publishers – who were also Wallace's – got cold feet and asked her to remove the character from the book. Ruck was in despair about the prospect of having to rewrite her entire story, so she picked up the telephone and called Wallace. He told her not to worry and to put whatever she liked in the book. He also said he would write to the publishers that same day to tell them that it was okay. 'All over the empire there are many people who can boast of kindnesses that have been shown in the hour of need by this master story-teller. I should doubt if any of them have felt more deeply grateful to him than I did, and do,' Ruck wrote.[10]

23

KING OF THE WEST END

The applause from the big audience was a deafening blast of sound that roared up to the Moorish roof of the Orpheum and came down again to the packed house like the reverberations of thunder.

Edgar Wallace, *The Feathered Serpent*, 1927

In 1927 there was a new and important addition to the 'Edgar Wallace Fiction Factory' team, a 23-year-old Russian woman called Jenia Reissar, who arrived in answer to Wallace's advertisement for an evening secretary. Years later, Reissar would describe Wallace as 'the greatest human being I have ever known'.

She remembered her first meeting with the, by now, very famous writer:

I was ushered in to see Edgar Wallace, and felt I'd never get the job. I really got frightened but he very soon put me my ease. And when he heard I was Russian, the first thing he said, well, you must like tea, so we'll have a tea and a chat. And there on we just worked together perfectly.[1]

In 1995 I met Jenia, then aged 91,[2] and the affection she had for her old boss was still very apparent. A warm, engaging woman with a twinkle in her eye, who later went on to become a highly respected casting director for films and television, I could understand why she and Wallace would have struck it off so quickly. Her role of evening secretary was soon extended. Officially she was employed from 8 a.m. to midnight, but she always started work at 7.45 a.m. to read the correspondence and to read and reply to the many begging letters herself, and often worked all through the night.

At 8 a.m. the non-begging letters would be replied to – sometimes Wallace dictated word for word, other times he gave Jenia the general idea of what he wanted to say. Then it was time for some breakfast, and after that Wallace would dictate an article, usually on the theatre – from 1928 onwards he was also writing a theatre column for the *Morning Post*. After the article was finished, it was usually more correspondence or back to work on a novel or serial. 'Plays were usually done at night, his favourite time was midnight to start on the first act,' she recalled.[3]

Jenia Reissar, Robert Curtis and Jim all had important, delineated roles in the Wallace production system. Wallace dictated some of his articles, chiefly on the theatre, a lot of his stories and his plays to Reissar, though he also wrote some plays by hand himself. All his novels were dictated and transcribed by Curtis, but Reissar also had to type copies of these. Jim was always there in case of emergencies, to help out with typing or checking through copy. Wallace also asked Reissar for advice about his whodunits. 'In the novels the question was can you guess who did it, and if I said yes, and told him, then he'd say well we must re-write this because it's too easy, if you've guessed it, it must be too easy for the public,' she said, 'And he would rewrite or insert pieces which made them more difficult.'

The work for Jenia was always varied: 'You really couldn't know what was going to face you during the day.' Another task was keeping Wallace's racing records – how his horses had fared, his bets and how his tips had got on.

A bond of loyalty and trust soon developed between Wallace and his new secretary. Reissar said:

> As an employer he really was a friend, he treated you as a friend, he treated all of us in the same way. Consequently, we worked all hours of the day and night and nobody minded because you wanted to do it for him, you wanted to repay his kindness, his consideration, his friendship, because he certainly gave that to all his employees. As for people outside, he could just talk to anyone in any walk of life and in a few seconds they would tell him their life stories and felt completely at ease with him. He had this great gift at putting you at ease, which is why also he made a good director in the theatre because actors liked him.

In fact, everyone who met or dealt with Wallace seemed to like him. In 1927, the journalist Beverley Nichols paid Britain's most popular writer a visit:[4]

> At a desk, lit by a green lamp a man sits writing. A long cigarette holder is in his mouth, and every few minutes the fag end of a cigarette is removed and scrunched on to the ashtray while another almost mechanically takes its place. The face of the writer is strangely like those faces of master crimi-nologists which adorn the paper jackets of popular detective stories … It bears an expression which one might be excused for calling inscrutable.

Nichols put it to Wallace that with his knowledge of crime, he could have made a first class criminal himself. 'Yes, I believe I should. I think, for one thing, I should have made a first-class confidence trickster. I could have worked some pretty burglaries, too.' Was Wallace not tempted to try his hand at some crime 'merely for the sake of it'?

> I might feel tempted if Scotland Yard were full of Sherlock Holmeses. The thing would be easy then. But the men at Scotland Yard are a good deal more dangerous than Sherlock Holmes. They're full of common sense. They're never put off the scent by fantastic clues. They're dogged. In fact, they're like good newspaper reporters. The principles are exactly the same. I'm a reporter myself. I was a crime reporter for nine years. I'm still a crime reporter. I shall never be anything else.

Nichols clearly warmed to his interviewee. 'I should like to be Edgar Wallace – like to sit back in that desk, with that long cigarette holder, pondering, with half-closed eyes, the ramifications of some baffling crime, and then going out into the highways and byways, engaging in many strange encounters, rubbing shoulders with many queer and furtive figures,' he enthused.

In 1927 no fewer than fourteen new books by Wallace were published. Among the most popular of the titles to appear that year were *The Squeaker*, which involved the hunt for a receiver of stolen goods who 'squeaks' i.e. betrays thieves to the authorities who take their loot elsewhere; *The Feathered Serpent*, in which visiting cards bearing an ancient Aztec symbol are left by an mysterious invisible caller; and *The Forger*.

'Mr Edgar Wallace to put it very mildly, gives us ample opportunity to become acquainted with his work, but if he can continue to be as thrilling and surprising as he is in *The Squeaker*, there is no fear that supply will exceed the demand,' *Punch* enthused on 28 September 1927.

Wallace also had a new racing column to write for in the *Star*, for which he was paid £3,000 a year, and which soon developed a huge following, helping to boost the newspaper's circulation. Meanwhile, he was still churning out pieces for a wide variety of publications. In the 16 December 1927 edition of *Popular Wireless*, he could be found waxing eloquent about his love of radio:

> I am getting all the joy which an unscientific man can secure from this greatest invention of the age … It is my joy to sit before this wonder box and by a turn of the wrist, listen as distinctly to a German delivering a lecture on hygiene as though I were in the next room. The slightest movement of the dial and I am in Roman, doing as the Romans do – enjoying an opera. And sometimes I wander off to Ireland, and Ireland has before now played the Irish bagpipes most beautifully for my amusement … To a busy man, and one who has very little time for good music and good lectures, the blessings of wireless are inestimable.

After he had switched off his Dictaphone – and his wireless – each evening, Wallace kept up his night-time play-writing activities. In addition to *The Terror*, two other plays by Wallace had their debuts in 1927: *A Perfect Gentleman* and *The Yellow Mask*, a musical which premiered in Birmingham, before transferring to London where, in February 1928, it became the second production to be put on at the new Carlton Theatre in Haymarket.[5]

Both plays were successful – *The Yellow Mask* chalked up 200 performances – but the fourth play Wallace wrote after *The Ringer* was not. *The Man Who Changed His Name* was an experimental thriller that was probably too experimental. Wallace's best stories were always just on the believable side of far-fetched, but the plot *of The Man Who Changed His Name* relied on too many coincidences. Wallace produced the play in partnership with the actor-manager, Robert Loraine, with Loraine making over his lease of the Apollo Theatre to Wallace at the rental of £450 a week.

It was to be an unhappy association. Loraine was domineering, egotistical and crassly insensitive to the feelings of others – Wallace once referred to him in a letter as a 'mad bastard'. When *The Man Who Changed His Name* was given a thumbs down by audiences and critics alike, both men rushed to blame each other. 'If there are many more like last night's performance this play is going to run for about two months,' Wallace wrote to Loraine, 'Last night's presentation was like an amateur performance played by the inmates of a lunatic asylum.' Wallace accused Loraine of trying to steal the limelight from the other actors: 'If you shine above all the other members of the cast, then the play must be a failure, because it is not written for a star.' Loraine sent a withering reply: 'Dear Edgar, your egregious self-complacence is only exceeded by your inability to write a play.'

A furious Wallace offered to buy Lorraine out, and the actor agreed. Meanwhile, Edgar's wife, Jim, found herself with a new role. Edgar appointed her his theatrical manager. She represented her husband at an emergency meeting of auditors and solicitors regarding the future of *The Man Who Changed His Name*. Wallace took over direction of the play and hired a new actor, Hartley Power, to replace Loraine. Alas, it made little difference and the play ended its run after just five weeks. It was a setback, but a record of one flop from five productions wasn't a bad one and Wallace was not greatly perturbed, especially as Jim was now part of his theatrical team.

His wife might not have known too much about the world of show business, but she was an extremely efficient organiser and it's easy to understand why Edgar preferred to trust her with the business side of his plays rather than appoint an outsider.

The first play that Edgar and Jim worked on together was *The Squeaker*. It was Jim who had suggested dramatisation of the popular novel. 'He was a little sceptical – but as my judgment had so far been pretty good, he decided to take a chance,' she noted. *The Squeaker*, unlike *The Man Who Changed His Name*, proved a hit with audiences and ran for six months, transferring from the Apollo to the Shaftesbury Theatre. Nothing was left to chance this time, with Wallace even taking the actor who was to play the reporter Joshua Colley down to the offices of the *News of the World* to watch the feverish activity on a Saturday night.

Wallace was overjoyed to have another West End triumph on his hands. He showed his appreciation to Jim by buying her a two-seater Rolls-Royce. Just one week after the opening of *The Squeaker*, another Wallace thriller debuted at the West End, *The Flying Squad*. That too ran for six months. Wallace could now bask in the knowledge that he was not only the nation's best-selling novelist, he also had three plays running simultaneously in the West End.

To celebrate, he held a joint party for the casts of his plays at the Carlton Hotel. There the champagne flowed, the cigarette holders were waved extravagantly in the air, and the dancing and fun went on well into the early hours. While no doubt there were many sore heads the next morning, after the party was over Wallace merely summoned his driver, got into his yellow Rolls-Royce and went home to start another day's work at the Fiction Factory, to devise yet more tales of mystery and adventure to keep the nation enthralled and entertained.

In the years 1925–1929, seventy-four books by Wallace were published – equating to one new title every three weeks. In 1928 it was claimed that one out of every four books sold in Britain, excluding the Bible, was by Wallace. In 1929, thirty-four Wallace books appeared. While there have been more prolific writers in terms of the number of books published (Georges Simenon, the Belgian creator of Maigret, wrote around 200, and British crime writer John Creasey is said to have written over 600), it is doubtful that any author had as many published in such a relatively short period of time as Wallace.

Unsurprisingly, Wallace's prodigious output became the subject of much affectionate humour. A cartoon in *Punch*, the leading satirical weekly, showed a bookstall salesman asking a customer, 'Seen the mid-day Wallace, Sir?' Wallace's friend, the author P.G. Wodehouse, wrote: 'Can you get anything to read these days? I was in the *Times* library yesterday and came out empty-handed. There wasn't a thing I wanted. To fill in the time before Edgar Wallace writes another one, I am re-reading Dunsany.'[6]

'He also very much enjoyed the stories told about him as his reputation for phenomenal speed at work increased,' said Pat Wallace of her father. 'One of his favourite and mine too, was of the man who telephoned him and was told "Mr Wallace is writing a book." "Right," said the man, "I'll hold on".'

There were also humorous references to the sheer variety of Wallace's output. This item appeared in *Theatre World* in October 1929:

On Sunday I write a three-act Drama,
On Monday I criticise the Tote,
On Tuesday I'm out
As a rival to 'The Scout!'
On Wednesday punters gloat!
On Thursday I do some special features;
On Friday a sketch for a Revue
And on Saturday I'm willing
If you'll only spend a shilling,
To freeze the blood of any one of you!

There were similar jokes about his theatre work and his domination of the West End. Here's Punch, from 6 July 1927:

Next week will be a fairly quiet for first nighters. Mr EDGAR WALLACE's Thirteen Stain makes its bow on Tuesday, and the premier of another of his new thrillers, The Spectre is announced for Thursday. It is a pity that this latter clashes with the first night of Broadmoor Jim, also by Mr WALLACE, but we understand that there is to be a repetition generale on Wednesday so that Mr WALLACE may be enabled to criticise it for the daily Press. For the rest there is merely a revival of The Horror – which is easily among the hundred best WALLACE plays – and the opening of the EDGAR WALLACE repertory season with that very sound crook-drama, The Crimp.

In May 1928, Wallace and the other prolific playwright of the day, Noel Coward, featured in an amusing write-up in *London Calling*. The publication informed that in the event of another General Strike all theatres, except those showing Wallace and Coward plays would be closed. It added that: 'This order would only affect the "Back to Methuselah" season at the Kensington Museum.'

All classes, from King George V downwards, had been bitten by the Edgar Wallace bug but the nation's addiction to Wallace did not go down well with everyone. For some literary 'highbrows', Wallace's amazing output and his enormous popularity counted against him. 'This prolific output inevitably inspired a considerable amount of jealousy, particularly among those writers who were then competing for the public's approbation,' records Wheeler Winston Dixon.[7]

In the *Evening Standard* of July 1928, Arnold Bennett wrote about reading Wallace for the first time: 'Well, I saw a new novel by Edgar Wallace ... and I said proudly to myself, "I will read that novel." I also said to my friends, "I am going to read Edgar Wallace." They were startled. They strolled around saying, "He is going to read Edgar Wallace. What next?" Such is our literary snobbishness.' Bennett goes on to say that he enjoyed *The Gunner* and that he preferred Wallace to Agatha Christie. But he concluded his article by saying that Wallace had 'a very grave defect'. 'He is content with society as it is. He parades no subversive opinions. He is "correct".' It is quite a generalisation to make from the reading of just one book. It is true that in his introduction to *People* Wallace had written:

> There cannot be much wrong with a society which made possible the rise of either J.H. Thomas and Edgar Wallace, that gave 'Jamie' Brown the status of a king in Scotland, and put Robertson at the War Office as Chief of the Imperial General Staff.

However, Wallace's novels do contain much criticism of contemporary society, particularly in relation to greedy, profiteering capitalists, such as the monopolist Montague Flake who appears in *The Brigand*. Wallace championed the feminist cause in *The Man Who Bought London* and *Barbara on Her Own*, while in *The Lone House Mystery*, a story in which an African and his mother travel to Britain to claim their rightful inheritance, he tackled the subject of racial prejudice.

While it's stretching things to call Wallace a radical, he did have great sympathy for the underdog. Robert Curtis even observed that had it not been for their implacable opposition to the British Empire, Wallace could quite happily have thrown his lot in with the communists.

In any case Bennett's criticism is harsh when one remembers that Wallace was writing to entertain. It would have seemed odd if his characters had suddenly come out with long speeches attacking the government, and his readers, eager for the villain to be unmasked and the heroine released from capture, probably wouldn't have thanked him for it.

Fellow crime writer Dorothy L. Sayers divided thrillers into the 'purely Sensational and the purely Intellectual,' with Wallace a prime exhibit of the former.[9] G.K. Chesterton, although he admitted to enjoying 'hundreds' of Wallace's stories, also questioned Wallace's entry to the elite club of detective writers. 'Even at their best Mr Edgar Wallace's stories are generally not detective stories, but adventure stories,' he wrote, and argued that the latter were far easier to write.[10] Praising Wallace's earlier South Africa sketches, Chesterton suggested, 'Perhaps he was a better writer before he was a best-seller.' Critic Q.D. Leavis also bemoaned Wallace's popularity, noting that if a librarian 'were to put two hundred more copies of Edgar Wallace's detective stories on the shelves, they would all be gone the same day.'[11] As a sign of how standards were declining, Leavis also cited a novelist who complained to her: 'I try to get my boys to read Dickens and Scott, but they won't read anything but magazines and Edgar.'[12] American critic George Jean Nathan, writing in 1935, was even more snobbish: 'True enough, he [Wallace] was popular, which is to say that thousands of inferior people admired what he wrote.'[13]

Wallace fired a salvo at his highbrow detractors in an article for *Britannia* magazine on 2 November 1928 entitled 'Amongst the Highbrows':

I am one of those old-fashioned people who believe in God, vaccination and the supreme genius of Rudyard Kipling. I believe in the decencies of family life, in normal vices, in horse-racing, women, good champagne, Charles Dickens, winter sports and fresh air. I like the picture that Tintoretto painted and the glorious music that Beethoven composed. I am partial to shower-baths, luxury travel, P.G. Wodehouse, and the down-trodden book-making class. In other words I am a lowbrow; so much so that you might say that the back of my literary neck begins at my literary eyebrows. I do not like the clever people who constitute the highbrow world, but it is because I do not understand them. I will be perfectly frank about it; I do not understand their painting, their poetry, their moral code, their queer predilections, their strange languages. I hate their clothes, their feet and their domestic animals. But it is only because I do not understand them.

Wallace didn't need to understand them. He had sales figures which his jealous rivals could only dream of, even if they claimed to be uninterested in such sordid details as sales figures. The poem 'I Like Edgar Wallace' by Reginald Arkell appeared in 1928[14] and summed up the national mood, although most Wallace fans would probably have taken issue with the last line:

I like Edgar Wallace,
His waistcoat is white,
He sits in his box,
When he has a first night,
And when I shout 'Speech!'
At the end of the play,
He always has something
Amusing to say

I like Edgar Wallace,
The Kipling of Crime,
I buy him in batches
Of ten at a time
I read all his stories
Of Squeakers and Crooks
I like Edgar Wallace
In spite of his books!

While Wallace could afford to ignore snobbish detractors, in March 1930 there came a potentially more damaging attack to his reputation – a claim that he had plagiarised another writer's work.

The work in question was a play about horse racing called *The Calendar*. Here's how it came about. After the success of *The Squeaker*, Wallace had next penned a comedy play called *The Lad*, written as a vehicle for the popular music hall comedian and pantomime star, Billy Merson. The plot involved a released prisoner who strays into a country house and is mistaken for a private detective. He finds he's fallen on his feet, as most of the household have secrets to conceal and he's given plenty of 'hush' money. 'Edgar Wallace has not yet written a pantomime. But he has written almost everything else, with a characteristic competence that abashes both praise and censure,' said the *Sunday Pictorial* in its review.[15] The play made a reasonable profit in Manchester, but was not a success when transferred to the Shaftesbury Theatre in London at Christmas 1928, and was taken off after just three weeks.

Wallace decided to return to a theme he knew very well for his next drama – horse racing. The plot of *The Calendar* revolved round the complicated 'Rules of Racing'. It had long been established that a horse entered for a 'Classic' would be automatically scratched from the race if its owner died before the race was run. The reason was to do with forfeiture fees, which were regarded as gambling debts, and therefore not enforceable by law from the estate of a dead owner. It was a situation which many thought unfair, and Wallace attempted to have the law changed. After consultation with the Stewards of the Jockey Club, racing's governing body, he entered one of his horses, 'Master Michael', in two races but did not run him. He was liable for forfeiture fees of £4, and invited the Jockey Club to take legal action, in the hope that he would lose, and a new law would be established. But to his dismay, he won the case. He decided to write a play in which the disqualification rule would figure.

The Calendar involves a racehorse owner who is dire financial straits. He decides to have his horse 'pulled' in a race in which it is the favourite at Royal Ascot, in order for it to run in another race where it will start at a bigger price and enable the owner to land some sizeable bets. Foolishly, the owner sends a letter to Lady Panniford, who he is in love with, telling her of his plans and warning her not to back his horse for the first race. But Lady Panniford is a cold-hearted villainess who keeps the letter and, after the hero sends her a further note to say that he has changed his mind about pulling the horse, decides to use the original letter to ruin him and get him warned off the turf. But her wicked scheme goes badly wrong, when the rules of racing come into play ...

After he had written his new drama, Wallace sent it off to Sir Gerald du Maurier, hoping that he would both produce and star in it, but the latter wrote a friendly letter back, addressed to 'Dear Old Edgar', to say that unfortunately he had other commitments. Wallace must have been disappointed to receive the letter, but thankfully he kept it as it was to prove to be an important piece of evidence in the court case which was to follow.

The Calendar went into rehearsal with a cast that included Nigel Bruce, Cathleen Nesbitt and Gordon Harker, and with the author himself as director. The cast enjoyed working with Wallace; 'At rehearsals I was enormously struck by his benign quiet concentration,' Nesbitt said.[16] 'He was never blustering, never ferocious, never sarcastic – he always saw everything what was going on.' The lead actress was also 'enormously impressed' at how Wallace was able to work on more than one project at the same time: 'One day I went to sit in the stalls, while the others were rehearsing a scene. Wallace was whispering dictation to his business secretary on his left, he was doing racing tips, I think, for the *Evening Standard* then, when suddenly he looked up and said "I wouldn't do that if I were you." They thought he was much too busy to notice what was going on.'

Once again, Wallace was keen to involve as many of his pals in the action as he could. He tried to persuade his jockey friends, Steve Donoghue and Michael Beary, to appear as extras on the opening night. They said that they would, but only if Wallace himself would appear as well. 'He accepted the condition, appeared heavily disguised with an enormous moustache, and was delighted that none of the three extras was recognised,' relates Donoghue's biographer, Michael Seth-Smith.[17]

Ironically, in February, the appeal in Wallace's forfeit case decision had been allowed, and the Jockey Club was able to change the rule about horses of dead owners being automatically scratched.[18] But the change in the rules of racing did not prevent *The Calendar* being a big success with audiences and critics alike. The author loved it too. 'I remember being in a box with him [Wallace], which incidentally was the only good racing play I ever saw,' wrote Jack Leach, 'I was very amused when he laughed heartily at all the jokes and led the applause with great enthusiasm, and I am certain he enjoyed the show more than anybody else in the house.'[19]

Wallace was able to enjoy the pleasure of having another West End hit, but six months after the opening he got a nasty surprise. He received a letter from a cardboard box manufacturer called Lewis Goldflam, accusing him in no uncertain terms of stealing the idea for *The Calendar*. Goldflam had written a racing novel called *Lucky Fool*, which had been published in April 1929. 'Yes, I am accusing you of having helped yourself to the material in the first half of my book – that which deals chiefly with horse-racing. ... To myself and many of my acquaintances who had read my book and witnessed your play ... you have exposed yourself to be nothing more nor less than a mean cribber!' Goldflam thundered. Wallace would probably have brushed the whole thing off, had it not been for his interlocutor's final, vindictive paragraph. 'I intend to forward copies of this letter to everyone of note in the theatrical and literary professions whom I think it will interest'.

Wallace was now dealing with a clear attempt to destroy his reputation. It would have been heartening for him that after hearing from Goldflam, the leading theatre critic, Hannen Swaffer, replied: 'You have made a great mistake in writing letters accusing Edgar Wallace. A man like Wallace never has to use other people's ideas. He is full of them, and anyway he is too vain to use other people's.' But that was Swaffer, who was always a law unto himself, and Wallace could not rely on others who received letters from Goldflam to dismiss his claims so easily. He had little option but to sue for libel.

In court, Wallace was represented by the distinguished barrister Sir Patrick Hastings KC, who had represented him in the Jockey Club case and who had become a close friend. 'Sir Gerald du Maurier and Mr Nigel Bruce gave evidence that *The Calendar* had been written, read, and made ready for production by December 1928, four months before Mr Goldflam's novel had been published,' relates Lane.[20] The letter that du Maurier had written to Wallace was produced as evidence in court. Hastings also said that *The Calendar* was no more like *Lucky Fool* than *Macbeth* was like *Charley's Aunt*.

Goldflam, however, refused to back down. He claimed that, although his book had only been published in April 1929, it had been in many publishing offices before then, and that Wallace must have found out about it. The judge had fun with what Goldflam was implying, 'That means that Mr Wallace, with the assistance of some of the people of the underworld, whom I believe he knows so well, may have made some clandestine visits to the offices of the publishers and read the manuscript in the night?' Goldflam's case had been destroyed, and judgement with costs was awarded against him. He was ordered to pay £1,000 in damages, but claimed he was broke and unable to pay anything. It would have understandable if Wallace had chosen to enforce his claim against a man who had tried to ruin him, but with characteristic generosity he decided to let his accuser off the hook. He did, though, make public an offer of £5,000 to anyone who could prove that he employed 'ghosts' to help him with his work, helping to scotch malicious rumours that had been circulating for years.

Wallace had conquered the worlds of journalism, fiction and drama and had put to bed false allegations about how he was able to achieve so much. By the time the 1920s were finished, he had succeeded in yet another arena – the motion picture industry.

24

EDGAR WALLACE: FILM DIRECTOR

In the small studio of the Knebworth Picture Corporation the company had been waiting in its street clothes for the greater part of an hour. Jack Knebworth sat in his conventional attitude, huddled up in his canvas chair, fingering his long chair and glaring from time to time at the clock above the studio manager's office.

Edgar Wallace, The Avenger, 1926

Wallace's fast-paced thrillers provided great material for the movies.

The first film to be made from one of his books was *The Man Who Bought London*, in 1916. In 1917, his *News of the World* serial, *Patria*, about 'The Last of the Fighting Channings and Her Struggle for Victory' was filmed in America. Between 1919 and 1925 a further fifteen films from Wallace books were released. In 1925 came the American-made serial of *The Green Archer*, which proved very popular in Britain and led to some interesting incidents. 'This story was running as a film serial in Leeds, where I lived at that time,' recalled Wallace fan Richard Kellerby, over fifty years later:

> The impact was so great upon certain members of the area, that 'Archers' were seen all over, the flights of imagination were so vivid, that a Yorkshire newspaper printed an 'Eye Witness' account of a farm labourer who had been suddenly confronted by a bowman but dressed in light coloured clothes in the grounds of a local squire – D'Arcy Wilson of Seacroft Hall. The next night, the grounds were swarming with ghost hunters, some were armed with weapons of all kinds, it was a very dark winter's night, and some were both jumpy and 'cosh happy' with the result that two or three of the hunters, became the hunted, on account of light-coloured raincoats, they were mistaken for the 'Archer' and finished up in hospital. After three of four nights of this, the authorities stepped in and put an end to it as it was getting out of hand.[1]

In 1926 Wallace decided to contact several film companies in the hope of selling them exclusive rights to his novels. Then in 1927 the Cinematograph Films Act led to a new opportunity. The act was designed to resuscitate the British film industry, which had been finding it hard to compete with American productions. A protectionist measure, it set a requirement for cinemas to show a quota of British films.

A consequence of the legislation was the formation of several new film companies. One of them, the British Lion Film Corporation, invited Wallace on to its board as chairman. Wallace didn't take much persuasion to accept the offer, but although it brought him back into the exciting world of movies – and the chance of fulfilling his long-held dream of directing films of his own books – the deal he signed with British Lion was not the best financial transaction he could have made at the time.

Wallace granted the company the exclusive film rights to everything he wrote. In return he received £10,000 worth of shares, £1,000 for every film made, 10 per cent of the gross receipts, and a director's fee of £500 a year. He made £26,000 from his five-year association with British Lion, yet would have earned much more had he negotiated the sale of film rights to his work on a book-by-book basis.

Once again, Wallace had thought short-term, going for money up front (no doubt to help him settle pressing debts), rather than doing deals that could have brought him higher long-term profits. Still, Wallace could now play the part of a movie mogul, and it was a role he was to greatly enjoy.

British Lion moved in to film studios at Beaconsfield in Buckinghamshire and, having got them renovated and re-equipped, film production was ready to start a few months later. From 1928–1929 British Lion made nine silent films from Wallace books, starting with *The Ringer*. *The Clue of the New Pin*, in 1929, starred a 25-year-old actor called John Gielgud as the baddie. He would go on to become world famous and would still be acting well into his 90s.

Not all the films received critical approval: 'Most of them were pretty awful,' was the view of James Cameron. Herbert Thompson, editor of *Film Weekly*, opined:

It is time that the British Lion Corporation realised that not all Edgar Wallace stories are suitable for filming. The Flying Squad, just privately shown, lacks coherence and plausibility. The direction of Arthur Maude is uninspired, and the acting on the whole no more than adequate, but obviously the principal fault lies with the producers who decided to produce a subject which gives no evidence of having been good film material.

It was perhaps because of this criticism that, in 1929, Wallace decided to direct the next British Lion film, *Red Aces* (a Mr J.G. Reeder mystery), himself. 'I shall make my first picture a commercial triumph,' he confidently predicted. *Kinematograph Weekly*, the leading trade paper, congratulated him, arguing that anything that brought the author into direct contact with the realities of film production was a good thing and suggested, in accordance with traditions, that he had his name painted on the back of his chair in the British Lion boardroom.

Wallace took his new responsibilities seriously; so seriously, in fact, that he even banned smoking on any part of the premises – a significant personal sacrifice for a man who smoked up to 100 cigarettes a day. 'For hours he went without a cigarette, the only time in his life, so far as I know, that he spent more than a few minutes without a lighted cigarette in his holder. He believed that smoke interfered with photography,' noted Jim. Instead of his usual chain-smoking, the director of *Red Aces* sucked toffees as he directed, bringing in two large tins of sweets to the studios.

Wallace saw his directorial debut as a great chance to involve old friends in his exciting new project. Nigel Bruce, who ten years later would be appearing as Dr Watson opposite Basil Rathbone's Sherlock Holmes, made his film debut. There were roles for Wallace's chauffeur, his butler, his valet – and for Robert Curtis too. 'I was told that everyone in Wardour Street (the part of London where all the film companies' offices are) was laughing at the idea of Edgar having such a lot of friends in the cast … but what Wardour Street ignored was that they were all excellent actors and, as it happened, the ones who had the least experience of film work had much the best results in the final showing,' noted Pat Wallace, in her report for *Picturegoer* magazine in August 1929.

Pat described her father's directing style and his skill at what, today, we know as multi-tasking:

> He didn't use a megaphone, and I don't remember him getting temperamental, though that is more or less expected of any film producer. While the cameras were turning on a scene he would sit as close to the action as possible, and direct, with the inevitable cup of tea in his hand. Between the shots he would explain the script of the scenario to people, or discuss new and startling methods of lighting, or be interviewed, or dictate a racing article.

Red Aces was an enjoyable experience for all concerned, but a big change was on its way – the arrival of the talkie.

Edgar Wallace's name features prominently in the early history of talking pictures. One of the first European talkies was the German version of

The Crimson Circle (Der Rote Kreis) which had been made as a silent film in 1928, but to which English dialogue was dubbed later. The aforementioned *The Clue of the New Pin* is thought to be the first British 'talkie', or at least the first film in which talking was used in part. Meanwhile, the first 'all-talking' picture to be shown in Britain, in November 1928, was a Hollywood version of Wallace's play *The Terror*, which was also the first ever horror-talkie.[2] Wallace had sold the film rights to Warner Bros for £3,000, the largest sum he had yet to receive for the film rights for any of his stories, but again he could have done better, as he hadn't noticed that the contract – which he thought had been for silent films rights only – included talking rights too. 'Never mind' he told Curtis when he found out his mistake, 'We'll make some talkies ourselves.'

For British Lion, getting 'wired for sound' meant major reconstruction work at Beaconsfield. The expense involved no doubt contributed to the company making a loss of almost £50,000 in 1929, but by February 1930, they were ready to make their first all-talking picture. Edgar Wallace would direct *The Squeaker*. 'Heavily seated in his canvas chair, his hat tilted back from his brow and a script in his hand, he enjoyed his new role so much that he would accept no money from the company for playing it,' Margaret Lane records.[3] Wallace as a director certainly looked the part, dressed in breeches and boots – the uniform of directors in the early days of Hollywood.

For his new film, Wallace was reunited with his actor friends, Nigel Bruce and Gordon Harker. Wallace seems to have found directing talkies easier than silent films. After all, what he was doing now was essentially filming plays. He revelled in his new public persona, that of Edgar Wallace, film director. Later that year, he could also claim to be a film actor too, as he had a small role in *The Crimson Circle*.

In addition to his work at the film studios, he was also by now writing regular articles on films for *Sunday News*. As always, any new success had to be celebrated with some very big spending. When he had first started to work with British Lion, he rented a furnished house in nearby Bourne End. In 1929, he went a stage further and bought a large house on the hill above Bourne End with a magnificent view of the Thames Valley. 'Chalklands'[4] cost Wallace £5,000, but he spent four times that amount adding two wings, a stable for his horses, and a planned garden. A permanent staff of servants was employed at great expense.

'Edgar Wallace, I hear, now has a Rolls-Royce and also a separate car for each of the five members of his family. Also a day butler and a night butler, so that there is never a time when you can go to his house and not find buttling going on. That's the way to live,' japed P.G. Wodehouse.[5]

At the age of 54 Wallace, the illegitimate son of a travelling actress who had been born in abject poverty, could now stand proudly on his terrace, admiring his beautiful garden and grounds, cigarette holder firmly clenched between his teeth and reflect on all he had achieved. It gave him great pleasure to have a house so close to the Thames, the river which had played such an important part in his life. He bought a motor-launch boat, called *Miss Penelope*, in which he would take his youngest daughter for rides up and down the river. 'Bernard Feeny [Wallace's chauffeur] would drive us down and drop us off, because neither of us were great with walking,' Penny recalled, 'and then we'd go with him talking all the time and we'd stop off at The Compleat Angler (in Marlow) and we'd have strawberries and cream, lots of cream, and lots of sugar, and terribly bad for both our figures.'[6] Wallace also liked to send his driver and the Rolls-Royce down to Brockley to bring his beloved foster sister, Clara, up to Chalklands, where they would sit and chat about old times.

Chalklands was at first used mainly at weekends, but there were changes too in Wallace's weekday living arrangements. In 1929, he moved himself and his family out of Portland Place for about six months, into even more luxurious surroundings – a large suite at the Carlton Hotel. 'Living at the Carlton suited Edgar's ideas of his own position better than anything else; it was his favourite hotel, and he enjoyed the mild sensation which he made when he appeared in the grill-room,' records Margaret Lane.[7]

Wallace had a private telephone line installed to connect his study at the Carlton to his service flat in Yeoman Place, where Bob Curtis and Jenia Reissar still worked, so that the pair could be summoned at any hour to collect the latest cylinders for typing. Lane also told how Wallace's yellow Rolls-Royce was kept almost permanently waiting at the door of the Carlton 'in case he should suddenly decide to go racing, or drive down to Chalklands'. Wallace would routinely telephone Wyndham's and ask what was in the till, and then send his chauffeur round to collect it. 'If he was going to the races he might tell the theatre manager to give him £2,000 from the safe. He regarded his future earnings as already in his pocket,' said Pat Wallace.[8]

It seemed that life couldn't get much better for Edgar Wallace. But there was still plenty of excitement and adventure to come.

25

ADVENTURES IN GERMANY AND AMERICA

From the broad balcony with its Venetian balustrading Tony Perelli could look down upon the city he was to rule. He loved Chicago, every stone of it.

Edgar Wallace, *On the Spot* (novel), 1931

Wallace's books weren't just registering phenomenal sales in Britain, they were also becoming immensely popular in many other countries across the world. 'One of the most amusing things for me is to see my stories come back translated into foreign languages, like Czechoslovakian and Danish. I never know which book it is till I have checked the names of the characters,' Wallace told an interviewer in 1926.[1]

He had already built up a loyal following in the US, where his books sold ¼ million copies annually between 1922–1932, and in the mid-1920s Germany fell under his spell too. Wallace's huge and enduring popularity in that country is rather ironic given the fierce anti-German line he took in the First World War. However, the jingoistic Hun-basher of 1914 changed his tune fairly soon after the end of hostilities and he wrote sympathetically about Germany and its people, following visits to the country.

Wallace's conquering of the German market began in 1925, when a translator offered the Leipzig-based publisher Wilhelm Goldmann a German translation of *Sanders of the River*. It was a great success, and Goldmann then commissioned the translation of *Bosambo*. The publisher realised that there was a vast back catalogue of Wallace detective stories and thrillers which could be translated into German, but was unsure of the legal position. So he decided to travel to London to meet the author himself. 'At this meeting I encountered immediately Edgar Wallace's generosity. He signed the contracts for the two African books and advised me to contact his literary agent with regards to further rights,' Goldmann said.[2]

It was to be the start of a profitable relationship for both Wallace and his new German partner. Wallace's books were devoured by the German public in the same way they had been devoured by the British. Wallace's books were devoured by the British. 'The long cigarette-holder of our Edgar Wallace must be also as well known to the inhabitants of central Europe as to those of the British Isles … there, as here, he is supreme in his own domain of fiction,' writes Cicely Hamilton in her book *Modern Germanies* (1931).[3] Wallace's work attracted the attention of the celebrated producer Max Reinhardt who, in 1927, produced *The Ringer* (*Der Hexer*) in the German Theatre in Berlin. 'This was the first thriller on a German stage and the success was astounding,' records Goldmann.[4] Other Wallace stage productions in Germany followed.

Wallace was thrilled with his popularity in Germany and greatly enjoyed his visits to a country where he had 'A-List' celebrity status. He enthused in a letter from Berlin:

> For some extraordinary reason there is a Wallace vogue in Germany. I don't think The Ringer started it. I have been sketched by the artists of half a dozen papers – and the pictures have appeared. If you saw the caricatures you would acquit me of boastfulness! But it is awfully astonishing to find oneself known in a strange land.

Berlin soon became Wallace's favourite city. 'He loved the place, primarily because he had great fondness for the Germans,' wrote Jim, though undoubtedly the Germans' love of Edgar Wallace also had something to do with it.

In a visit in 1928, he saw mystery from the very start of the trip:

> There was a shabbily dressed woman in the Pullman going down to Dover who had a little square blue card which she kept in her hand. Pinned to it was a large brooch at which she glanced continuously. She was rather pretty. She had been crying. I saw her at Calais – she was on the Nord Express. She was sitting in the corner of the sleeper, smoking a cigarette, and was reading, with every evidence of amusement, a letter which obviously she had opened on the train. At Brussels she left us.

Then, in Berlin, Wallace saw the woman again:

> Looking down from my window at the Adlon, which commands a view of Unter den Linden, I saw her driving in a Rolls, magnificently attired. She was with another woman, apparently a maid or some sort of servant. What did it mean – the brooch, the tears, the letter, the change of attire? To me, drama. To somebody else, a very deep sex story.[5]

One of the Berlin newspapers asked Wallace if he could be photographed in the streets with a local policeman. 'I hate that sort of publicity but I was obliging,' he wrote, 'the policeman was a fine specimen of a man. An ex-sergeant major. Most of the police in Berlin are ex-NCOs – that is why they are the smartest and most efficient uniformed police in Europe.'

Edgar Wallace, the great crime writer and author of *Der Hexer*, wasn't just in demand for photographs with law enforcers in Germany, but was also enlisted to try and solve a real-life murder mystery. The industrial city of Dusseldorf had been the scene of a series of grisly murders. Wallace was approached by a Berlin newspaper and asked to investigate, and then to pen an article on the crimes and who their perpetrator might be. In the piece he provided his own pen portrait of the killer, detailing his character, tastes, habits, even what he looked like. Unfortunately, when the man was eventually arrested, Wallace was shown to have been way off the scent. 'Not one single detail which Wallace had supplied was found to be correct,' Curtis noted. Wallace had discovered that it was one thing to write detective novels, it was quite another to solve real-life murder cases.

In 1929 he travelled to Leipzig to be the godfather at the christening of Wilhelm Goldmann's son. At the station around 400 people, including a posse of journalists, were waiting for him. One reporter said: 'Mr Wallace, I know your name, but I have never read one of your books.' Wallace turned to his publisher and muttered: 'Dear William, is this gentleman illiterate?'

Occasionally Wallace had time to relax on his trips to Germany, but usually he worked as hard there as he did at home, as Wilhelm Goldmann recalled:

Once he arrived in Berlin at the Stettiner Bahnhof and said in his taxi on the way to the Hotel Adlon that he did not want to be disturbed during the next two days. On his journey to Berlin he had worked out a plot for a play. As a matter of fact, during the next three days, Edgar Wallace hardly slept, but smoked several hundred cigarettes, and ordered no less than eighty pots of tea. With a triumphant gesture he showed me quite a stack of notepaper of the Hotel Adlon. On the top sheet, in his hand, was written: 'The Man Who Changed his Name.'

Once Wallace returned from Germany with more than just presents for his family. His daughter Penny recalled:

I think a story which typified my father as a man, concerned his German publishers, who suggested that he engage a bilingual secretary. He agreed and the publisher found a suitable girl for him to interview. He returned to England with the girl's younger sister because the prospective candidate was worried that this younger sister was getting involved with the emergent Nazi party. All might have been well but the younger sister had no secretarial training and could not speak a word of English. To his incredulous personal secretary, Jenia, he suggested that the girl might do the filing.[6]

In the autumn of 1929, Wallace returned to the United States. His American agent, George Doran, encouraged him to pay another visit to New York, where he could not only meet with newspaper and magazine editors, but also take advantage of the publicity he was sure to attract. On his earlier visit in 1921, he had gone on his own. This time he decided to take his entire family with him, together with a friend of Pat's, and Penny's governess too. He decided that the whole entourage would travel in the most luxurious (and expensive) way possible – in a royal suite on the liner SS *Berengaria*.

On board, Wallace enjoyed chats with the captain and worked on a desk which had been brought for the use of a prime minister. At quarantine, around thirty reporters came on board to meet America's famous guest, who treated them to champagne and whisky.

On shore, there was a hectic programme of meetings and functions to attend in New York. 'It was only to be expected that he was invited to all sorts of literary parties and I went to those which were only just "literary",' wrote Pat Wallace in her write-up of the trip for *Pearson's* magazine.[7]

Wallace and Pat found that 'Prohibition' in America didn't mean that you couldn't buy an alcoholic drink, only that the price of one had rocketed. At dinner one day Wallace told his eldest daughter that he fancied some champagne – which, apart from ginger beer, was the only alcoholic beverage that he ever touched. Pat quietly asked the waiter if he could oblige. 'A moment later, the "forbidden" booze appeared. When the bill came it included an item: "Minerals – 10 dollars."'

It was Prohibition, of course, which had led to the rise of famous gangsters like Al Capone. Wallace had become increasingly fascinated by the American criminal underworld, and was keen to visit Chicago, Capone's city and where several sensational gang murders had recently been committed. Wallace took the train to the 'windy city' and on the way immersed himself in literature about racketeers. When he arrived, he was given a 'gangster' tour of the city by a Lieutenant of Police. He visited the garage which had been the scene of the St Valentine's Day Massacre; Hotel Lexington, where Capone had his HQ; the flower shop where Dion O'Banion had been put 'on the spot' and the state jail.

He returned to New York after his thirty-six hour stay in Chicago, totally enthused by what he had seen. 'We sat round open-mouthed while he told us the most exciting gangster news,' wrote Pat. Wallace spent the journey back to England deep in thought.

'During his stay in America, Mr Edgar Wallace gave eighty-three interviews, wrote six articles and three stories. He has now returned home to start work again,' joked *Punch*. But America would seem like a holiday compared with what was to come. As soon as he arrived back in Britain, Wallace told

Jenia Reissar that he had a wonderful new idea for a play. What happened next was classic high-speed Wallace, as Reissar relates:

> At midnight, I think it was a Tuesday, he rang up from Chalklands and said: 'The car is on its way. I'm going to start the play now' – so I came down – it was about 1 o'clock. He started dictating. I knew roughly what the characters were but he acted the parts and you just guessed who they were once he got into dictation. He finished dictating the first act and went to bed and I typed it. When he got up in the morning he dictated the second act, and while I was typing he corrected the first one. Then he had another nap in the afternoon and then he dictated the third act. While I was typing that he was correcting the second act. By midnight of that day we had the whole play in draft.[8]

By Friday lunchtime Reissar, fortified by drinking endless cups of black coffee, had the work collated and, on the car journey to London, she and Edgar sat frantically stapling together the pages. Incredibly, one week later, the play was in rehearsal at Wyndham's. *On the Spot*, a play about Chicago gangsters, proved to be Wallace's most critically acclaimed drama. 'Without doubt it is Wallace's best play, and perhaps the finest melodrama of our time,' wrote Margaret Lane in 1938.[9]

The lead role of Tony Perelli, the charismatic Italian gangster chief modelled on Al Capone, was played by Charles Laughton, who went on to become a leading Hollywood star.[10] Wallace had heard good reports about the Scarborough-born actor following his performance in *The Man With Red Hair*, and wrote to him. In response, Laughton called to see Wallace in his flat. Elsa Lanchester, Laughton's wife, later described the meeting. Her husband arrived to see Wallace sitting at a 'large desk surrounded on three sides by big glass screens' and wearing 'a rich-looking dressing gown over an ordinary suit' and, of course, with his now legendary long cigarette holder in his mouth. Wallace got straight down to business, 'Laughton, I have written a play for you about an American gangster.' He described the role of Tony Perelli, 'his cold-blooded shootings, his many mistresses, and the floral funerals he gave to people he bumped off'. He told Laughton how Perelli's mistress would be 'unusual, exciting, exotic'. Lanchester reported that her husband came home 'pale and tired' and told her 'I believe Edgar Wallace has written the play of his career.'[11]

Laughton received a copy of *On the Spot* two days later. Despite his enthusiasm for the play, Laughton did have doubts that he was the right man to play the macho womaniser, Tony Perelli:

When I was rehearsing *On the Spot*, in which I had to wear smart clothes and go around the stage kissing the women, I came home one night in a state of despair, sullen and nasty, and said to Elsa: 'I know they won't stand for this. I've got a face like an elephant's behind, and in this play I've got to do the big sex act.' She turned on me like the proverbial tiger-cat and whipped out: 'How dare you presume you are unattractive! Hold your shoulders back, keep your head up and smile, so that I can hold my head up with other women.' Can you beat that? I owe her plenty.[12]

After the triumphant first night on 2 April 1930, which brought critical praise not only for Laughton but for the young Welsh actor Emlyn Williams[13] who played Angelo, Tony Perelli's henchman, there was a breakfast party for the cast and crew at a Lyons Corner House. To show his appreciation for the way she had helped him get the play written up so quickly, Wallace presented Jenia Reissar with a beautiful diamond clip.

About the only person who wasn't celebrating was 7-year-old Penny Wallace. She was usually given a given a seat in the royal box at Wyndham's to watch her father's first nights, but for *On the Spot* she wasn't allowed because Tony Perelli and Minn Lee weren't married. 'I was awfully annoyed,' she later recalled.

The play ran in London for almost a year and then, with Laughton still in the lead role, made a successful tour of the provinces. Wallace was understandably very proud of the play's success. On 24 June 1930 he wrote to his great idol Rudyard Kipling from the Carlton Hotel:

My dear friend,
How nice and characteristically kind of you to send me 'The Mission that Failed'. When are you and Mrs Kipling coming to town? I want you so much to see 'On the Spot' which is such a big success.
My thoughts and homage to you
Yours sincerely
Edgar Wallace

In 1931 *On the Spot* also opened on Broadway, starring Anna May Wong as Perelli's Chinese mistress, and brought in £3,000 a week. The reviews were excellent, and when it opened in Chicago even real members of 'the mob' were impressed – sitting in the stalls, they sent a note on stage for the author saying that he had 'told it as it was.' Despite the expense of hiring the royal suite in the *Berengaria*, Edgar Wallace's second trip to America had proved very profitable indeed.

26

HATS OFF TO EDGAR WALLACE!

So hats off to Edgar Wallace,
Now look what he's done for me,
I want to hear horrible shuddering screams,
I want to be frightened to death in my dreams,
I long to hear somebody's body fall with a sickening thud
So hand me the shivers, and let me
See Rivers of Blood, blood, blood!

Song by Stanley Lupino, first performed in the musical play,
So This is Love, 1928

At the end of 1929, Wallace could look back at a decade of remarkable achievements. He was not only firmly established as Britain's best-selling novelist, but a highly successful playwright, and a film director too. His reputation was now an international one. He had become one of the most famous and most recognisable men on the planet.

There was no sign of readers becoming tired of his books, or the genre in which he specialised. 'The extraordinary popularity of detective stories shows no sign of diminishing,' proclaimed an advertisement in *Hush Magazine* in 1930. 'The late Prime Minister has confessed that he enjoys them, eminent men and women of every branch of life find them a mental stimulus. There is room for the Detective Story Club Limited, founded to issue stories from the best detective writers from Gaboriau to Edgar Wallace at a uniform price of 6*d*.' As the 1930s dawned, Wallace was in greater demand than ever before. There seemed no reason why he couldn't enjoy another decade at the top of the tree.

In the series 'Letters to Living Authors', Robert Lynd penned a fulsome tribute to 'The Author who never gets tired':

Sir – At the age of fifty-five you are already a legendary figure. You have accomplished feats of writing that in an earlier age, would have been generally explained by the existence and assistance of a fairy godmother. Two years ago, it was said that, besides plays and short stories, you had written at least a hundred and forty novels, containing in all about nine million words. You yourself have declared that you seldom take more than eight days to write a book. One of your plays you are said to have written in fourteen hours. And, apart, from your fiction and your work for the stage, you contribute to the Press a mass of articles on racing and, indeed, on any subject on which an editor approaches you, which is probably equal in bulk to the output of an ordinary journalist working full-time. You are obviously one of those rare human beings who never get tired and who can use any spare half-hour of the day to dictate another thousand words.

But Wallace's success had not come cost-free, the years of hard work, of waking up early in the morning to dictate his latest serial or book, and then starting to dictate a play at midnight, were beginning to take a toll on his health. People who met him remarked on his grey pallor. 'I used to call Edgar (behind his back) the Man with No Face. His face had no expression, no colour, no anything except those restless eyes, summing up everyone and everything,' recalled Jack Leach.[1] 'He looked unhealthily flabby, with a grey face,' observed Sir Rupert Hart-Davis, a guest at Chalklands.[2]

Wallace, to his credit, knew he wasn't in the best physical condition and did try to rectify things. In the rear advertising section of *Strand Magazine*, November 1928, he endorsed 'Abplanalp' – described as 'a new and simple apparatus for losing weight.' 'My dear Abplanalp,' he wrote (in a letter dated 28 September 1928):

> I am in the middle of your exercises. As you know, I am physically the laziest man in the world. For twenty-five years I have walked, on average, three or four miles a year. I took up the Abplanalp system in June last, never dreaming that I should perform the exercises for more than one week – if I lasted so long! It is now the end of September, and I feel fifty percent more efficient than I did in the summer.

Alas, Wallace didn't keep it up. The problem was not just laziness, but that he genuinely believed that expending physical energy would mean his reserves of mental energy would be depleted too. If he did start going out for long, strenuous walks, or take up golf or tennis, then he would be too tired to work. His self-description as 'physically the laziest man in the world' was not too much of an exaggeration, as his electrician and maintenance man, Harry Sargeant, later related:

He told me that he averaged two miles a year and so I was astonished one day when he walked out of the house and started to walk down the road dressed as though he was going for a long, long hike – with walking stick and the lot. He went about 150 yards and he sat in a seat, waved to one of the gardeners who was cutting the lawn, the gardener came over, he sent him back to the garage for the Rolls, the Rolls appeared, Wallace got into the car and came back to the house. And that was his walk.[3]

Neither Wallace, nor those closest to him, believed his incredible consumption of cups of sweet tea and his chain-smoking was injurious to his health. 'Thirty or forty cups of tea was his average and I imagine he smoked about 80–100 cigarettes through his famous 10 inch holder,' wrote Robert Curtis. 'He did not inhale the smoke, so I do not suppose the habit did him much harm.'

Whether it was caused by his heavy smoking or not, Wallace was suffering more from chesty ailments, and began to be plagued, from his mid-fifties, by bronchitis and colds that he couldn't shake off. And unbeknown to him, he also had diabetes.

Domestically too, things were not as happy as they first appeared, nor as they were a few years earlier. Friction had developed between Jim and Jenia Reissar. Jim, it seems, was jealous of the woman who had replaced her as her husband's secretary, and saw her as a rival for Edgar's affections, perhaps even fearing that the young and engaging Russian could one day become Mrs Edgar Wallace Number Three. One night Wallace entered the room in Chalklands where Reissar was busy typing away, and noticed that she was sitting on a very small, uncomfortable chair. Kind-hearted as ever, he bought her a new one. Reissar recalled:

> One of the following days his wife came looking for him, noticed the chair and asked 'what is that beautiful chair doing in your room?' I answered, 'I don't know, Mr Wallace bought it and had put it there.' 'I will check that' she answered, 'because it is a very expensive chair.' At night Wallace came to me and said: 'Don't pay attention to her, the chair belongs to you, you ought to sit more comfortable when you work for me.' She, however, never forgave me and always said it was the most expensive chair he ever bought. It simply wasn't right, she was constantly afraid, that he might leave her.[4]

Wallace told Reissar that he had had eight different secretaries in a few months because of the jealousy of his wife. In a television interview broadcast in 2000, Reissar didn't mince her words when talking of the second Mrs Edgar Wallace. 'This woman could be really unpleasant, and I think Wallace thought so too, because he always said to me: "Don't pay attention to her when she asks any questions, just don't answer her." She couldn't stand another woman in the house. She was terrible.'

Yet, according to Reissar, it was Wallace who had more grounds to feel jealous than his Jim. 'One day he was looking for his wife. I said that she was in the theatre. "How do you know?" he asked and I was inclined to say "because so-and-so- is also there." But then he already said himself: "I think she has got a lover." "Oh, really," I answered.'

Of course, articles about the Wallaces painted a picture of domestic bliss. In 'Housekeeping for a Genius', a piece on 'the world's hardest working author', which appeared in *The New London Magazine* in December 1930, journalist Jim Gliddons visited Chalklands. 'My husband may be a genius, but I can assure you that he does not in the least live up to the popular idea that geniuses are difficult people to 'manage'; he is neither erratic, temperamental, or even very unpunctual, and any wife will appreciate what a blessing that means,' Jim told the reporter.

Gliddons gave his readers a peek at the engine room of the Edgar Wallace Fiction Factory. Wallace's study had soundproofed double-glazed windows, with 6in between the panes. There was also a heavy padded door. 'In the middle of the room is Edgar Wallace's desk. He works with his back to the windows, facing the cream-painted wall. To avoid having to bend over his manuscript a piece has been cut out of the oak desk, so that he can't sit upright in his chair and have his paper in a direct line.'

We were told that Wallace started work at 4 a.m. every morning using a small room on the first floor where he slept when he decided to cut the night short. 'My husband has that lucky gift of being able to sleep at will,' said Jim, 'If he feels tired, he comes up here and takes one or two hours sleep and wakes up the minute he wishes to. I think that's why he is able to keep going at the rate he does.'

In *The Secret of My Successful Marriage*, a collection of essays by the wives of famous people, published by John Long in 1930[5], Jim stressed her role in helping her husband unwind:

> We don't always work. There are times when we spend whole days together in our country house at Bourne End. Then Edgar lies stretched luxuriously on a deckchair doing nothing at all save pulling Penelope's gold curls and I remonstrate or encourage as I think fair … I encourage Edgar to take off-days. Perhaps this is where I have helped him most – for Edgar never knew when to stop working, and I made him realise the truth of the old saying 'All work and no play makes Jack a dull boy' – which even applies to the indefatigable Edgar Wallace.

No doubt Wallace would have loved to have taken things easier, but he was caught in a trap. His high levels of spending, his incredible generosity and his heavy gambling meant that he simply had to carry on working at a ferocious pace simply to pay the bills. The reputation he had obtained for his prodigious output had also become an albatross round his neck – if he didn't have a new book coming out every few weeks, a new play on the go, or a new film project, he felt he would be letting his enormous legion of fans down.

As he passed his mid-fifties, he should have been slowing down and enjoying the fruits of his extraordinary labours. In fact, he was having to work as hard as ever. The theatre occupied much of his time in 1930. The success of *On the Spot* was followed by another failure, *The Mouthpiece*. The plot involved a group of crooks who decide to marry one of their number to a young girl who doesn't know she's an heiress to a large fortune. Wallace offered the lead role to Charles Laughton, but this time the actor declined. Professionally, it was the right thing to do, though Wallace was disappointed by Laughton's decision, believing he could have shown him more loyalty after the success of *On the Spot.*

On its opening night, *The Mouthpiece* was booed by the audience and there was even a shout of 'none of your rubbish'. Wallace realised quickly the play was doomed and at one of the intervals he mentioned to his friend, Sir Patrick Hastings, that he had another idea for a new play which he would start writing as soon as he got home and would have ready for the stage in just three weeks. Almost all the reviews of *The Mouthpiece* were scathing, except one from a journalist in a provincial newspaper who actually claimed it was Wallace's best work. 'I showed Wallace the cutting and saw his eyes light up,' recalled Robert Curtis. '"Send this fellow a wire," he said and dictated a long and expansive telegram congratulating this lone voice upon being the only critic in England with a sense of dramatic values!'

Smoky Cell, which did indeed open three weeks after *The Mouthpiece*, was another gangster drama set in the US, but was not really in the same league as *On The Spot*. It lacked the compelling central character of Tony Perelli and relied on too many shootings, bombs and police sirens: Lane notes that the loud noises 'bruised the ears of the audience from the first act to the last.' Its first night, which Wallace missed because he was in Germany, was even more disastrous than that of *The Mouthpiece* – indeed, it must rate as one of the most catastrophic opening nights of any play that has appeared in London's West End

Actor Harold Huth forgot his lines and the revolver of another actor, Bernard Nedell, went off in his pocket during a speech, causing him great pain and the audience to shriek with fear. It was all too much for poor Jim, who usually was a bag of nerves on first nights anyway, and she departed the royal box for the retiring room where she sat with clenched fists in the dark. During the next interval she was found unconscious.

Wallace, on hearing about how things had gone, radically rewrote the play and introduced a heroine into what had been an all-male cast. 'A play without a girl is a dull business, however successful it may be from the box-office point of view,' he admitted. The changes helped *Smoky Cell* recover, and it lasted for four months, not a bad run considering how badly it had all started.

As we have seen, in February 1930, Wallace made his debut as a director of talking pictures with *The Squeaker*. He was, of course, still writing books, serials and newspaper articles and demonstrating his wonderful versatility. He worked as drama critic of the *Morning Post*, while in the spring of 1930 he returned to the pages of the *Daily Mail*, to write a daily racing column. In addition, he was continuing to file his twice-a-week racing articles for the *Star*.

Easter 1930 brought some racing news to celebrate, as Wallace's horse King Baldwin won the Welbeck Handicap at Lincoln by a short head at odds of 9–1, helping to land some good bets in the process. 'Wallace invested on the horse that day, but I remember that it comprised fivers and tenners for nearly everybody closely associated with him. That was Edgar Wallace. His losses were his own, but his rare wins must be shared with his friends,' remembered Robert Curtis.

For the launch of the fiction page of the new *Daily Herald*, in March 1930, Wallace provided a new serial, 'The Clue of the Silver Key', another classic murder mystery which begins with a murdered burglar being delivered to Scotland Yard in a stolen taxicab.

Wallace was in demand from everyone and, perhaps mindful of the times when he struggled to get his work published, he never liked to say 'no' to any commission or offer of work. Loyalty played its part too. For those he regarded as his 'old pals', like H.A. Gwynne, the man who had given him his first big break at Reuters in South Africa, and who was now editor of the *Morning Post*, he was happy to work for well below the rate he could command elsewhere. It was easy to see why Wallace was so popular with commissioning editors. He could write about virtually subject under the sun and do so in a way that always engaged readers – and of course like the old pro he was, he always filed copy in time.

He was now firmly established as a public figure, and his views were eagerly sought out on a wide variety of topics. In the late summer of 1929 he had engaged in a lively debate in the pages of the *Sunday News* with Sir Arthur Conan Doyle, the creator of Sherlock Holmes, over the latter's belief that clairvoyants could help police catch criminals. Conan Doyle was a firm believer in spiritualism, but Wallace expressed his scepticism about mediums. 'The average professional medium is a liar, who says that, if you sing enough hymns and hold enough hands and get enough dark into the room, she can produce all these mysterious manifestations with the same ease as the housewife can produce a pound of butter by telephoning to the dairy,' he wrote. In reply, Conan Doyle questioned Wallace's knowledge of the subject: 'I am prepared to sit at that gentleman's feet when it comes to racehorses and to follow him in many of his multifarious activities, but, in psychic questions I do not know that he has done sufficient reading or had sufficient experience to justify him in laying down the law.' Wallace then called Conan Doyle's allusion to him as 'very rude and silly.' Conan Doyle assured Wallace he had no intention of being rude, and suggested that Wallace had been overworking and had become too sensitive.

There may have been some truth in the claim, but Wallace, however tired or overworked, never lost his sense of humour. A young journalist, Herbert Harris, was writing an article entitled: 'What I owe to my Parents'. One of the celebrities whom he asked to reveal what he owed to his parents was Edgar Wallace. The reply came surprisingly quickly, but even more surprisingly it was written in Edgar's rather large round handwriting on an open postcard. It said simply – 'Sorry, cock, I'm a bastard.'

With plays, films, books, articles and newspaper columns you might have thought that Wallace had enough on his plate as he celebrated his 55th birthday in February 1930. But he was now to embark on yet another new challenge – a career in politics.

27

EDGAR WALLACE MP?

One excellent result followed Tony Newton's 'election' to Parliament. He had secured for himself an extraordinary amount of publicity and the consequences of this advertisement were to prove both exhilarating and profitable.

Edgar Wallace, *The Brigand*, 1928

Edgar Wallace was a man without strong party political affiliations and neither, for that matter, did he have too much interest in politics in general. In 1908 he had written:

I have no politics. Trade statistics leave me unmoved. Our decaying British industries arouse only the faintest interest: threatened war upon the 'trade' and the possibilities of prohibition alike bore me. Home Rule (has Ireland got Home Rule, by the way, I can never keep up-to-date in these things) doesn't cut ice so far as I'm concerned; and the ultimate fate of the House of Lords exercises no influence upon the smooth current of my daily life.

Yet in the spring of 1930, the man who had no politics was revealed as the Liberal Party's prospective parliamentary candidate for the seat of mid-Buckinghamshire. Just two years earlier, when the *Daily News* reported that he had been asked to stand as a Liberal candidate in the next general election, he had cabled the newspaper with a strong denial, saying that he had 'yet to generate any wild enthusiasm for any party'. But in early 1930, when he was asked by Mr Goss, the Liberal agent for Aylesbury, if he would consider being the party's candidate for mid-Buckinghamshire, he said 'yes'. Was it flattery that made him change his mind? Perhaps. Or it could simply have been that he was a man who loved to try out new things and thought it was about time he gave politics a go.

The Liberal Party in 1930 needed Edgar Wallace more than Edgar Wallace needed the Liberal Party. Having won a landslide election victory in 1905, the party had, for various reasons, declined in the years following the First World War and, in the 1920s, had been replaced by Labour as the main party of opposition to the Conservatives. In the general election of May 1929 they had won just fifty-nine seats. The party clearly hoped that having a man as famous – and as popular – as Edgar Wallace on their side would boost their flagging fortunes.

Wallace's election campaign began in April 1930, with a village bazaar in Aylesbury opened by Lady Samuel, wife of party bigwig Sir Herbert Samuel. Wallace joked about why he had entered politics. 'I am in politics because I think this is the moment when any man who has any leisure – and everyone knows that I have nothing to do for at least one hour a day – should give himself and whatever talents he has to the service of the country.'

Miss F.M. Pugh acted as Wallace's general assistant. 'He was a very busy man and wanted someone to represent him in the constituency and work up the local association, while he would come to public meetings, socials and so forth. He summoned me to the Carlton Hotel for an interview. I was interested and thrilled to find the famous writer clad in a super dressing gown and smoking his cigarette in the well-known holder.'[1]

In June, Pugh arranged for Wallace to address a meeting of around 1,000 women constituents at the Pavilion Cinema in Aylesbury. 'It is a real pleasure to me to meet so many women especially from this charming town,' he began; 'You may not know it but I have never been a politician before – up to now my life has been honest!'

Wallace's campaign looked to have got off to a flying start and his cause was enthusiastically supported by a newly launched local newspaper called the *Bucks Mail*. The support wasn't surprising, considering that Wallace had set up the paper himself and wrote most of the articles. One week, he penned a leader about a notorious murder which had recently taken place. 'This thrilled the local populace and the circulation went up sharply,' remembered Miss Pugh.

Wallace also used British Lion film studios in his campaign. A nationwide contest to discover a new British female film star was launched, which got not only British Lion but Wallace's prospective candidacy, plenty of publicity. Yet by early 1931, Wallace's enthusiasm for fighting mid-Bucks for the Liberals was waning. Despite his great efforts, it was clear that Conservative sentiments in the constituency ran high. His party was also badly divided, and was splitting into different factions. He had also made one bad mistake which lost him local support. He had been billed to speak in Great Missenden, but had to cancel owing to a cold. The meeting was rescheduled, but on the night he sent another message to say he was sorry and couldn't come, leaving Miss Pugh to stand in for him. Alas, a local Conservative discovered that Wallace had been enjoying himself that night in London at the Jockey Club Dinner. 'This was not well received in Great Missenden', noted Miss Pugh.

In April, Wallace announced he was withdrawing his candidature. It was not, however, the end of his political ambitions. He would instead stand as an Independent Lloyd George Liberal in Blackpool. Being MP for the Lancashire seaside resort undoubtedly appealed more to Wallace than being MP for a Home Counties seat. Blackpool was bright, breezy and cheerful, just like him. The slogan 'A Showman for a Showman's Town' made great appeal.

In October 1931 Wallace would head north for what he firmly believed would be a successful election campaign. Before that, though, he still had plenty of other projects to concentrate on. The Edgar Wallace Fiction Factory was still continuing to turn out thrillers to keep the nation – and readers across the world – entertained, though because of Wallace's other commitments, the number of them had dropped significantly compared to the mid-to-late 1920s.

The Man at the Carlton, published by Hodder & Stoughton in July 1931, had first appeared as a serial in the *Daily Express* earlier in the year. Sir Rupert Hart-Davis and his wife Peggy Ashcroft were staying at Chalklands while Wallace was writing it:

> We asked if we could see him at work and he readily agreed … owing to his other commitments he was only 24 hours ahead of the serialisation. Wearing his famous dressing-gown, he switched on the dictaphone, into which he spoke all his books and started hesitantly, having forgotten the characters' names. After a few minutes of rambling narrative, he said into the machine; 'Cut out all that and start again'. By then he was back in the groove, and the complicated story flowed from him without pause or hesitation … Wallace worked through Sunday night, and when we left after breakfast on Monday we took with us cylinders containing seven thousand words, which we delivered to Curtis in London.[2]

Wallace loved to entertain at Chalklands, but often the only time guests saw him was at dinner, as at all other times he would be working away in his study. Sometimes he didn't even make it to dinner. Sir Patrick Hastings was a guest during the weekend when Wallace wrote an 80,000-word novel, *The Devil Man*, a fictionalised account of the life of the Sheffield murderer Charles Peace, in just sixty hours. Hastings had difficulty in sleeping on the Friday night, and had gone to Wallace's study where he found him dictating. He sat and watched him for two hours and was enthralled by the way Wallace worked. By nine o'clock on the Monday morning, Wallace had completed his task, which earned him £4,000 in serial rights alone. He then went to bed for two days to make up for the sleep he had missed.

It wasn't all work though. Wallace was always in demand as a party guest and in the summer he had attended, along with other celebrities of the day, a lavish midnight party at the Savoy Hotel in honour of William Randolph Hearst, the American media magnate. 'There were Hore Belisha [a government minister], Rebecca West [novelist] and Marion Davies [Hearst's actress wife] and the Baroness Ravensdale and Edgar Wallace, complete with cigarette in 8-inch holder,' wrote Tom Clarke, in his 1939 book *My Lloyd George Diary*.

At British Lion, talking versions of Wallace's classic thrillers were continuing to be made, and although the author was no longer directing them, he still enjoyed his involvement with the studio.[3] In 1931 the production of *The Ringer* began, directed by Walter Forde. John Croydon, location accountant on the set, remembers the impact the author had when he came to watch the filming:

> About twice during the shooting Edgar Wallace himself visited the set. Naturally, as the junior, I never had the opportunity to speak with him, but his well-known flamboyance was exemplified by his Stetson hat, cravat, riding jacket and jodhpurs, and his long, black cigarette holder. Even at a distance, he conveyed his dynamic personality.[4]

Harold Brust, an ex-Special Branch detective who attended some of the shooting, was similarly impressed. 'Edgar was a grand man to work with, utterly unspoiled despite the tremendous publicity which attached to his name, and as friendly with the lowest messenger boy and odd-job man of the studio as he was with the directors of the film company.'[5]

In 1931 Wallace's voice could be heard regularly on the wireless.[6] On 26 April he broadcast an appeal for King's College Hospital for the 'Week's Good Cause' and in July he began a series of weekly talks for the BBC, under the general heading 'The World of Crime', which ran until November. There were factual talks, (in one he gave advice on how people could protect their homes from burglars) and two short stories featuring 'The Sooper'. They were a big hit with listeners and critics alike. Raymond Postgate wrote in *Reynolds News*:

> Like a lot of the rest of England, I suppose, I made a point of staying in on Monday to hear Edgar Wallace. I was disappointed because – if I may put it that way – he was too good. Mr Wallace was acting the part of a retired 'Super' who was yarning about his experiences ... Mr Wallace's impersonation was superb. He had the exact intonation and phraseology of a Superintendent, the slight same pomposity, the tendency to verbiage, and the same stock of would-be profound reflections.[7]

Wallace, with his easy, conversational manner and calming voice, was a natural for the wireless. Today, sadly, just one recording of Wallace's voice is thought to survive – a commercial recording, made on a 78rpm disc, on 25 September 1928, of Wallace reading 'The Man in the Ditch', a short six-and-a-half minute story which had not yet been published in printed form. 'I am going to tell you the story of the man in the ditch. I was returning from Cheltenham by road once wintry night and as I came through the village of Winthrone I very naturally slowed my car …' Wallace begins – and after only a few seconds the listener is hooked.

Wallace was on the airwaves and, in early 1931, he was also back in the editor's chair of a national newspaper, the *Sunday News*.[8] It was a struggling title and Wallace did his best to try to revive it. He wrote much of the copy himself, bringing back tipster 'Nick O'Lincoln' for the racing pages, and also contributed leaders, articles and theatrical gossip, plus puff pieces on British Lion film productions.

He also used the paper as a vehicle for fighting a rather unseemly feud with the theatre critic, Hannen Swaffer,[9] the man who had defended him against Lewis Goldflam, but who had later savaged a play Wallace had put on at Wyndham's.

The play in question was *Charles III*. Wallace had been renting Wyndham's for the sum of £408 a week. In 1930 he was offered a new seven-year lease at £200 a week, and decided to accept. He was confident that he could put on plays that would be profitable, either his own work or someone else's. He thought that in *Charles III*, a play about a runaway novice nun which had been a big hit in Germany under a different title, he was on to a winner. This was something very different for Wyndham's – a play adapted by Edgar Wallace, but one which had nothing to do with criminal gangs and detectives, and featured nuns instead of guns. Sadly, *Charles III* proved to be another flop.

Rupert Hart-Davis, whose wife Peggy Ashcroft played the novice, remembered Wallace being in a bad mood after the dress rehearsal: 'I was sitting in Peggy's dressing-room with her friend Diana Wynyard. Suddenly, the door burst open and in strode Wallace, wearing his hat, smoking a cigarette in a long holder, and with a face of thunder. "Those bloody nuns are no good; they'll have to go,"[10] he said fiercely.' Wallace's fears proved to be well-founded and the play was taken off after a week.

It was condemned by Hannen Swaffer, but the way Wallace responded – by launching a campaign against the critic in the *Sunday News* – was quite out of character. Perhaps Wallace pursued Swaffer because he could – previously, when his productions had been attacked, he hadn't been a national newspaper editor. Or perhaps it was because he was overworked, tired and with his nerves on edge, he had become too sensitive.

He certainly appears to have been genuinely hurt by Swaffer's criticism. He believed that Swaffer had been a pal, not a close one perhaps, but one who would never fire his most poisonous arrows in his direction. In 1929, in his foreword to the book *Hannen Swaffer's Who's Who*, he had written: 'I shall like all the unpleasant things he says about people I dislike, and hate his reference to my friends. I hope he has written nothing about me because we are, just now, on speaking terms.' Now though, the gloves were off:

> Swaff has made enemies because he hurts people [he wrote]. Of course he hurts people! If he didn't he wouldn't be noticed and that would be death to him. He has no acutely aggressive qualities; in real life he is rather a timid man. What appears in him to be senseless malignity is merely part of his defence, like the stink of the polecat. He has got himself regarded as the theatrical terrorist and he loves it.

In one piece, Wallace said that when he first knew Swaffer he hadn't a penny to his name, but now he was earning £10,000 a year. When Rupert Hart-Davis, who also knew Swaffer, said to Wallace 'Surely he can't be earning anything like that,' Wallace answered, 'Of course not, but it may provoke some awkward questions from the Inland Revenue.'[11]

The Sunday News also mocked Swaffer's belief in spiritualism, but Wallace's anti-Swaffer campaign ended in dramatic fashion when he claimed to experience a 'visitation' himself. He woke up early one morning to see a woman, whom he recognised as Swaffer's dead sister-in-law, sitting in the blue velvet chair in the corner of his study. The woman offered him condolences on recent gambling losses at Newmarket and then vanished into thin air. He also claimed to have heard, the night before, a voice in his room saying that he ought to be ashamed of himself for making fun of Swaffer over his views on spiritualism.

The experience was enough for Wallace, the great sceptic, to change his tune. 'I shall no longer sneer at spirits,' he pledged in an article which followed. Did he make up the story in order to give him an excuse to drop his campaign against Swaffer, or did he genuinely believe he had been contacted from 'the other side'? Margaret Lane says that he had heard rumours that Swaffer was planning to sue him for libel, and that the letters page of the *Sunday News* showed that his anti-spiritualist stance wasn't going down well with readers. She also comments that he refused to discuss his experience even with his own family.

Given the circumstances, it seems likely that Wallace had invented the whole thing, but another possibility is that he had been dreaming about Swaffer and had confused his dreams with reality, at least in relation to the ghostly apparition. It might be significant that during the week in question he had been very tired following a heavy attack of bronchitis, and was on medication.

Ghosts or no ghosts, Wallace was determined once again to bounce back from a West End flop. He would go back to writing his own plays for Wyndham's, but unfortunately his next effort, a comedy thriller called *The Old Man*[12] only lasted ten weeks in London, before going out on tour. Most people would, by now, have grown disillusioned with the theatre, but Wallace, to his enormous credit, refused to be downhearted. He decided to return to the type of play he did best – a good, old-fashioned thriller. 'I am going back to playing unadulterated English drama on *The Ringer* lines,' he informed *Sunday News* readers.

The Case of the Frightened Lady was a welcome return to form, and showed that Edgar Wallace, the playwright, had not lost his touch. Rehearsals were enjoyable, with the lead roles played by Wallace regulars Cathleen Nesbitt, Emlyn Williams, who had starred in *On the Spot,* and Gordon Harker. The play concerned mysterious goings on at Mark's Priory, home to the aristocratic Lebanon family. It had all the classic Wallace ingredients, an old dark house, secret passages, a heroine in mortal danger, an idiosyncratic and rather comical policeman (a part Wallace wrote specifically for Harker) and a cleverly concealed serial killer whose identity is not revealed until the very last scene. It was scary, wildly entertaining and also, with its unsympathetic portrayal of the upper-class Lebanons, subversive – further evidence that Wallace was not the complacent conservative that some of his critics accused him of being.

The Case of The Frightened Lady opened at Wyndham's on 18 August 1931, and was well received by audiences and critics alike, running for 188 performances in the West End. Edgar Wallace had another theatrical hit on his hands, his biggest since *The Terror, a*nd not long after the opening night of *The Case of the Frightened Lady*, there was more exciting news – an offer of two months' employment as a scriptwriter in Hollywood.

The offer from Hollywood was very tempting. RKO studios had offered him £600 a week for a two-month contract, with the option of a further two months at a higher salary. Should he go or should he stay? Wallace had no doubt that he'd be able to produce good work in Hollywood, and that his contract would be extended. He had also long expressed a desire to go to Hollywood, by now firmly established as the centre of the global film industry. The experience he gained there would be invaluable when he came back to British Lion. So what was holding him back?

Firstly, there were ties of family. Did he really want to leave his family for as long as three months? Jim, busy with her role as Wallace's theatrical manager, would not be able to go with him, and neither would his children. There were also concerns over Jim's health and Wallace was worried that she might have to have what she described as a 'serious operation'.[13] Then there was the upheaval. Wallace in his later years had become more and more of a home bird, he loved his house at Chalklands and had started to resent time spent away from it.

He was also feeling tired; his health, like Jim's, was not good, and if anything he desired rest, not another demanding assignment. Wallace couldn't make his mind up. He decided to take a holiday to give him time to think things over. 'I'm going to Rome on Thursday to have a complete rest,' he told a reporter. 'I shall also visit Naples – just in case. Last week, I had a touch of bronchitis, and I said to myself, 'I must see Naples before I die.' Little did Wallace know that he only had a few months to live and that he would not see Naples before he died. He didn't have much of a rest in Rome, and spent his time seeing all the sights, and confounding the tour guide with his extensive knowledge. Wallace encountered a problem on the trip because the hotels were reluctant to change his sterling into Lira, following Britain's fall from the Gold Standard, but he was still able to buy his daughter Penny a plaque of Raphael's *Madonna of the Chair*, his favourite painting. He wrote to Jim from Rome:

> This American trip is, of course, dependent upon "other things being equal" – upon you and your health for one thing and the nature of the contract for another. I am feeling quite well and bright and really have had a wonderful week. I shall hate going away to Hollywood but haven't gone yet.

In the end Wallace decided to postpone the decision on going to America until after the forthcoming general election. The year of 1931 was a dramatic one in British politics: the Labour government was split on how to deal with the economic crisis and in August, Prime Minister Ramsay Macdonald effectively betrayed his comrades by deciding to form a cross-party national government. Liberals, led by Sir Herbert Samuel, served in the new government, but the Lloyd George faction opposed it.

A general election was scheduled for 27 October. On 11 October, Wallace telegraphed Lloyd George, confirming his candidature. 'I am fighting Blackpool as a plain Lloyd George Liberal and am going to win it from the food-taxers. I feel that nobody is more competent to expose this national confidence trick which is gulling the country than one who has made a study of this form of crime.' Lloyd George replied, gratefully accepting Wallace's support and saying that there had never been a time when Liberalism stood more in need of fighting men and not funks.

Wallace travelled north in mid-October full of hope. His enthusiasm was not shared by Jim, however. Politics was of even less interest to her than to her husband. She had no ambition to be an MP's wife and accompany him on official duties. The one occasion she had spoken at an election meeting in

Aylesbury she had been terrified, and had cried hysterically in the car on the way back home.

Wallace set up base in Blackpool at the seafront hotel, Metropole. 'The unique profile, the long cigarette holder, the yellow Rolls; these became overnight the icons of a cult,' wrote Henry Hodgkinson, 'The legends spread, above all, of an unruffled, soft-spoken hero in silk dressing gown, who, in the most luxurious suite of the Hotel Metropole, dictated campaign literature out of one corner of his mouth and novels out of the other.'[14]

Wallace believed that his fame would win the day. He was, however, up against a number of obstacles. Firstly, Blackpool was not a traditional Liberal seat. The Liberals had won it in 1923, but had lost it again to the Conservatives one year later. The trouble for Wallace was that it wouldn't be working-class holidaymakers and seaside promenaders who would be voting in the election, but Conservative-leaning hotel and bed and breakfast owners.

Secondly, there were Wallace's own views. He didn't have many strong political beliefs, but support for free trade was one of them. The Conservatives had lost the 1923 general election on the subject of tariffs, but by 1931 the tide had turned and many believed that introducing some measure of protectionism was the only way to save declining British industries.

Thirdly, there was Wallace's candour. If a professional politician had been asked at a public meeting what he would do to revive the cotton industry, he would have at least attempted to show he had an answer. Wallace simply said that he didn't know, and that it was a subject he would have to study more closely.

Throughout his campaign, Wallace refused to shape his comments to this audience. Addressing members of the Fleetwood Congregational Church he declared: 'I am a sinner. I go to racecourse and mix with coarse men who use coarse language. I make money out of the theatre and lose money in it.' At another church meeting he admitted he was 'not a church member' and had 'never give a bob to a church in my life'. It was hardly the most tactful thing to say, yet at the same time we can only admire Wallace's honesty, and wish that our politicians today were are as frank.

As he had done in Buckinghamshire, Wallace set up a newspaper – the bi-weekly *Wallace's Blackpool Banner* – to boost his campaign. Organisation of it was mainly down to Robert Curtis who had accompanied Wallace to Blackpool to help with the election. Also assisting him was a young newspaper reporter called Hugh Cudlipp, who later became a Fleet Street legend himself.[15] Cudlipp witnessed Wallace's frustrations at first hand: 'Edgar Wallace knew absolutely nothing about politics and even less about the machinery of politics. The hecklers gave him hell – he was only there for a fortnight and I have never seen a more unhappy man for a consistent period – he was in a constant state of fury – a smouldering rage I think is the right way to describe it.'[16]

Wallace probably found corresponding to prospective constituents more enjoyable than addressing fractious public meetings. He was asked by a Mr Gaskell of Cleveleys what his view was on the cuts in the salaries and wages of public employees which had been imposed by the national government. 'In view of the increased cost of living, I think the cuts suffered by the police, the civil service and the teachers must be considerably modified,' he replied, showing once again his concern for the plight of ordinary people.

By the time polling day arrived, Wallace was exhausted. He had put everything into his campaign and now it was up to the electors of Blackpool. Just after 1 a.m. on the morning of 28 October 1931, the returning officer announced the result. Wallace, Richard Horatio Edgar, had polled 19,524 votes. His National Conservative opponent, Captain Clifford Charles Alan Lawrence Erskine-Bolst, had got 53,010 votes.

The Tories had held Blackpool with a big majority, but the result was not as bad as it first appeared, bearing in mind the circumstances. The national government had been widely promoted in the media as the only way Britain could be saved from further economic crisis. Anyone who stood against National candidates had a very hard job in October 1931, and the truth was that it would have taken a miracle for Wallace to win the seat, even allowing for his celebrity status. 'Having regard to the cyclonic conditions, your achievement was a remarkable one,' Lloyd George wrote in a letter to him on 6 November. 'My majority was not swept away because I was sheltered by very formidable mountain barriers which broke the force of the hurricane, but you stood in the open of the tornado beating down upon you, and you managed not merely to face it out, but to rally 20,000 men to your banner.'

However, in the early hours of the morning following his defeat, it was hard for Wallace to be philosophical about what had happened. He sat up drinking champagne and listening to the radio broadcast of the election results, cursing the national government. The next morning he was up early to pack his bags and prepared to leave town. His unhappy stay in Blackpool was to have no happy ending. 'Edgar Wallace shook my hand and prepared to enter the famous Yellow Rolls-Royce,' remembered Cudlipp; 'as the car started slowly off he turned down the window and waved to the crowd. A voice said "Goodbye and good riddance". Wallace unfortunately heard this, ordered the car to swerve around in the road, re-entered the scene, stepped among the crowd and said "Who said that?" There was no reply. And Wallace said, "I thought so, a coward". He went back into the Rolls and swept off the station at high speed and that was the last that Blackpool ever saw of Edgar Wallace.'[17]

28

EDGAR GOES TO HOLLYWOOD

I get on terribly well with these executive people, and I believe they are awfully pleased with me. If I get this big story over it will be grand.

Edgar Wallace, *My Hollywood Diary,* 1932

The defeat at Blackpool was a crushing blow to Wallace's pride. 'The result of that election was, I think, the bitterest disappointment Edgar ever had,' wrote Jim. Wallace now had no real excuse not to accept the offer from RKO Pictures.

So he cabled his acceptance to the offer, checking first that British Lion, whom he was under contract to, had no objection. However, a week later he had changed his mind again. He went to see Sam Smith, managing director of British Lion to ask him to cable to Hollywood to say that he was under exclusive contract to the studio, and that he could not be released. A few days later, and Wallace changed his mind yet again, deciding that he must go to Hollywood. Smith was asked to send another telegram, rescinding the first.

Why did Wallace, a man known for his decisiveness, find it so hard to make his mind up on whether to go to America? His age and health no doubt played their part; ten years earlier and he would have jumped at the chance. As we have already seen, he also had worries about Jim's health. In addition there was his ever-growing jealousy of Jim too – he may have entertained fears that in his absence she would fall in love with another man. In the end though, it was the money which proved decisive. His debts were growing all the time and he owed around £20,000 to the Inland Revenue. In the circumstances, a two-month contract at £600, plus the very real possibility of further work to come, was too good to turn down. Robert Curtis recalled the day Wallace finally made up his mind: 'One morning he called me into his study. "Bob, we've got to go. I'm not exactly broke but I owe a lot of money and it's time I squared things up. We'll make eight thousand pounds in the next four months and come back with money in the bank".'

The night before he was due to sail to America, Wallace's yellow Rolls-Royce was seen in Brockley, outside the house of Clara Freeman, his foster sister. Whether he had a premonition that he would never return alive from America, we don't know, but he certainly thought it was important to say goodbye.

Edgar Wallace set sail for America on the cruise ship *Empress Of Britain* with Robert Curtis and his valet, Robert Downs, on Saturday 21 November 1931. It was a grey and gloomy day. Pat and Bryan went to Southampton to see their father off. Stewards handed out paper streamers among the passengers and Wallace took his, and wrote on the end of it in pen 'Goodbye, Edgar Wallace' before throwing it overboard. 'It is rather sad going away – sadder than anybody knows – and more unreal than any sailing I have ever made,' he wrote to Jim.[1]

In theory, the six days of the voyage gave him a great chance to unwind. But although he didn't do much work on the first three days, he was soon back in harness. 'Wallace ... assured me that, with the exception of five articles, the opening instalment of a serial story and the rough draft of a scenario, which he had in mind, he could spend the six days in absolute idleness!' wrote Curtis. Already, before he had left, Sir Gerald du Maurier had agreed to produce Wallace's new play *The Green Pack* at Wyndham's. Once on board, Wallace got down to revising it. 'My intention when I started was to do at least sufficient work to pay for my passage and I think I have just about done that,' he told Jim, 'My record since last Monday week ... is one novel-length story, one 20,000 word story, one three-act play [*The Green Pack*], one scenario written, sixteen articles, one broadcast, there is something else I can't remember.'

On Friday, 27 November 1931, six days after departure, the *Empress of Britain* arrived in American waters. 'There was the usual long delay at quarantine ... there was also the inevitable incursion of reporters and photographers, who lined up on the deck, but this time they had to shoot in the dark with flash-lamps,' Wallace recorded. He gave interviews to about thirty journalists, his caused not helped by a troubling sore throat.

It was around 7.30 p.m. when the ship finally berthed and Edgar was met by his agent Carl Brandt. Even at this stage, Wallace had not given up hope of making a quick return to his family. His RKO contract was due to be signed in New York, but in case the deal fell through at the last minute he had already made plans to come back on the *Empress of Britain*, sailing to Madeira, Gibraltar and Monte Carlo, before travelling to Caux where he would be reunited with Jim for Christmas.

Wallace sat up late discussing projects with Carl Brandt, his other American agent Harold Freedman, and his old friend the actor Nigel Bruce, who had moved to America. 'Carl thinks he can sell *The Frightened Lady* but that will mean holding up the English publication … He also thinks I can get a big sale with the *Saturday Evening Post* … I told them the story of *The Green Pack* and they were enthralled.'

The next morning at 7.30 a.m. he put through a transatlantic call to his wife. At breakfast, he received a wire from Jim about the big race in England that day, the Manchester November Handicap. After breakfast it was time to 'battle out' the contract with the lawyer from RKO. Wallace duly signed up – announcing the deal to be 'satisfactory' and told Jim he would be leaving on Tuesday to go to Chicago, and after that to the 'woolly West'.

Wallace had little time to relax in New York: 'I have a terrific lot of work to do to keep my articles going. By the way, I am doing three articles for the *Daily Mail* on Hollywood.' On Sunday morning, Nigel Bruce and fellow actor Leslie Banks, who had starred in the original stage version of *The Ringer*, joined Wallace for breakfast. 'Leslie is terribly nice. He is looking after Nigel like a father and I must say Nigel is devoted to him,' wrote Wallace. On Monday, Wallace met up with actress friend, Heather Thatcher, who told him that Hollywood was 'full of scandal, the directors wives have nothing to do except sit around and tell stories,' he told Jim.

On Tuesday, Wallace boarded the train to Chicago. He spent the journey working, despite still nursing a cold. Just six hours out of New York, and Wallace had already completed three articles. He sent Jim his impressions of the journey from Chicago to California. He thought the Mississippi was 'quite a thrill. It was almost as imposing as the Congo, though naturally the vegetation was not green but a shade of cinnamon brown.' He thought Missouri 'much more prosperous-looking and better organised than the state of Illinois, or even, if truth be told the state of New York.'

As the train approached Las Vegas he wrote, 'In many ways the country strongly resembles South Africa; the same, vast rolling pampas with mountains on the skyline, and the same flat-topped hills.' When he finally arrived in Los Angeles, he was met by more reporters and posed for photographs on the steps of the train, with his trademark cigarette holder.

He was not overawed by his first sight of Hollywood. 'Hollywood seems to consist of filling stations, fruit markets and drug stores. I suppose we passed forty filling stations on our way here. In fact my first impressions are not exceptionally favourable.'

Wallace was keen to hit the ground running, and start work straight away. The following day – a Saturday – he arrived at 10 a.m. at the RKO studios. The executives were surprised to see him: 'They had imagined that no Englishman works on a Saturday or Sunday, and that he would not dream of visiting the studios until the Monday morning,' recalled Robert Curtis.

Wallace met with the studio chiefs, including the 'big noise' producer David O. Selznick, and was given a secretary and his own room. He was delighted to hear that he only had to ring up the transportation department to get a car whenever he wanted one. He was told that the studio wanted him to write a 'horror picture'. Wallace returned back to his base, the Beverly Wilshire Hotel, determined to show Selznick and his associates what he could do.

'All right,' he said to Curtis, 'You're not going to see much of Hollywood this weekend. We're going to turn in a complete story by Monday morning.' Wallace and Curtis worked throughout the rest of Saturday and Sunday, and on Monday morning a complete story was delivered to the studios. 'There you are,' said Wallace as he handed it to RKO executive and director Merian C. Cooper, 'If that isn't what you want, I'll get another one done for you in a day or two.' The Edgar Wallace Fiction Factory had arrived in Hollywood.

Edgar was off to a flying start, but it wasn't long before he realised that the Beverly Wilshire had one serious drawback which would affect his productivity. As we know, there were only two things that Wallace needed in order to work at his usual breakneck pace – an endless supply of cigarettes, and tea. The former were no problem, but the latter was. He simply could not get a decent brew at the Beverly Wilshire. 'The faithful Robert had tried to remedy this deficiency by going down to the service pantry and making it himself, but as Edgar demanded tea at all hours of the day and night this unorthodox practice was soon severely discouraged,' records Lane.[2]

Wallace decided to leave the hotel and rent a house, where he would feel more at home and could organise his own tea-making. He found what he thought was the ideal property – No. 716 North Maple Drive, Beverly Hills, at a rent of $350 a month – and moved in along with Robert Curtis, his valet Robert Downs, a Japanese gardener and a cook.

Even though his tea problem was now sorted, Wallace was still homesick and greatly missed Jim and his children. Christmas was fast approaching, and for the first time in many years he wouldn't be spending it with his family at Caux. He spent a small fortune on transatlantic telephone calls (the cost was around £20 for nine minutes) to keep in touch with Jim. On Christmas Day he woke up at 6 a.m. and found it to be raining heavily. It set the tone for the rest of the day. 'It was so dismal that I didn't feel like working,' Edgar told Jim.

He had a visit from Merian C. Cooper: 'We talked over the big animal play we are going to write – or rather I am going to write and he is going to direct. He has just had an approval from New York, and I am going to turn him out a scenario.' The 'big animal play' was to be *King Kong*.

Later, Wallace went over to his friend Guy Bolton's for a cocktail, before returning home for a roast turkey and cranberry sauce Christmas dinner. 'We opened a bottle of champagne at dinner, but it would have taken a dozen to relieve the deep depression centred off North Maple Drive,' Robert Curtis wrote in a letter to his wife, 'Edgar wouldn't admit to being thoroughly bored, although I know he was.'

With Christmas over, Wallace got down to work. He had already impressed RKO and other studios too, with his output. 'Edgar Wallace's speed as a writer is well known, but Hollywood is still gasping with the scenario he brought in completely finished in one day. "If this won't do," he had scrawled across the bottom, "I'll write you another one tomorrow." Since the average time required by local scenario writer is five weeks to turn out a pearl of thought, no wonder there is consternation in the ranks,' reported the *Motion Picture Herald*.

Wallace, though, was disappointed in the way his scenarios, which he had worked so hard on, just disappeared, and said of Hollywood that 'in some ways it is rather like living in a madhouse'. He confided, in December, to Jim that he hoped that the scenario that he was working on would be made into a film with a major star – he envisaged Constance Bennett – and that he would be asked to direct it himself. 'That's my secret ambition and I whisper it into your ear so that I may have all the sympathy if it doesn't come off.' Alas, it didn't come off, but Wallace still had more than enough work to keep him busy.

Given his commitments, the last news he wanted to hear was that Sir Gerald du Maurier believed that significant changes were required for *The Green Pack,* which was now in rehearsal at Wyndham's. Wallace fired off an angry telegram suggesting that he would rather abandon the whole project than rewrite the play, but when he had calmed down he agreed to make changes. On 30 December, Wallace went to the RKO studio for further discussions on his 'big animal play'. He also saw how the giant ape would be portrayed on stage. 'I went into the animation room and watched the preparation of the giant monkey … Its skeleton and framework are complete.' Wallace worked at his usual pace and completed his scenario for 'Kong' on 5 January 1932.

There was a pleasurable diversion from writing the following week-end when Wallace, with his friends Guy Bolton and Virginia Bedford, a young actress Joan Carr, and his two jockey pals Michael Beary and Steven Donoghue, headed for a weekend jaunt to Agua Caliente, Mexico, where there was both a racetrack and a casino.

When he reached his hotel, Edgar sent this charming rhyme to Penny, who was then at Caux:

My dearest dear, I'd have you know
I'm writing this from Mexico
When I arrived at seven twenty
At Agua (Ogwa) Caliente
And to say that you too may be able
To say 'I've been there' here's a label
To stick upon your little trunk,
Forgive this little bit of bunk,
The ride was long but quite amusing
(What grown up language I'm using!)

Steve Donoghue and Michael Beary
Are staying here – the latter weary.
Well, I must finish – hope you're well
And that your tummy's life a bell
(By which I hope that it is sound
And not loud noises rumbling round).
Daddy with love.
Two extra labels – one for Mike.

The Saturday was to be one of Wallace's most enjoyable days ever at the races; to his great delight he learnt that the second most important race on the card had been called 'The Edgar Wallace Stakes'. He also could do little wrong with his bets, backing five winners and winning the equivalent of £80. Wallace travelled back across the border in high spirits. Little did he know that it was the last time that he would ever go racing, but at least, at the very end, the sport which he had loved so much had been kind to him.

29

THE FINAL CHAPTER

Kong opens his eyes, picks the girl up, holds her to his breast like a doll, closes his eyes and drops his head.

Edgar Wallace, 'Kong', final lines of his scenario

After weeks of uncertainty, on 3 February 1932 Wallace finally learnt that his contract with RKO would be renewed. He looked forward to Jim's visit in the spring – he promised her a wonderful holiday, and told her of his plans to rent a large house and transport the entire family to Hollywood for the following winter. He was now really beginning to enjoy his time in America. He had quite a large circle of friends, and was always delighted to meet the top stars of the day. He was flattered that, when he was introduced to the actress Norma Shearer, she exclaimed, 'I don't believe it!' 'She said she had heard so much about me but never dreamt we should meet,' he told Jim.

The Green Pack was due to open on 9 February at Wyndham's. Wallace obviously couldn't be there, but he had hit on a great idea as to how he could establish personal contact with the audience. He would broadcast to the theatre from Hollywood before the rising of the curtain. The broadcast never happened, for on the night *The Green Pack* opened, its author was fighting for his life.

It all started with Wallace making the mistake of sleeping with the windows open on a cold, wet and windy night. 'I woke at five, coughing, due to the very strong east wind that blew in on me,' he wrote on 3 February. The following day he reported that he had a 'slight sore throat', which soon developed into a cold. A couple of days' rest would surely have sorted things out, but for Wallace there was no let-up in his busy schedule.

On 6 February he held his own *Green Pack* party. His guests met at Wallace's for cocktails, and then went on to the Embassy Club. The party lasted until around 2.30 a.m. and, despite it being another cold night, Wallace foolishly carried his overcoat home instead of wearing it. The next morning, a Sunday, was spent writing letters. He started to complain about having a headache, saying it was the worst he had ever had, and sent his valet to the local drug store to buy some medicine. Wallace dosed up, and spent much of the afternoon resting in his bedroom.

According to an account of Steve Donoghue, written in 1938, Wallace, instead of going to bed that evening, carried on working, despite his worsening fever. Donoghue's source was 'an American girl' – presumably Anne McEwen – whom Wallace had taken on as a secretary, and mentioned earlier in his Hollywood diary:

> This American girl noticed that he kept taking these aspirins thinking that he was not counting the number he was consuming or that in his abnormal state he was not really clear as to what he was doing; she mentioned to him that he had taken an enormous number throughout the evening and night. He smiled at her and told her he was used to them and put two more into his next cup.[1]

Donoghue says that Jim telephoned from England and Wallace spoke to her, but that he was not talking sense. Wallace, having taken twenty-seven aspirins, collapsed and the doctors could not save him.

However, the version of events according to Margaret Lane was rather different. Wallace didn't go to bed early on the evening of 8 February, not because he was working, but because he had invited a young actress, with whom he had become besotted, round to dinner that evening. Lane doesn't name the lady concerned, but does say that 'he had said little of this new acquaintance in his letters to Jim' and that 'she had dined at his house several times in the company of friends'.[2] If we hold Lane's account to be accurate, then who was the mystery actress?

From a close reading of Wallace's *My Hollywood Diary*, by far the most likely 'suspect' was a glamorous young lady called Sari Maritza[3] who was 21 at the time, and who Wallace admitted to liking, dining with and taking home to her 'artistic apartment' after a party one evening. On 6 February 1932, a *Pittsburgh Post-Gazette* feature on Ms Maritza informed readers: 'She loves backless dresses with trains. She always wears evening sandals without toes. She never drinks and when smoking always uses a long, black holder given to her by Edgar Wallace, English novelist'.

It was an infatuation which would have probably worn off as soon as his beloved Jim arrived in Hollywood; however, it was one which would have disastrous consequences for Wallace. The actress telephoned at around 5 p.m. to cancel, but said that she would call to Edgar's house after dinner. Wallace got up and ate his dinner, combining the food with large amounts of aspirin and numerous cigarettes.

Despite his headache worsening he stayed up, waiting for his lady friend to arrive. At eleven he told Robert he was going to bed, but asked him to wake him up if anyone called. At midnight, Robert went round to lock the doors and windows of the house and was shocked to see his master, wearing his silk dressing gown pacing up and down in the street outside, apparently looking out for a car. 'He immediately offered to bring his master's overcoat, since the night was extremely cold; but Edgar answered him abruptly, saying that it was too hot already, and refusing the offer of the coat,' says Lane.[4]

The next morning, when Robert went into his master's room, he found that he was seriously ill. He hurriedly called a doctor. Meanwhile, a prear-ranged telephone call to Jim in London was due to be put through. Curtis, knowing that Edgar was too ill to talk, spoke to Jim himself and told her that her husband had a headache and would try and call her later. 'I felt instinc-tively that something was very wrong,' Jim later admitted, 'I knew that Edgar would never book a call to me from six thousand miles and allow a headache to stand in the way of his talking to me.' An agitated Jim then sent her hus-band a cable, before heading off to Wyndham's for a final dress rehearsal.

By the time that Dr Fishbaugh, a well-known Hollywood physician, had finally arrived Wallace had slipped into a coma. He examined the patient and diagnosed sugar diabetes. Curtis replied to Jim's cable thus: 'Mr Wallace has headache and slight temperature. Sleeping now. Will cable doctor's report immediately I get it. Feel sure nothing to worry about.'

But Wallace's condition continued to worsen throughout the day, and by mid-afternoon double pneumonia had set in. He was then given oxygen, and regained consciousness. On waking, he asked if he was going to die and pleaded that Jim be informed that he was seriously ill. The following morning Jim received another cable from Curtis: 'Mr Wallace critically ill pneumo-nia.' A few hours later he cabled again, 'Condition unchanged wants you sail Bremen Friday. Will keep you informed. Curtis.' Jim prepared to sail the fol-lowing day from Southampton.

Meanwhile, theatregoers arriving at Wyndham's for the opening night of *The Green Pack* were met with newspaper contents bills at the entrance which proclaimed 'EDGAR WALLACE GRAVELY ILL'. Among the famous people in the audience that night were the retail millionaire Mr Selfridge, Prince Ali Khan and the Hon. Mrs Esmond Harmsworth, wife of the propri-etor of the *Daily Mail*. Ironically, in the theatre programme, Wallace, who was lying on his deathbed 6,000 miles away, appeared in an advertisement for du Maurier cigarettes, described as:

… The healthiest cigarette you can smoke. Edgar Wallace discovers the clue to throat safety and enjoys sixty du Mauriers in one day. He writes: 'The du

Maurier is the perfect Virginia cigarette and the filter tip draws absolutely freely. It has a perfect flavour and is a suave smoke. I smoked 60 of them yesterday with the greatest leisure.[5]

Wallace's friends waited nervously for the latest news. Actor Emlyn Williams, who had appeared in several Wallace plays, was working at a theatre close to Wyndham's, 'We all gathered together absolutely spontaneously – people who had worked with him and the cast of *The Green Pack*, in a bar. I realised that we were like children who were gathering around to wait for news of father.'[6]

At the end of the play, Jim telephoned Curtis. He told her that her husband was now in a coma with periods of consciousness. When awake, Wallace seemed to think that if only he could put on his dressing gown and slippers and have a cup of tea all would be well again. The doctor allowed Robert to make him some tea.

Jim, meanwhile, had made it on to the *Majestic*. Though ill himself and in a nursing home, Prime Minister Ramsay Macdonald sent a telegram to Jim before her departure, expressing his hope for her husband's recovery. The boat had just pulled out of Southampton on 10 February, when Jim received another telegram from Curtis. It simply read 'Mister Wallace passed away peacefully four forty-five a.m.'

Wallace's valet Robert Downs, Robert Curtis, and his actor friend Walter Huston and his wife had been in the sitting room downstairs, grouped around Wallace's desk, when the doctor told them the devastating news. 'The only thing he said during the time that I was at the house Tuesday morning was to ask Robert for a cup of tea,' Huston wrote in a letter to Bryan Wallace. 'He made no remarks to anyone … He understood on Tuesday morning before he went into a complete coma that Mrs Wallace was coming, and signified merely by nodding his head.'

30

EDGAR WALLACE LIVES ON

He was a man who has warmed both hands in the fires of life and got slightly scorched.

Edgar Wallace, *Sergeant Sir Peter*, 1932

Emlyn Williams remembered how shocked he was when he first heard the news of Wallace's death:

I came out of rehearsal and saw a poster saying 'EDGAR WALLACE DEAD' I was stunned and I looked at people – literally you could call them 'the man in the street' and they were looking at the poster as I had. To me it was like seeing a great steam engine, which had been stoked with wonderful fire and sparking away for years, on its side and empty and wheel going round with nothing working. You realised that it was over.[1]

In the *Daily Mail*, Sir Gerald du Maurier described Wallace's death as 'a nightmare experience' for the cast of *The Green Pack*.

Others, too, were stunned by the news. '"Old Edgar Wallace is dead!" "Edgar Wallace – dead? No! Why he was made of iron." It ran around Fleet Street yesterday; shouted from the placards. Wallace was one of the best reporters who ever trod Fleet Street; and reporters don't die. Not like this,' wrote 'A Reporter' in the *News Chronicle*.

Newspapers and journals were fulsome in their tributes: 'For some years the name of Edgar Wallace has been one of the few which everybody in England knows and a synonym for success. Abroad his fame has become as nearly universal's as any man's,' said the *Daily Telegraph*. The *Daily Mail* described their former reporter as the 'man who drove care from millions. Few men of world-wide fame will be so universally mourned as Mr Edgar Wallace. Novelist, playwright, film scenario writer, and racehorse owner – he was a man whose very name came to stand for a particular type of enterprise and energy.'

'The popularity of Edgar Wallace was a proof of the sound taste of our people, for he was read by everybody from bishops to barmen. He wrote plain, clear English, and he had far more literary skill than most people realise,' said the *Spectator*.

'The world has lost a great man,' wrote Francis D. Grierson in the March 1932 edition of *The Bookman*, 'For Wallace was great – not merely because he wrote some one hundred and fifty novels and thirty plays, and film scenarios, pen pictures and newspaper articles by the score; but because of the indomitable spirit that made a little newsboy into one of the most amazing figures of his generation and a very fine gentlemen withal'.

Morning Post editor H.A. Gwynne, the man who had given Wallace his first big break by appointing him a Reuter's correspondent in South Africa thirty-three years earlier, praised Wallace's human qualities: 'Edgar Wallace was a genial-hearted, kindly man, always on the lookout for opportunities of helping dogs over stiles. He was a good friend, and I doubt whether he ever made an enemy.'

Three of Wallace's children, Pat, Michael and Penny, were staying at Caux when their father died, and Bill Linnit, the manager of Wyndham's, had the unenviable task of relaying the news, though the *Daily Mail* revealed that Penny would not be told until she saw her mother.

Meanwhile, Jim was involved in a drama of her own when the *Majestic* was caught in a blizzard off Cherbourg which lasted for thirteen hours. There was nearly a double tragedy, when the tender taking her and other passengers ashore was hit by a German liner during the gale. The tender managed to make it ashore, and Jim, unsurprisingly, given her ordeal over the past forty-eight hours, was described as being 'utterly worn out by grief and fatigue'.

Meanwhile, dressed in his favourite suit, and wearing the gold cufflinks that Jim had given him, her husband was lying in state in a little memorial chapel in Los Angeles.

Then the man who had travelled the globe in search of excitement and adventure made his last journey. Ivor Novello, the Welsh songwriter and actor, who had just finished writing the dialogue for *Tarzan the Ape Man* for MGM, was returning across the United States by train to catch the boat home from New York. A porter told him that a fellow British writer was on the same train. 'Oh, ask him if he'd like to have a drink with me,' said Novello. 'That's gonna be kinda difficult boss,' replied the porter. 'He's in the box car in the coffin.'[2] It was Edgar Wallace, going home for the last time. His coffin was carried on to SS *Berengaria* draped with a Union Jack and when the ship sailed into Southampton Water, her flag was lowered to half-mast. The bells of Fleet Street tolled for one of its legends, and the lights went out at Wyndham's.

In accordance with his wishes, Wallace was buried in the churchyard at Little Marlow, which he could see from his windows at Chalklands. His funeral was attended by celebrities of stage and turf, including the colourful racecourse tipster, Prince 'I Gotta Horse' Monolulu, who placed a wreath with the words: 'On the Turf and under it, all men are equal.'

A memorial service was also held at St Bride's Church in Fleet Street.

In his will, Wallace left a sum of £2,000 to Jim, whom he appointed his executor and trustee, and £1,000 to each of his children, but when details of his estate were published there was a shock for all concerned – he had assets of £18,000, but debts of around £140,000, a large enough sum today but a huge one for 1932. Almost everything had to be sold: the Rolls-Royces, the house at Chalklands and the racehorses. The racehorses fetched only £3,800 – one of them went for a measly £10.

Jim and Penny moved into a three-bedroom flat in Kensington. Despite her radically changed circumstances, Jim refused to criticise her husband for his profligacy. 'I am rich because Edgar, by his superlative goodness, engendered in others a genuine love for everything and everybody. If only those who criticise him for leaving his wife and children worse than penniless realised the value of his bequest to us, they would perhaps curb their tongues,' she said. In just two years, the royalties from Wallace's work had cleared all the debts. 'He died broke, and his ghost picked up the royalties and laughed,' mused James Cameron.

Alas, Jim was not there to see it. Devastated by her husband's death, she became stricken with cancer in late 1932 and died aged just 36, in April 1933. A wreath from her mother, at her Kensington burial, read: 'To the sweetest girl.' Poor Penny Wallace had lost both her parents before she had reached her 10th birthday.

In the spring of 1933 *King Kong*, billed on posters as 'Edgar Wallace's last story', opened in cinemas in the UK. However, Wallace literally did not get the credit he deserved for the part he had played in the production of the picture. In his *Hollywood Diary* on 6 January 1932, he had written:

> If this big film gets over that Cooper is doing it's going to make a big difference to me, for although I am not really responsible for the success of the picture, and really can't be since the ideas were Cooper's, I shall get all the credit for authorship and invention which rightly belongs to him.

But that was Wallace being modest – and in the end, his contribution was minimised, not exaggerated.

The opening titles said that the film came 'From an idea conceived by Edgar Wallace and Merian C. Cooper', but the screenplay was credited to

James Creelman and Ruth Rose – aka Mrs Merian Cooper. Cooper later said of Wallace, 'Not one single scene, nor line of dialogue in *King Kong* was contributed by him.' Fortunately, a copy of Wallace's 110-page scenario exists which gives the lie to that assertion. Although the first half of the film does differ from Wallace's original script, the second half follows it quite faithfully, including the dramatic New York finale. It's Wallace who has Kong climbing to the top of the Empire State Building and catching the wing of an aeroplane which comes too close – a scene that has become part of film folklore; and it's Wallace who develops the beauty-and-the-beast theme that gives the story such pathos. The attempt to play down Wallace's contribution to a twentieth-century cinematic masterpiece after his death was shameful, though thankfully now the record has been set straight.[3]

There were no statues of Wallace erected, but in 1934 a plaque was put up in his memory in Ludgate Circus in London, over the spot where he sold newspapers as a boy. 'He knew wealth and poverty, yet had walked with kings and kept his bearing. Of his talents he gave lavishly to authorship – but to Fleet Street he gave his heart,' the inscription reads.[4]

For the decades which followed his untimely demise, the popularity of Edgar Wallace showed no signs of abating. New generations of readers across the world continued to be enthralled by his stories. In 1958 the *Sunday Express* reported 'a boom in the sale of Edgar Wallace crime novels' and ¼ million copies had been sold in 1957 alone, with sales still going up.

In 1965, it was claimed that sales of Wallace's work had topped 50 million, with his books translated into twenty-eight languages.

In 1977, Wallace expert W.O.G. Lofts wrote:

> Hodder & Stoughton's, Edgar Wallace's foremost publisher estimated some years ago that they had printed no less than 28 million copies of his books. Taking into account his other twenty-one publishers, books printed in their millions in America – usually under other titles – together with translations into dozens of foreign languages Germany alone being reputed to be bigger in sales than the USA, it would be no exaggeration today that the total sales of his books must have exceeded over 100 millions.[5]

In Germany alone, Goldmann Verlag sold over 43 million Wallace books between 1926–1982, amounting to nearly 800,000 a year.[6]

In 1990, it was claimed by John Hogan, organiser of the Edgar Wallace Society, that total sales of Wallace's work had exceeded 200 million.[7]

Wallace's work dominated other mediums too. By 1973, over 200 films had been made from his material, making him one of the most filmed authors of all time. Among the most famous was the Korda brothers' 1935 *Sanders of the River*, with Paul Robeson as Bosambo and Leslie Banks as Commissioner Sanders.[8] The German series of films, by Rialto Films, which began with *Der Frosch mit der Maske* (based on *The Fellowship of the Frog*) in 1959, and starring the likes of Gert Fröbe and Klaus Kinski, proved hugely popular. In 1986 a showing of *Der Grüne Bogenschütze* (*The Green Archer*) on German television was watched by 17.07 million people.

In Italy, Wallace's works also had cult status as 'giallo' novels[9] while Wallace's son, Bryan, collaborated in the early 1970s with Italian giallo director, Dario Argento.

Wallace never lived to see the development of television, but his work proved ideally suited to the new medium. From 1959–1960, those classic heroes *The Four Just Men* came to British television screens in thirty-nine half-hour television episodes, starring Dan Dailey, Jack Hawkins, Richard Conte and Vittorio De Sica. From 1960–1965 forty-six films were made in the *Edgar Wallace Mysteries* series, with each programme starting with a bust of the author revolving to the tune *Man of Mystery*, by The Shadows. While from 1969–1971, Thames TV showed sixteen hour-long mysteries in their series *The Mind of Mr J. G. Reeder*.

Wallace's works continued to be referenced in popular culture and in politics too. In the debate on the May 1966 Budget, Shadow Chancellor Ian Macleod, talking about the British government's turnover tax on betting, suggested that the chancellor of the exchequer, James Callaghan, read Edgar Wallace:

> I am afraid that the opportunities for evasion are very large indeed, and if I might recommend to the chancellor some leisure reading next weekend, now that his budget is out of the way, he might care to get hold of a copy of a book by Edgar Wallace called *The Calendar* ... which became a film and a play. If I remember rightly, Gordon Harker was in it and the whole plot, the whole story is about a method of beating the turnover tax [on betting] as it then existed in this country.[10]

A cartoon showed Callaghan, government minister George Brown, and Prime Minister Harold Wilson poring over *The Calendar*, with Macleod in the background. A month later, the *Sunday Mirror* reported 'soaring sales' of a new paperback edition of *The Calendar*. 'Apparently all the bookmakers, or at least many of them, rushed off to buy a copy, and perhaps a lot of tax inspectors and MPs too,' said a spokesman from the publishers.

In January 1969, Penny Wallace established the Edgar Wallace Society, and soon it had hundreds of members from countries across the world. In 1976 the 'Essex Head' pub off Fleet Street was renamed the 'Edgar Wallace', and remains an unofficial Wallace museum today.

But, while we've had remakes of *King Kong* in 1976 and 2005, and a smash hit stage musical, Wallace's other works have tended to be neglected in recent years. His extraordinary popularity in the 1920s, and afterwards too, has also been overlooked. Incredibly, Wallace's name has been absent from a number of recent histories of Britain between the First and Second World Wars. There was no inclusion of Wallace, either, in the 2005 book, *20th Century Crime Fiction* published by Oxford University Press. In his 1965 work, *English History 1914–45*, A.J.P. Taylor did acknowledge Wallace's existence, but only in the most dismissive way: 'The masses had their own form of cultural satisfaction. High-grade literature was beyond them. Low-grade literature – the novels of Nat Gould or Edgar Wallace – hardly improved on its nineteenth century predecessors.'

Is the modern downplaying of Wallace due to ignorance, snobbery or a misguided political correctness? Or is it due to the old highbrow prejudice that someone who wrote so much, and was so enormously popular, couldn't be any good and therefore isn't worth mentioning? Whatever the reason, it's time Wallace was once again given the acclaim that he so richly deserves. His books are fast moving and vital, perfect escapism for the stresses and strains of modern living. They entertain and excite, and have more wisdom and philosophy in them than the work of many more pretentious writers.

If this book does generate renewed interest in this remarkable man and his works, then its author's job will have been done. As I hope I've proved, it is impossible not to be thrilled by Edgar Wallace.

NOTES

Introduction

1 Gifford, Denis, *A Pictorial History of Horror Movies*, Hamlyn, 1973, p.100.
2 Lane, Margaret, *Edgar Wallace: A Biography*, 1938, with a revised edition published in 1964 (unless otherwise stated all quotes from 1938 edition).

2. *The Story of Polly Richards*

1 Lane, op. cit. p.5.
2 Ibid., p.5.
3 Ibid., p.7.
4 Richard Edgar and Jenny Taylor had five children. Interestingly, Edgar Wallace was not the only child of Richard Edgar to make his name in the world of entertainment. George Marriott Edgar, born in 1880, dropped his first name, and as Marriott Edgar wrote musical comedies, songs and pantomimes. His most famous monologue was *The Lion and Albert*, written for Stanley Holloway, about a 'grand little lad' who is eaten by a lion in Blackpool Zoo, and which is still performed today. He also worked on films, co-writing the scripts for classic Will Hay comedies such as *Oh, Mr Porter!*, *Good Morning, Boys* and *Ask a Policeman*. Edgar Wallace's half-brother died in 1951.
5 Ibid., p.16.
6 www.freebmd.org.uk.
7 Lane, op. cit. pp.16–17.
8 *People*, 1926 (later republished as *Edgar Wallace*, by Edgar Wallace (1929), and *Edgar Wallace by Himself* (1932)). Unless otherwise stated, all quotes from Wallace are from *Edgar Wallace by Himself*, Dodo Press reprint. This quote comes from p.1.

3. *A Docklands Childhood*

1 *Edgar Wallace: The Man Who Made His Name*, first broadcast on 1 April 1976, the 101st anniversary of Wallace's birth. Unless otherwise stated, all quotes from James Cameron are from this programme.
2 Letter to Penelope Wallace, published in *The Crimson Circle*, magazine No. 104 of the Edgar Wallace Society, November 1994.
3 Lane, op. cit. p.26.
4 There had been a fish market at Billingsgate wharf during the sixteenth and seventeenth centuries, and, in 1850, the first purpose-built market building was constructed. It proved to be inadequate for the amount of fish being brought to market, and was replaced by a new, enlarged building, Italianate in style and designed by Sir Horace Jones. This was formally opened in 1877.
5 George Freeman's job as a fish porter was a hard one, but it was also prestigious. Only fish porters were allowed to move fish around, the role being officially recognised by the Corporation of London in 1632. The fish porters' monopoly lasted for many centuries; it wasn't until 2012 that the ancient role of the licensed fish porter was ended.

6 The first such schools were set up by Congregationalist chapels in Wales in 1697. The first Church of England Sunday school was opened at Catterick, in Yorkshire, in 1765.

7 Lane, op. cit. p.32.

8 Ibid., p.32.

4. *The University of Life*

1 *John O'London's Weekly*, 19 June 1926.

2 Lane, op. cit. pp.38–39.

3 Ibid., p.39.

4 Ibid., p.40

5 Edmund Pook, son of the master of the house where Jane Marie Clouson had worked, was arrested and found guilty of the murder in the coroner's court, but was acquitted when the case went to the Old Bailey. Later, a labourer in Australia called Michael Carroll confessed to the murder, but the British authorities did not believe him to be guilty. No one was ever brought to justice for the terrible crime.

6 Lane, op. cit. p.40.

7 Ibid., p.49.

8 Ibid., pp.50–51.

9 Ibid., pp.52–53.

5. *'I'll be a Great Man One Day!'*

1 James Keir Hardie (1856–1915).

6. *The New Recruit*

1 Lane, op. cit. p.57.

2 Kent was one of the four counties of England which were split to form more than one regiment. The others were Lancashire, Surrey and Yorkshire.

3 Lane, op. cit. p.64.

4 Article in *Kentish Mercury*, 1932.

5 The battleship sank after it was accidentally rammed by HMS *Camperdown* close to Tripoli, Lebanon, on 22 June 1893. In all, 358 crew lost their lives, including Vice-Admiral George Tyron, commander of the British Mediterranean fleet. It remains the Royal Navy's biggest peacetime disaster.

6 An 1811 battle during the Peninsular War in which Britain, Spanish and Portuguese forces fought the French near the village of Albuera in the south of Spain.

7 Arthur Roberts had a different account of how he came to accept Wallace's song. He said that a young private in the RAMC (i.e. Wallace) had come to see him at the theatre and presented his work. Roberts read through the song. He asked the soldier how much he wanted for it. 'Ten shillings,' Wallace replied. Roberts said that he wouldn't give him 10s for it but £10. 'I sang that song and it was a great and immediate success.' Arthur Roberts, *Fifty Years of Spoof*, The Bodley Head, 1927, pp. 57–60.

7. *Off to South Africa*

1 Lane, op. cit. p.72.

2 One of the two Boer-run states, the other being Orange Free State.

3 Lane, op. cit. p.75.

4 Ibid., p.76.

5 Ibid., p.78.

6 Ibid., pp.91–92.

7 Wilson, G.H., *Gone Down the Years*, Howard Timmins for Allen & Unwin Ltd, 1947, p.90.

8 Ibid., p.90.

9 Ibid., p.91.

10 Ibid., p.91.

11 *Cape Illustrated Magazine*, vol. 8, no. 8, April 1898.

12 Lane, op. cit. p.103.

8. *Edgar Wallace: War Reporter*

1 Sibbett, 'Edgar Wallace – War Correspondent', published in *The Crimson Circle*, magazine of the Edgar Wallace Society, No. 87, May 1988.

2 Vulliamy, C.E., *Outlanders*, Jonathan Cape, 1938, p.313.

3 Ibid., p.314.

4 Sibbett, op. cit.

5 Lane, op. cit. p.131.

6 As cited by Christopher Lowder, in 'Odds and Ends', Edgar Wallace Society Newsletter No. 46, May 1980.

7 *The Spectator*, 13 July 1901, p.2.

8 *Hansard*: HC Deb., 11 June 1901 Vol. 97, cc72–73; cc73–74; 74–75.

9 Lane, op. cit. p.156.

9. *A Husband, a Father and a Newspaper Editor*

1 Lane, op. cit. p.144.

2 Ibid., p.158.

3 There's a different version of how Wallace got the job. Three candidates, including Wallace, were made to toss a coin for the position by Freeman-Cohen, and Wallace won. This was according to Colonel Eric Thomson of Johannesburg, son of Ernest George Thomson, one of the candidates.

4 Lane, op. cit. pp.161.

5 Ibid., pp.162–63.

6 One of the actors who appeared on the Johannesburg stage at this time, and who subsequently became famous, was a young Godfrey Tearle, whose father, Osmond, was in partnership with Rayne. Tearle became a great Shakespearean actor and film star, and was knighted in 1951. Perhaps his most famous film role was as the enemy agent 'Professor Jordan' in Alfred Hitchcock's 1935 version of *The 39 Steps*.

7 Lane, op. cit. p.165.

8 Ibid., pp.165–66.

10. *The Special Correspondent*

1 Read, Donald, *Edwardian England*, Harrap, 1972, p.60.

2 In *The Edwardians*, 2004, p.414, Roy Hattersley describes how the sales of another Harmsworth-owned title, the *Evening News*, saw its circulation rise from 187,000 to 390,000 in seven days, as a result of the way it covered the execution of James Canham Read in 1894.

3 Lane, op. cit. pp.167–68.

4 Gibbs, Philip, *The Pageant of the Years*, Heinemann Ltd., 1946, p.42.

5 Ibid.

6 From Greene's introduction to the 1964 edition of Margaret Lane's biography, *Edgar Wallace*.

7 Lane, op. cit. pp.168–69.

8 'Edgar Wallace and his Mother', by Margaret Lane, *The Crimson Circle* (magazine of the Edgar Wallace Society), November 1987, No. 76.

9 Lane, op. cit. p.177.

10 Falk, Bernard, *Bouquets for Fleet Street*, Hutchinson, 1951, p.60.

11 A reference to John Thadeus Delane 1817–1879, who became editor of the *Times*, at the age of 23 in May 1841, and held the position for thirty-six years until his retirement in 1877. An obituary in the *Spectator* magazine, published on 29 November 1879, described him as 'perhaps the ablest newspaper editor who ever lived'.

11. *The Four Just Men*

1   Lane, op. cit. p.181.
2   *Hereford Times*, 16 December 1905.
3   *Four Men in the Same Boat*, by Frank Richardson, Printer's Pie, 1906.

12. *In Deepest Africa*

1   'Nine Terrible Men', *Weekly Tale-Teller*, 24 August 1912.
2   Cited by Margaret Lane, op. cit. p.213.
3   Ibid., pp.213–14.
4   Ibid., pp.214–15.

13. *Captain Tatham and Commissioner Sanders*

1   Lane, op. cit. p.218.
2   Liveing, Edward, *Adventures in Publishing: The House of Ward Lock*, Ward Lock & Co., 1954, p.79.
3   Sir Harry Johnston 1858–1927, British colonial administrator, commissioner of Uganda 1899–1901. He is credited for helping to identify the okapi as a separate species; the animal's taxonomic name is *okapia johnstoni*.
4   Lane, op. cit. p.224
5   'The Story of Sanders', by Edgar Wallace, *John O'London's Weekly*, 11 July 1925.
6   Ibid.

14. *Back on Fleet Street*

1   Lane, op. cit. p.228.
2   Dunn, James, *Paperchase: Adventures in and out of Fleet Street*, Selwyn & Blount, 1938, p.22.
3   Edgar Wallace Society Newsletter No. 34, May 1977.
4   Falk, op. cit.
5   He also used this pseudonym for at least one poem, 'Out of It', published by the *Story Journal* on 9 June 1913.

15. *The Curious Case of the Confession of Dr Crippen*

1   Neil Clark, 'A Century later, was Dr Crippen innocent?' *Daily Express*, 22 November 2010 (link to article: http://www.express.co.uk/expressyourself/212959/A-century-later-was-Dr-Crippen-innocent.
2   'My Murderers' by Edgar Wallace, printed in Vol. 2, No. 2 of November/December issue of *Criminology* magazine, 1964. Later reprinted in *The Crimson Circle*, the magazine of the Edgar Wallace Society, No. 87, August 1990.
3   Ibid.
4   Ibid.

16. *More Bright Ideas*

1   Lane, op. cit. p.240.
2   Falk, op. cit.
3   *Press Club Bulletin*, 1912.
4   *The Novel Magazine*, No. 86, May 1912.
5   Other examples of 'Invasion literature' were *The Riddle of the Sands* by Erskine Childers (1903); *The Invasion of 1910* by William Le Queux, published in 1906 and serialised in the *Daily Mail*; *When William Came – A Story of London under the Hohenzollerns* by Saki (1913); and the play, *An Englishman's Home* (1909) by Guy du Maurier.
6   Lane, op. cit. p.230.
7   Ibid., p.231.

8   Ibid., pp.249–50.

9   Born in Lancashire in 1869, Hulton's father, 'Ned', had been a compositor on the *Manchester Guardian*, who then set up two newspapers of his own – the *Sporting Chronicle*, which rivalled the *Sporting Life* as Britain's leading national horse racing daily and the *Athletic News and Cyclists Journal*, a weekly sports paper. By 1913, his son's newspapers included the *Daily Sketch*, the *Daily Dispatch* and the *Manchester Evening Chronicle*.

10 Wilson, A.E., *Playgoer's Pilgrimage*, Stanley Paul, 1948, p.139.

11 Thaw, Evelyn, *The Story of My Life*, John Long, 1914.

12 In *Bouquets for Fleet Street*, Bernard Falk relates how, a few weeks before his death in 1925, Sir Edward Hulton was accidentally met at Ascot by the journalist Hannen Swaffer. Swaffer congratulated Hulton, saying that he looked much better. The newspaper magnate shook his head, 'You are wrong,' he said, 'I am dying and I am the most miserable man on earth.'

17. *For King and Country*

1   Read, op. cit. pp.249–50.

2   'Odds and Ends' by Christopher Lowder, Edgar Wallace Society newsletter, May 1980.

3   *Town Topics*, 19 August 1916.

4   Booth, J.B., *Life, Laughter and Brass Hats*, T. Werner Laurie, 1939, pp.315–16.

5   Booth, J.B., *A Pink Un' Remembers*, T. Werner Laurie, 1937, p.192.

6   Lane, op. cit. p.251.

7   McCormick, Donald, *Who's Who in Spy Fiction*, Elm Tree Books (Hamish Hamilton), 1977, p.183.

8   Nowadays published as *The Weekly News*, the paper has been in production since 1855.

9   From *Ten Divisions and a Red-Haired Girl*, 1918.

10 Wallace was one of the original members of 'The Legion of Frontiersmen', founded in 1905 by Captain Roger Pocock. Pocock's idea was to have an organisation of men willing and eager to serve Britain and its empire on any frontier of the world. Other members included Winston Churchill, and the writers Sir Arthur Conan Doyle and H. Rider Haggard.

11 Edgar Wallace Society Newsletter No. 38, May 1978.

18. *Jim*

1   Curtis, Robert, *Edgar Wallace: Each Way*, John Long, 1932. Unless otherwise stated, all further quotes from Curtis are from this source.

2   Robert Curtis 1889–1936. 'In 1921 he went on a tour of the USA … lecturing and demonstrating for the Woodstock Typewriter Company, typing at the rate of 134 words a minute without error from unfamiliar material and whilst answering questions.' 'Robert George Curtis', by John A. Hogan and Marjorie Fowler, *The Crimson Circle*, magazine of the Edgar Wallace Society, No. 74, May 1987.

3   Lane, op. cit. p.256.

4   Mrs Edgar Wallace, *The Secret of My Successful Marriage*, John Long, 1930.

5   Wallace, Ethel V., *Edgar Wallace, by his Wife*, 1932. Unless otherwise stated, all further quotes from Violet King, aka 'Jim', are from this source.

6   Dixon, Wheeler Winston, *The Transparency of Spectacle*, State University of New York Press, 1988, pp.79–80.

7   The burial place is now a major tourist attraction in China, and is home to the famous terracotta army – 10,000 members of the emperor's army immortalised as life-size terracotta figures. The burial place has been described as the most remarkable archaeological site in the world.

8   W.O.G. Lofts, 'Collecting Edgar Wallace', *Antiquarian Book Monthly Review*, Vol. 4, No. 8, Issue 40, August 1977.

9   Lane, op. cit., p262.

10 Booth, op. cit.

11 Lane, op. cit. pp.263–64.

12 Morland, Nigel, 'A Day with Edgar Wallace', Edgar Wallace Society Newsletter, February 1981.

13 Lane, op. cit. p.258.

14 Ibid., p.257–58.

15 Ibid., p.267.

16 Ibid., p.268.

17 Ibid., p.269.

18 Ibid., p.270.

19. *The Fiction Factory*

1 Lane, op. cit. p.269.

2 Ibid., p.274.

3 Ibid., p.277

4 Peter Coussee, 'He Only Wrote the One', *The Crimson Circle*, magazine of the Edgar Wallace Society, No. 9, July 1994.

5 Lane, op. cit. pp.280–81.

6 Dixon, op. cit. p.79.

7 First published in the US by Small Maynard, and published by John Long in Britain, in 1923.

8 The stories first appeared in the *Windsor Magazine*, published by Ward Lock in 1920–1921.

9 Interview in *Edgar Wallace: The Man who made his Name*, BBC Documentary, first shown 1 April 1976.

20. *Thrilling a Nation*

1 In 1980, Penny Wallace emulated her father by being elected chairman of the Press Club of London. She was the first woman chairman.

2 Obituary by Jack Adrian, the *Independent*, 11 February 1997.

3 Interview in *Edgar Wallace; The Man who made his Name*, BBC Documentary, first shown 1 April 1976.

4 As late as 1970 it came second in a poll of favourite Wallace books by members of the Edgar Wallace Society.

5 The extent of the royal family's devotion to the works of Edgar Wallace was revealed in 1985 by John Hogan, who had just become organiser of the Edgar Wallace Society, 'They have a superb collection beautifully bound. In my younger days I wrote to them saying I would be interested if it was ever for sale. I got a short note back saying there was no question of that.'

6 H. Douglas Thompson, *Masters of Mystery*, Collins, 1931.

7 From newspaper obituary of Wallace in February 1932.

8 Tom Pocock, 'A Name to Live Up to', *Evening Standard*, 9 June 1967.

9 Leach, Jack, *Sods I Have Cut on the Turf*, Gollancz, 1961, p.118 (republished by J.A. Allen, 1973).

10 Dunn, op. cit.

11 Lane, op. cit. p.296.

12 Ibid., p.302.

13 Leach, op. cit. p.116.

14 Barrie got his nickname for ringing the changes on a number of horses, by use of paints and dyes. A 'ringer' in racing terms is a substituted racehorse, i.e. one disguised to look like another horse.

15 First appeared as the serial 'The Fellowship' in *The People*, 1923–4.

21. *Enter the Ringer*

1 Nigel Morland, Edgar Wallace Society Newsletter No. 30, May 1976.

2 Interview in BBC TV documentary, op. cit. Dickson lived to the ripe old age of 102, dying in September 1995, almost seventy years on from appearing in *The Ringer*.

3   The building later became the embassy of the People's Republic of China.
4   'When Edgar Wallace Kidnapped Me', by Patricia Wallace, *Pearson's*, 16 March 1929.
5   Penelope Wallace, *Edgar Wallace – The Man and the Writer*.
6   Patricia Wallace, op. cit.
7   Du Maurier, Daphne, *Myself when Young*, Virago, 2004, p.107 (previously published under the title *Growing Pains: The Shaping of a Writer*, Gollancz, 1977).
8   Ibid., p.109.

22. *People*
1   Three years later the book was republished as *Edgar Wallace* by Edgar Wallace, and in 1932 as '*Edgar Wallace by Himself*'.
2   *The Bookman*, December 1926, p.193.
3   Morgan, Janet, *Agatha Christie: A Biography*, Collins, 1984, pp.145–6.
4   Lane, op. cit. p.312.
5   From interview in *Kentish Mercury*, 1932, as later Campbell quotes.
6   'Fred Bason's Diary', cited in *The Crimson Circle*, magazine of the Edgar Wallace Society, No. 79, August 1988.
7   Hichens, Robert, *Yesterday*, Cassell, 1947, p.308.
8   Greene, op. cit.
9   Lane, op. cit. p.370.
10 Ruck, Berta, *A Story-Teller Tells the Truth*, Hutchinson, 1935, pp.222–3.

23. *King of the West End*
1   Transcript for BBC TV documentary, op. cit.
2   Reissar died, aged 96, in October 2000.
3   Interview in BBC TV documentary, op. cit.
4   Nichols' portrait of Wallace entitled 'The Burglar's Friend', appeared in his book *Are They the same at Home?*, a collection of celebrity interviews published by Jonathan Cape in 1927.
5   Wallace wrote the script, but the music and lyrics were written by Vernon Duke and Desmond Carter respectively.
6   Wodehouse, *Performing Flea* (entry 10 March 1928), originally published by Herbert Jenkins, 1953. Also in *Wodehouse on Wodehouse* collection by Hutchinson, 1980, p.271.
7   Dixon, op. cit.
8   Bennett, 'I Read a Thriller – and Startle My Friends', *Evening Standard*, 19 July 1928.
9   Sayers, D.L., *The Omnibus of Crime*, Gollancz, 1928.
10 Chesterton, *Come to Think Of It*, Methuen, 1930, pp.29–33.
11 Leavis, Q.D., *Fiction and the Reading Public*, Penguin, 1932, Harmondsworth, 1979, p.20.
12 Ibid., p.45.
13 Nathan, *Passing Judgements*, 1975, Alfred A. Knopf, 1935, pp.165–6.
14 Arkell, *Meet these People*, with caricatures by Bert Thomas, Herbert Jenkins, 1928, p.41.
15 'In the Limelight' review, *Sunday Pictorial*, 30 December 1928.
16 Interview in BBC TV documentary, op. cit.
17 Seth-Smith, Michael, *The Life and Times of Steve Donoghue*, Faber & Faber, 1974, p.205.
18 Wallace's lawsuit enabled Cameronian to win the 1931 Derby. As Michael Seth-Smith explains in his biography of Steve Donoghue: 'Lord Dewar [the owner of Cameronian], a bachelor, had died in April 1930 and but for Wallace's lawsuit Cameronian's nomination for the Derby would have been void', p.208.
19 Leach, op. cit., p.119.
20 Lane, op. cit. p.338.

24. *Edgar Wallace: Film Director*
1   Letter to the Edgar Wallace Society Newsletter No. 42, May 1979.

2   *The Terror* was Warner Bros' second 'all-talking' picture, but is now sadly a lost film.

3   Lane, op. cit. p.360.

4   The house, since 1977, has been the Ramakrishna Vedanta Centre, the only centre in the UK affiliated to the Ramakrishna Order of India. More details here: http://www.vedantauk.com.

5   Wodehouse, op. cit, p.272, 1980, Hutchinson edition.

6   Penelope Wallace, *Edgar Wallace – the Man and the Writer*.

7   Lane, op. cit. p.365.

8   From *A Name to Live Up To*, op. cit.

25. *Adventures in Germany and America*

1   'The Human Machine', *The London Mail*, 13 March 1926.

2   From a transcript of television interview. All other quotes from Goldmann are from the same source.

3   Cicely Hamilton, *Modern Germanies*, J.M. Dent & Sons, 1931, p.239.

4   On 9 April 1928 *The Ringer* also opened in Sweden to good reviews.

5   'Edgar Wallace, Master of Mystery, writes of Two Holiday Mysteries', Berlin, in *Titbits*, 4 August 1928.

6   Penelope Wallace, *Edgar Wallace –The Man and the Writer*.

7   'With Edgar Wallace in America' by Pat Wallace, *Pearson's*, 21 December 1929.

8   Interview in BBC TV documentary, op. cit.

9   Lane, op. cit. p.342.

10 Charles Laughton 1899–1962. Among his most famous film roles were Captain Bligh in *Mutiny on the Bounty* (1935) and Quasimodo in *The Hunchback of Notre Dame* (1939).

11 Elsa Lanchester, *Charles Laughton and I*, Faber & Faber, 1938, pp.75–76.

12 From Charles Laughton's introduction to *Charles Laughton and I*, p.8.

13 Emlyn Williams 1905–1987. Celebrated actor and dramatist, and author of *Night Must Fall* and *The Corn is Green*.

26. *Hats off to Edgar Wallace!*

1   Leach, op. cit.

2   Hart-Davis, Rupert, 'Writers Remembered: Edgar Wallace', *The Author Magazine*, Summer 1988.

3   Interview in BBC TV documentary, op. cit.

4   From an interview with Jenia Reissar on German television (ZDF), broadcast in December 2000, two months after her death. All quotes from Reissar in this chapter are from the same source.

5   Among other contributors were Lady Conan Doyle, and Lady Baden-Powell.

27. *Edgar Wallace MP?*

1   'Recollections of Edgar Wallace', by Miss F.M. Pugh, *The Crimson Circle*, Magazine of the Edgar Wallace Society, February 1986.

2   Hart-Davis, op. cit.

3   In 1931 Wallace also wrote the dialogue for the first talkie version of Gainsborough Pictures' *The Hound of the Baskervilles*.

4   From *Armchair Detective*, Vol. 18, No. 1, winter 1985.

5   *I Guarded Kings*, by ex-Detective Harold Brust, Stanley Paul, 1936, p.260.

6   Wallace's first radio broadcast had been on 6 June 1923. He gave a talk entitled 'Impressions of the Derby'.

7   'World of Wireless' column, *Reynolds News*.

8   Formerly known as *Lloyd's Sunday News*. The paper was incorporated into the *Sunday Graphic* in 1931.

9   Hannen Swaffer (1879–1962) 'Swaff', like Wallace, was one of the greatest characters in British

journalism. A socialist, spiritualist and bohemian, he wrote for various newspapers and was nicknamed 'The Pope of Fleet Street'.

10 Hart-Davis, op. cit.

11 Ibid.

12 Later novelised as *The Coat of Arms.*

13 Wallace, Ethel V., *Edgar Wallace by His Wife*, 1932, p.244.

14 'Libs Wha Hae' by Henry Hodgkinson, Edgar Wallace Society Newsletter No. 44, November 1979.

15 Hugh (later Baron) Cudlipp, 1913–1998. Cigar-smoking editor of the *Sunday Pictorial*, managing editor of *Sunday Express*, editorial director of the *Daily Mirror*, and later chairman of the Mirror Group. Described as 'the superstar of Fleet Street, the editor with the greatest charisma' in 1998 obituary in *The Independent.*

16 Interview in BBC TV documentary, op. cit.

17 Ibid.

28. *Edgar goes to Hollywood*

1 Wallace's letters home to Jim were later edited and published in *Edgar Wallace, My Hollywood Diary*, 1932. All quotes from this and the following chapter from Wallace are from letters to Jim or diary entries.

2 Lane, op. cit. p.401.

29. *The Final Chapter*

1 Donoghue, *Donoghue Up!*,1938, p.206–07.

2 Lane, op. cit. p.408.

3 Sari Maritza 1910–1987, real name Dora Patricia Deterding-Nathan, born in China to a British father and Austrian mother. Usually cast in vampish/femme fatale roles.

4 Lane, op. cit. p.409.

5 On Wallace's death, he was replaced by the actress Evelyn Laye in the du Maurier cigarettes advert. Laye, unlike Wallace, lived to a ripe old age, dying aged 95 in February 1996.

6 Interview in BBC TV documentary, op. cit.

30. *Edgar Wallace Lives On*

1 Interview in BBC TV documentary, op. cit.

2 Story told in *A Stupid Boy*, by Jimmy Perry, Century, 2002, p.80.

3 For more on this controversy, see 'Who was the father of Beauty and the Beast?' by Janet Morgan, *Financial Times*, 4 December 1982. A copy of Wallace's original script is in the Bodleian Library, Oxford.

4 Years later, when he was rich and famous, Wallace went back to the spot where he sold newspapers. The man to whom he sold his pitch was still there, and told him that he had made a mistake in selling, as the business was going well.

5 Lofts, op. cit.

6 'Edgar Wallace in Germany: The Eighth Decade', by Thomas David, *The Crimson Circle*, magazine of the Edgar Wallace Society No. 86, May 1990. German translations of Wallace's work even found their way into Egyptian prisons. A future president of Egypt, Anwar el-Sadat, learnt German with the help of an Edgar Wallace novel when imprisoned in the early 1940s. El-Sadat, Anwar, *In Search of Identity*, Collins, 1978, p.47.

7 Ibid., Editor's Note.

8 The film also featured as an extra Jomo Kenyatta, the future leader of Kenya.

9 Giallo were/are crime mystery novels, so called because of their yellow cover background.

10 *Hansard*, HC Deb, 4 May 1966 vol. 727 cc1637–762.

SELECT BIBLIOGRAPHY AND FURTHER READING

Booth, *A 'Pink 'Un' Remembers*, T. Werner Laurie, 1937.

Booth, *Life, Laughter and Brass Hats*, T. Werner Laurie, 1939.

Brust, *I Guarded Kings – the Memoirs of a Political Police Officer*, Stanley Paul, 1935.

Curtis, *Edgar Wallace – Each Way*, John Long, 1932.

Denham, *Stars in my Hair*, T. Werner Laurie, 1958.

Donoghue, *Donoghue up! The Autobiography of Steve Donoghue*, Collins, 1938.

Dixon, *The Transparency of Spectacle, Meditations on the Moving Image*, SUNY Press, 1988.

Du Maurier, *It's only the Sister*, Peter Davies, 1951.

Du Maurier, *Myself When Young*, Virago, 2004 (previously published under the title *Growing Pains: The Shaping of a Writer*, Gollancz, 1977).

Dunn, *Paperchase: Adventures in and out of Fleet Street*, Selwyn & Blount, 1938.

Falk, *Bouquets for Fleet Street*, Hutchinson, 1951.

Gibbs, *The Pageant of the Years*, Heinemann, 1946.

Gifford, *A Pictorial History of Horror Movies*, Hamlyn, 1973.

Glover, *Looking for Edgar Wallace: The Author as Consumer*, History Workshop Journal, No. 37, 1994.

Hastings, *The Autobiography of Sir Patrick Hastings*, Heinemann, 1948

Hichens, *Yesterday: the Autobiography of Robert Hichens*, Cassell, 1947.

Lanchester, *Charles Laughton and I*, Faber & Faber, 1938.

Lane, *Edgar Wallace: the Biography of a Phenomenon*, Heinemann, 1938 (Revised and republished by Hamish Hamilton in 1964).

Leach, *Sods I Have Cut on the Turf*, Gollancz, 1961 (republished by J.A. Allen, 1973).

Liveling, *Adventures in Publishing: the House of Ward Lock*, 1854–1954, Ward Lock Co., 1954.

McCormick, *Who's Who in Spy Fiction*, Sphere, 1979.

Monolulu, *I Gotta Horse: the Autobiography of Ras Prince Monolulu*, Hurst & Bracket, 1950.

Nichols, *Are They the Same at Home?*, Jonathan Cape, 1927.

Rickman, *On and Off the Racecourse*, George Routledge & Sons, 1937.

Roberts, *Fifty Years of Spoof*, John Lane, 1927.

Ruck, *A Story-Teller Tells the Truth*, Hutchinson, 1935.

Seth-Smith, *Steve: The Life and Times of Steve Donoghue*, Faber & Faber, 1974.

Wallace, Ethel V., *Edgar Wallace by his Wife*, Hutchinson, 1932.

Wallace, Edgar, *People*, Hodder & Stoughton, 1926 (republished as *Edgar Wallace* by Edgar Wallace in 1929 and *Edgar Wallace* by himself, in 1932).

Wallace, Edgar, *My Hollywood Diary*, Hutchinson, 1932.

Wilson, A.E., *Playgoer's Pilgrimage*, Stanley Paul, 1948.

Wilson, G. H., *Gone Down the Years*, Howard B. Timmins for Allen & Unwin, 1947.